T0304581

An Economic History of India

This book offers a major new economic history of India from the reign of Akbar in the sixteenth century to India's post-independence integration into the global economy. Using concepts and theories from economics and economic history alongside extensive new data, Bishnupriya Gupta builds a new framework for understanding the economic impacts and legacies of British rule. She charts India's transition from precolonial economy to colonial rule and evaluates its economic performance from a comparative perspective, particularly in the context of the Great Divergence between Europe and Asia. Finally, she examines India's post-independence economy and the evolution of social and economic inequality through to the turn of the twenty-first century. By taking a long view, the book sheds new light on the persistent effects of historical institutions as well as the impacts of policy-driven changes. It will be essential reading for anyone seeking to understand the long-run evolution of the Indian economy.

Bishnupriya Gupta is Professor of Economics at The University of Warwick and the research director of CAGE Research Centre. She has published widely on industrial development in colonial India, gender norms in India and is a key contributor to the debate on the Great Divergence.

Cambridge Studies in Economic History

Editorial Board

Gareth Austin: *University of Cambridge*
Stephen Broadberry: *University of Oxford*
Naomi R. Lamoreaux: *Yale University*
Sheilagh Ogilvie: *University of Oxford*
Şevket Pamuk: *Bogaziçi University*

Cambridge Studies in Economic History comprises stimulating and accessible economic history which actively builds bridges to other disciplines. Books in the series will illuminate why the issues they address are important and interesting, place their findings in a comparative context, and relate their research to wider debates and controversies. The series will combine innovative and exciting new research by younger researchers with new approaches to major issues by senior scholars. It will publish distinguished work regardless of chronological period or geographical location.

A complete list of titles in the series can be found at:
www.cambridge.org/economichistory

An Economic History of India

Growth, Income and Inequalities from the Mughals to the 21st Century

Bishnupriya Gupta

The University of Warwick

CAMBRIDGE
UNIVERSITY PRESS

CAMBRIDGE
UNIVERSITY PRESS

Shaftesbury Road, Cambridge CB2 8EA, United Kingdom

One Liberty Plaza, 20th Floor, New York, NY 10006, USA

477 Williamstown Road, Port Melbourne, VIC 3207, Australia

314–321, 3rd Floor, Plot 3, Splendor Forum, Jasola District Centre, New Delhi – 110025, India

103 Penang Road, #05–06/07, Visioncrest Commercial, Singapore 238467

Cambridge University Press is part of Cambridge University Press & Assessment, a department of the University of Cambridge.

We share the University's mission to contribute to society through the pursuit of education, learning and research at the highest international levels of excellence.

www.cambridge.org
Information on this title: www.cambridge.org/9781108491624

DOI: 10.1017/9781108869065

© Bishnupriya Gupta 2025

This publication is in copyright. Subject to statutory exception and to the provisions of relevant collective licensing agreements, no reproduction of any part may take place without the written permission of Cambridge University Press & Assessment.

When citing this work, please include a reference to the DOI 10.1017/9781108869065

First published 2025

A catalogue record for this publication is available from the British Library

A Cataloging-in-Publication data record for this book is available from the Library of Congress

ISBN 978-1-108-49162-4 Hardback
ISBN 978-1-108-79873-0 Paperback

Cambridge University Press & Assessment has no responsibility for the persistence or accuracy of URLs for external or third-party internet websites referred to in this publication and does not guarantee that any content on such websites is, or will remain, accurate or appropriate.

For
Dhruva, Cherry and Anirban

Contents

Figures

Maps

Tables

Acknowledgements

This book brings together my work on colonial India and my understanding of the country's long-run economic development. Many people have helped in this journey. Among them are my co-authors, Steve Broadberry, Latika Chaudhary, Johann Custodis, James Fenske, Dilip Mookherjee, Kaivan Munshi, Cora Neumann, Tirthankar Roy, Mario Sanclemente, Anand Swamy, and Song Yuan.

To Monobina Gupta, I owe the inspiration to embark on this book project. To Steve Broadberry, I owe the conceptualization and measurement of the Great Divergence between Europe and India, which forms the core of Chapters 1 and 4. I owe many friends and colleagues for their intellectual input into various research projects and for many discussions over the years. Among them are Jean Pascal Bassino, Sascha Becker, Nick Crafts, Kyoji Fukao, Mark Harrison, Debin Ma, Takashima Masanori, Sharun Mukand, Sevket Pamuk, and Debraj Ray.

The pandemic put a brake on excursions to libraries and access to data, books, and the old notebooks in my office. I thank the weekly virtual happy hour community of colleagues – James Fenske, Dennis Novy, Herakles Polemarchakis, Giacomo Ponzetto, and Claudia Rei – for keeping discussions alive and staying afloat.

I thank Didi Egerton Warburton for her careful reading of the chapters, Cathy Humphrey for reading the final draft and Viswarajan Pillay for his help with the bibliography. I thank Joerg Baten, Guilhem Cassan, Latika Chaudhary, James Fenske, Kyoji Fukao, and Sun Go for sharing their data and Tim Goodfellow for drawing the maps. I thank Eric and Doreen Anderson and Robert and Cynthia Swanson of Arc Indexing for doing the index of the book. I am grateful to the CAGE Research Centre for financial support and to Michael Watson at Cambridge University Press for his patience and helpful suggestions. I thank an anonymous reader of the book draft for valuable comments. My biggest debt is to James Fenske for reading the first draft and to Steve Broadberry for many conversations and joint projects on the economic history of Asia and Europe. The errors are mine alone.

Introduction

The economic history of India has been a contested field. The nationalist and the imperialist historiography was useful to get us started in thinking about different aspects of colonization and economic development in colonial and pre-colonial India. There have been important contributions from a large number of historians and economists. Economic historians Naoroji (1878) and Dutt (1906) made an economic argument against British rule using the concept of drain of wealth from India and the disproportionate influence of the imperial power in different spheres of the economy. This was a product of the time and an effective political weapon to make an economic case for independent economic policy that would prioritize economic development of the country rather than imperial interests. An imperialist view of colonial India in recent work comes from Niall Ferguson in *Empire: How Britain Made the Modern World* (2012). Ferguson sees British imperialism as playing a crucial role in bringing modernization to the colonies. The idea of modernization is defined as integration into world trade and financial markets and building of modern infrastructure. Very little is said about growth in per capita incomes and improvements in living standards. More recently, there has been a revival of the nationalist approach in Shashi Tharoors's *Inglorious Empire: What the British Did to India* (2018); this narrative contests the imperialist view. Without colonization, India would have prospered. Without the destruction of traditional industries, India would have become an industrial nation.

Neither Ferguson nor Tharoor use data as evidence. Neither say anything concrete about the fiscal capacity and technological capabilities in pre-colonial India and how to think about measuring living standards. For Ferguson the benefits flowed from Britain to the colonies, and for Tharoor there was a drain of resources from India to Britain.

Many of the conclusions from this literature have not stood up to empirical scrutiny. For example, the magnitude of economic drain has been debated. The economic impact of the railways has been shown to be more beneficial than merely a transportation network that served imperial interests of trade. By the early twentieth century the network criss-crossed the country and connected markets and towns. The claim that colonial policy stopped industrialization does not square up with the evidence from subsequent research. A large import substituting cotton textile industry developed with Indian ownership. The interwar years saw a diversification of the industrial sector under Indian entrepreneurship and the entry of multinational corporations. Deindustrialization in the nineteenth century is flagged up as evidence of impoverishment, and specialization in agricultural exports is considered to be the cause of underdevelopment. Yet Indian GDP per capita declined in the eighteenth century when the textile trade prospered and stagnated in the nineteenth century rather than declined as India became an agricultural exporter. Data show that the main economic decline coincided with a booming trade in traditional textile exports.

British rule impacted on the Indian economy in significant ways. Without quantitative evidence it is difficult to understand which areas of the economy became underdeveloped and which areas developed, or which policies had a detrimental effect and which did not. There is an overarching moral critique of occupation of one country by another. This would not diminish in importance, should there be evidence of economic prosperity. Political freedom is factored into measurement of living standards today. By that yardstick, being a colony feeds into the index of underdevelopment. There are examples of economic growth under colonization, such as Malaysia in Asia and Senegal in Africa. A moral critique would still make a case against colonization, whereas an economic critique may not.

There is a rich literature using empirical evidence at the regional level to illustrate the impact of colonization on regions, communities, and social groups. Among them are contributions by Sugata Bose, Rajat Datta, Sumit Guha, Dharma Kumar, and David Ludden. There are rich evidence-based narratives of industry in the work of Amiya Bagchi, Morris David Morris, Rajat Ray, and Indrajit Ray. An evidence-based approach to an economic history of India was adopted in the work of historians of Mughal India such as Irfan Habib, Shireen Moosvi, and Najaf Haidar, and in the work on the colonial economy by Dietmar Rothermund, Tirthankar Roy, and B.R. Tomlinson. In the last twenty years there has been a revival of interest in Indian economic history. Data digitization has made it easier to build large data sets and researchers have used new granular data. New data, new sources, and digitization has made it possible to think of new questions and provide new perspectives.

This book brings together old and new research and offers a historical perspective on how we can think of India's economic development. It aims to build a narrative based on the new empirical evidence to understand the nature of economic development or a lack of it in a large colonial economy, using concepts and theories from economics and economic history. It aims to use the available empirical evidence to understand the impact of British rule on the economy. It takes a long view to understand the changes from the pre-colonial economy to colonial rule and puts a timeline on what has come to be known as the *Great Divergence* between Europe and Asia, with a focus on India. Finally, it attempts to understand India's post-independence development from the perspective of an economic historian of colonial India. By taking a long view, the book explores persistent effects of historical institutions as well as policy-driven changes after independence in 1947.

I.1 Data on Colonial India

The East India Company and the colonial government produced detailed records on different aspects of the economy. Evidence on exports and imports from India, wages, and prices were documented carefully by the East India Company. Regional surveys produced evidence on the state of agriculture and industrial and service sector activities, occupation structure, and other aspects of living standards and quality of life. These resources have documented wages paid to workers in different occupations as well as prices of goods traded in the internal market and the records of fiscal spending. This information is patchy. From the time of Crown rule, we have more systematic data on population, production, disease environment, government revenue, and expenditure. The decennial censuses from 1872 made available district level data on population, occupations, civil condition, education, and other aspects of the economy and society. District gazetteers and sectoral reports provide more granular data. The reports of the Sanitary Commission provide heath and demographic data. Agricultural censuses from 1891 recorded acreage under different crops, livestock, and irrigation at the level of districts. Yield per acre by crop was estimated for these districts. Investors manuals, business directories, and reports of industrial associations provide information on firm ownership, capital, the number of workers, and profits. Over the last two decades new research by economic historians has analysed this data using rigorous statistical methods and has brought new insights, some of which question existing views in the literature on the colonization of India.

Historical data can never be as good as contemporary empirical evidence. Still, it is possible to compile the evidence available and evaluate it statistically. This book is an attempt to look at the economic impact of colonial rule through the lens of recorded empirical evidence. I use data collected in my research on Indian living standards covering several centuries.

The book presents empirical evidence, old and new, based on the agricultural statistics from the nineteenth century and trade and production statistics for industry to discuss deindustrialization in the nineteenth century and the rise of modern industry. I have used primary sources of the data and evidence from secondary sources for my own research to put forward an evidence-based perspective. I also borrow from the research of others over the last decades to understand different aspects of India's long run development.

In the following chapters I use insights from research based on the empirical evidence to assess the response of economic agents to the process of colonization, the role of institutions in creating unequal access to resources, and the factors that shaped economic policy. The approach will be to study how economic agents in different sectors (farmers, labourers, entrepreneurs, and traders) responded to the changing environment of policy making. I evaluate the modernization of the economy through investment in physical and social infrastructure such as the railways, irrigation, and education, and the impact of integration into the global network of the British Empire. The book covers a long span of history from the time of Emperor Akbar to the reign of the East India Company and the period of Crown rule and, finally, Nehru's vision of a new India and the policies of regulation and subsequent economic reforms in independent India. The choice of dates is determined by the availability of data for long run comparisons. It ends roughly in 2000 as the consequences of history become less relevant given the momentous changes in Indian economic policy and outcomes. The chapters are organized thematically and traces the historical origins of different aspects of economic development.

I.2   Defining India over the Long Run

In this book, India is not the same unit over time. Mughal India covers the boundaries of the Mughal Empire. British India includes the modern states of India, Pakistan, and Bangladesh. 'India' after 1947 refers to only one country. Most historical discussions on economic change cover the area now included in India, Pakistan, and Bangladesh. The two longlasting empires, the Mughal and the British, unified large parts of the country under one political entity. The term 'India' will be used to refer to the political entity at a given point in time. Therefore, the borders and the area termed 'India' will not be the same as I move through centuries. Mughal India, British India, and independent India will form the changing contexts and geographic boundaries.

The Indian subcontinent is diverse in geography, the people that inhabit this region, the languages they speak, their religious practices, and the cultural heritage they own. In political terms, neither the Mughal nor the British Empire ruled over the entire region of today's India. Parts of Southern India remained outside the Mughal Empire and the princely states in British India were ruled by local elites, remaining outside the political boundary of the British Empire. In the year 2000, India, Pakistan, and Bangladesh were three separate countries. India after independence lives the shared history of the region. An analysis of post-independence economic changes in Pakistan and Bangladesh remains outside the scope of this book.

I.3   Geography

Geographically, the region can be divided into four zones – the Himalayas, the Indo-Gangetic Basin (the floodplains of the Ganges and the Indus), the arid or semi-arid areas of north-west-centre and south, including the Deccan Plateau, and the littoral (Gupta and Roy 2017). The southern part of South Asia has a tropical climate, while the northern part is more continental. The region depends on the south-west and north-east monsoon rains, which provide water for agriculture. Map I.1 also shows the regional variations in rainfall and highlights the extensive dry regions in the north-west and on the Deccan Plateau.

I.4   The Timeline of Empires

The Mughal Empire was established by Babur in 1526. The territory expanded under the reign of Humayun (1530–1540, 1555–1556), Akbar (1556–1605), Jahangir (1605–1627), Shah Jahan (1627–1658), and Aurangzeb (1658–1707), when it reached the largest geographical boundary (see Map I.2). After the death of Aurangzeb, the Empire began to crumble. The eighteenth century brought wars and conflict over territorial control, disrupting economic activity. The peak in prosperity in this Empire was reached during the reign of Akbar.

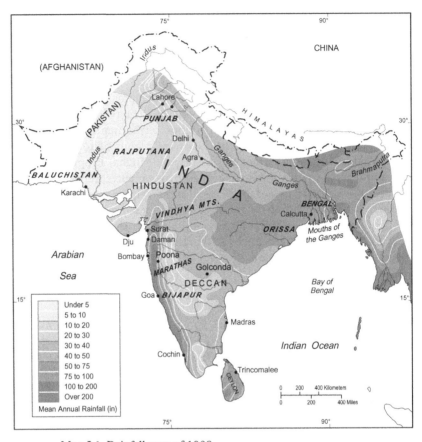

Map I.1 Rainfall map of 1908

The European trading companies began to arrive in India in search of spices and other exotic products. The Portuguese, British, Dutch, French, and Danish monopoly trading companies entered into trading contracts with the local rulers and set up trading posts in various parts of the country. The trading posts dotted the western and eastern littoral and various spots along the river Hooghly in Bengal. The companies bought textiles in India and exported them to Europe and other markets.

In 1757, the ruler of Bengal was defeated by the English East India Company and thus began the Company's rule of Bengal. From a trader, the Company transitioned into a fiscal consolidator and expanded its reign to other regions of India. By the middle of the nineteenth century, it looked more like a ruler than a trading firm. Map I.3 shows the timeline of the conquest by the Company. In 1858, India came under

Map I.2 Mughal India

Crown rule. The transition to Crown rule integrated India into the economic project of the British Empire. The princely states were ruled by
local princes and coexisted with British India although they remained
outside its political control (see Map I.4).

The independence of India came at the cost of a partition of the country. The movement for independence had been led by the Congress
party under the leadership of Mohandas Gandhi, Jawaharlal Nehru, and
Vallabhbhai Patel. The Muslim League, formed in 1906, came to see a
separate state for the Muslims as their political goal. By the 1940s their
support had grown and the colonial government accepted the demand
for a two-state solution for independence.

The political boundaries of India and Pakistan were drawn in an arbitrary fashion. Cyril Radcliffe, a British barrister, was assigned the task

Map I.3 Political conquest by the East India Company

of drawing the dividing line. This was his first visit to the country and he had five weeks to do the job. On the western side the region of West Pakistan and on the eastern side East Pakistan were carved out to form the new state of Pakistan. British India was partitioned on lines of religion and its end was one of the bloodiest episodes in the history of the subcontinent. Map I.5 shows the partitioned state of British India and the presence of the two largest religious groups, Hindu and Muslim. In 1971, East Pakistan became the independent country of Bangladesh. At the time of independence, the numerous princely states became a part of India. In 1952, the newly independent state of India became a republic.

Jawaharlal Nehru, the first Prime Minister, adopted policies that were very different from the path followed by the colonial government of the

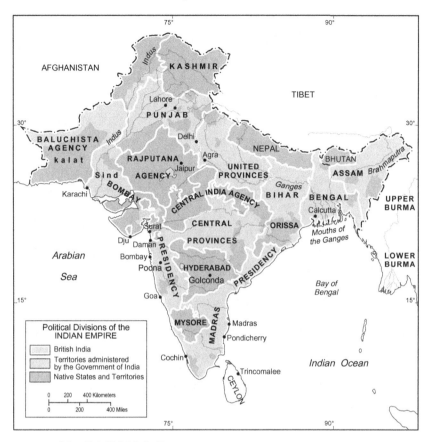

Map I.4 British India

British Empire. Colonial India had been a part of a globally connected economy. India after independence became one of the most inward-looking economies in the world. The Nehruvian policies of state that directed development have come under much criticism. However, any evaluation of the policies after independence without considering the policies under colonization and their implication for the economy ignore the context in which the post-independence policies were made and how their impact should be evaluated. By taking a historical perspective, this book will look at economic outcomes before and after 1947 and reflect on the continuity and departure from the past. The book will end with a comparison with the East Asian economies of South Korea and Taiwan that gained independence from Japanese colonization around the same

Map I.5 Partition of India

time in order to understand the historical differences that may explain
their differences in economic performance as independent countries.

I.5   A Narrative of Colonial Underdevelopment

In this book, I have used empirical evidence to understand the economic
outcomes in pre-colonial and colonial India. My analysis differs from
much of the existing literature in the following aspects. First, I argue that
the role attributed to colonial policy on the decline of traditional industries and lack of development of a modern industrial capability need
rethinking. Second, the stagnation in colonial India was not because
of developments in industry but because of the stagnation of the main

sector of the economy, which was agriculture. The provision of agricultural infrastructure was low and resulted in declining yield per acre in many parts of the country. Third, the emphasis on secondary and tertiary education rather than on an extension of primary education had consequences for the development of human capital and provided an advantage to the service sector, but deprived industry the benefit of a literate workforce.

The overall narrative of an agricultural decline is consistent with the findings that GDP per capita began to decline from the middle of the seventeenth century from a highpoint in 1600. The decline in Mughal India may be explained by falling yield per acre in agriculture as marginal land came into cultivation. The decline coincided with the rising trade in traditional textiles. The colonial government did not do enough to stem the decline in agriculture output. The changes in GDP per capita track changes in per capita agricultural output in the nineteenth century. Industry, on the other hand, did not see a systematic decline or stagnation after 1850. Modern industries in jute, tea, and cotton began to develop, assisted by the colonial state in the case of export industries but despite the colonial policies towards import substituting industries. After the First World War, the attitude of the colonial government towards import substituting industries began to change and several new industries emerged in the interwar years. A comparison with the South Korea and Taiwan emerging from Japanese colonization at the same time points to the differences in policies towards agriculture and education to understand where India lagged behind and what might explain the different outcomes in the two East Asian economies and India after 1950.

Chapter 1 provides a long view of the living standards and economic growth from the Mughal Empire to the end of British rule, followed by economic changes in independent India. Living standards are measured in terms of income categories such as average wages and estimates of per capita incomes. What was the effect of colonization on these indicators? How prosperous was Mughal India? Does the picture of the opulence of the elites in pre-colonial times and the vibrancy of urban centres represent how the average Indian lived? I show that Indian per capita GDP was 60 per cent of British level in 1600. But Indian per capita GDP began to decline from the seventeenth century, well before the conquest of Bengal by the East India Company. It stabilized in the nineteenth century and even grew a little in the latter half. The first half of the twentieth century showed stagnation and increasing divergence with Britain.

How did the economy change after independence? The policies of Nehru's government are analysed in the context of a failure of colonial policies to bring about modern economic growth and in the context of the theories of underdevelopment put forward in postcolonial settings in different parts of the world. The chapter argues that the economy moved from stagnation to positive economic growth after independence. Although the rate of growth was low compared to recent decades, it marked a structural break with its historical trend and set India on the path of modern economic growth.

Chapter 2 focuses on the largest sector of the economy, agriculture. The rural economy produced most of the output in Mughal India and British India and 85 per cent of the population lived in rural communities. How did this sector evolve over the centuries as population increased and less productive land came under cultivation? The chapter considers the successes and failures of agricultural policies before and after 1947. The economic history of India has a rich narrative of regions, of introduction of new institutions, and integration of the cultivators into commercial exchange of food and raw material at the regional level. This chapter brings together an overall narrative of the regions and explains why some regions prospered while others declined. It sees the role of infrastructure as an important part of this discussion, that is, the impact of the railways and irrigation. While British investment in irrigation and new technology in agriculture was inadequate and can explain agricultural stagnation in different parts of the country, the railways played an important role in integrating markets. The chapter ends with a discussion of the building of agricultural infrastructure after independence and the *Green Revolution* of the 1960s and it importance in economic growth and development.

Chapter 3 is about industry. In the discussion of colonization, the decline of the traditional textile industry is seen as a major cause of economic decline under colonial rule. This chapter takes a different view. The world textile market underwent significant changes with the industrial revolution in Britain and new technology in the production of cotton textiles. The effect on the traditional textile industry in India was devastating. However, this industry was a small part of the Indian economy. So, its rise in the eighteenth century and decline in the nineteenth century had significant effects in some regions, but its effect was negligible on the average living standards measured by GDP per capita. A modern industrial sector developed from the middle of the nineteenth century, which was more productive than the traditional sector and it grew rapidly. In 1947, the shares of the modern and the traditional sectors were roughly the same. Entrepreneurship and capital for the modern import substituting cotton textile industry came from the Indian trading communities. British investment in industry was initially in the export sectors, such as tea and jute, and later in the interwar period in modern import substituting new industries. I have argued in this chapter that lack of industrialization was not the major consequence of colonial policy. This sector saw a reasonable growth in productivity and size and in 1945 did not look very different from the industrial sectors in East Asian countries. Most of the industrial production was in consumer goods. The intermediate and capital goods production was limited.

After 1947, India adopted a strategy of intermediate and capital goods-led industrialization. The process of industrialization was led by the public sector with highly interventionist policies towards trade and industrial location. The role of the private sector was constrained. Yet, the industrial conglomerates owned by family-based enterprises of the Tatas and the Birlas and other industrial houses prospered and dominated the industrial sector in the second half of the twentieth century. Several of these groups had come into industry in the colonial period and grew in size and shape by venturing into new sectors.

Chapter 4 discusses the origins of India's service sector advantage. Although modern industries developed in the colonial period and the policy of public sector-led industrialization after independence led to the development of industries producing consumer, capital, and intermediate goods, the share of the sector in employment has remained low. Industry in India did not play the same role in structural transformation as it did in the context of European industrializers and in China today. The service sector in India has been the most productive sector historically. Labour productivity in services in the early twentieth century was higher than in industry. Labour productivity in industry grew faster until the 1980s and thereafter the service sector has led productivity growth. The service sector today has a concentration of workers with secondary and tertiary education, but this was also the case historically. The caste level literacy data from the colonial censuses shows high literacy in the trading castes and other upper castes, who were typically engaged in service sector occupations including medical and financial services and the civil service. The service sector-led growth in India today has historical origins. The education policies in colonial India prioritized secondary and tertiary education for a few at the cost of universal primary education. This continued after independence. Only in recent decades has expansion of primary education become a priority. India continues to spend a large share of the education budget on higher education.

No discussion of growth and development is complete without understanding the distributional consequences. Chapter 5 focuses on four different aspects of economic and social inequality. The first is regional inequality. There were historical differences in levels of economic development across provinces. The Bombay Presidency was one of the richest parts of colonial India and had been the centre of activities for several Indian trading communities involved in the Indian Ocean trade and China trade. It was also the region where the first modern cotton textile industry developed. Maharashtra and Gujarat today are among the richest provinces in India. Punjab saw investment in irrigation in colonial India and agricultural growth. It was the first region of the Green Revolution and today it ranks among the rich provinces. The poorer regions in colonial India, such as the United Provinces and the Central Provinces, rank among the poorer regions today. The regional differences in colonial India persist in many different contexts.

The second aspect is the trend in income inequality from the early twentieth century. Income inequality was high in the 1930s and 1940s and the first decades after independence saw a decline in inequality following the policies of public sector-led development. Since the economic reforms of 1980, income inequality has increased but it is not as high as in the colonial period. Unlike in many other colonies, Indians always had a substantial share in top incomes reflecting the economic prosperity of urban communities of traders and industrialists.

Third, the chapter discusses caste inequality by looking at indicators in literacy and heights in colonial India and changes in outcomes in education and jobs after the introduction of affirmative action for the lowest castes after independence. Upper castes were healthier and more literate in colonial India. There is continuity in caste inequality in many dimensions, but also changes. Lower castes have better access to education and jobs as a consequence of policies of affirmative action. However, big differences in economic and social outcomes remain.

Finally, the chapter looks at an aspect of gender inequality that is specific to India: the preference for sons. I discuss this by using the standard measure from the literature: missing women in the population, measured by sex ratio. There was a regional variation in son preference in colonial India. Biased sex ratios and female deficit was more prevalent in the north-west compared to the south and the east. The difference emerged in the early years of life, but was most pronounced in adolescence. I discuss the persistence of regional variation in sex ratio. Regions of son preference in the early twentieth century continue to have male biased sex ratios today. However, the share of missing women by age groups has shown some changes over the century. Maternal mortality in adolescence has declined, but there are more missing girls at birth due to the availability of sex-selective abortion.

Chapter 6 discusses the policies of colonization in India in a comparative perspective with Korea and Taiwan under Japanese rule. The slow growth in India after independence has been compared with the high growth in East Asia. This comparison rarely looks at the historical context, with the exception of Kohli (1994). In this chapter, I take a historical approach and consider the differences in policies of colonization. At the time of independence, the share of industry in total GDP was not very different in the three countries. Modern industries had developed in India, Korea, and Taiwan during the colonial period. The two big differences in colonial policies were with respect to agriculture and education. First, Japan imported essential food grains from the colonies, which prompted investment in improvements in agriculture to raise productivity. A large proportion of land came under irrigation in both colonies, enabling the introduction of new varieties of seeds. The British government in India did relatively little to raise agricultural productivity. Second, Japan as a colonizer expanded primary education. A large proportion of industrial workers became literate. In India, as a result of the emphasis on higher education, it was mainly the service sector occupations that benefitted in terms of human capital. The chapter argues that the history of colonization may have contributed to the divergent paths of the two regions.

In this book on Indian economic history, I offer a long run perspective on India's economic development. I analyse India's development path, bringing in data as evidence and offering a comparative perspective. The book discusses the timing of the *Great Divergence* between India and Britain and the impact of colonial policies on measures of economic development. The book also offers a comparative perspective with East Asia under a different colonizer and different policies. The first thirty years of slow growth in independent India is assessed with a historical perspective.

1 The Decline and the Rise
of the Indian Economy

In the year of independence, after 200 years of British rule, India was one of the poorest countries in the world. India was poor not just in comparison to industrialized countries; it was poor even by the standards of other developing countries. Figure 1.1 shows that Latin American countries were richer than countries in Asia and Africa. Latin American countries, such as Brazil, Argentina, and Mexico, had gained independence in the nineteenth century and therefore had designed their own policies for a century. Within Asia, Indian per capita GDP in 1990 International Geary-Khamis dollars was 619 in 1950, compared to 817 in Indonesia, 854 in South Korea, 916 in Taiwan, 1559 in Malaysia, and 1253 in Sri Lanka (see Figure 1.1). Indian GDP per capita was comparable to several countries in Africa in 1950. These countries were among the poorest in the world.

Figure 1.2 shows changes in Asian and Latin American countries between 1910 and 1950. The independent countries in Latin America grew faster, whereas the colonies grew more slowly. In particular India and Indonesia show stagnation.

Colonial rule began with the conquest of Bengal by the East Indian Company in 1757. India formally became a part of the British Empire in 1858 with a transition to Crown rule. Crown rule lasted until 1947. Did the long years of colonial rule impoverish India? Was India prosperous before the conquest by the East India Company? How can we measure prosperity in the seventeenth and eighteenth centuries?

Urbanization is often used as a measure of economic development the further we go back in history. The agricultural surplus needed to sustain cities is a measure of development. City size, city growth, and share of the urban population in a country have been used by economic historians to measure development in the context of Europe, China, and other parts of the world. Historians have suggested that India was more urban in the eighteenth century compared to the end of the nineteenth century (Roy 2013, chap. 6). The share of the urban population in India during Akbar's reign has been estimated at 15 per cent (Habib 1982a). In 1901,

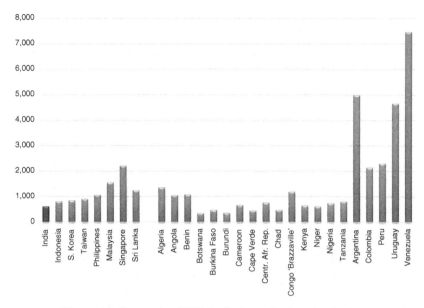

Figure 1.1 Per capita GDP in India and other developing countries
(1950) (1990 International Geary-Khamis dollars)
Source: Maddison Project database

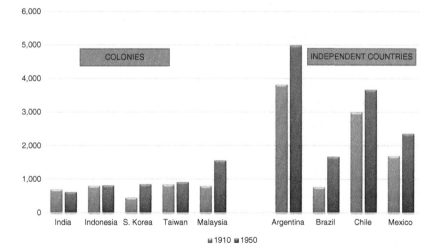

Figure 1.2 Changes in GDP per capita in Asia and Latin America
(1910–1950) (1990 International Geary-Khamis dollars)
Source: Maddison Project database

the urbanization rate was 10 per cent (Visaria and Visaria 1983). The sixteenth-century urbanization rate was not attained again until after independence. Did the decline of the urban economy suggest a decline in living standards during colonial rule?

In this chapter I explore another measure of economic development, the changes in GDP per capita. Estimates of GDP per capita for India going back to 1600 are available in the work of Broadberry et al. (2015). They allow a comparison of the average living standard in India across time starting from the reign of Akbar until the end of the nineteenth century. They also make possible comparison with other countries. After the industrial revolution, Britain was the most industrialized economy and also among the most urbanized. This chapter will look at Indian living standard in comparison with that in Britain to understand the timing of the economic divergence between India and Britain. Was the standard of living in Britain before the industrial revolution the same as in India? Did India and Britain have comparable average incomes before colonization? Due to data constraints, it is not possible to use some of the other indicators of economic development, such as life expectancy or literacy, before the late nineteenth century. I will focus on changes in real wages of unskilled urban workers as evidence as this is more easily available and provide evidence on newly estimated GDP per capita to understand the changes in the standard of living in India over four centuries.

I start with qualitative accounts of living conditions followed by quantitative evidence on real wages and estimates of per capita GDP. I evaluate the possible impact of colonial rule in economic decline and stagnation and low per capita GDP. The final section of the chapter offers a historical perspective of the changes in Indian per capita GDP after independence evaluated in the context of available evidence over 400 years.

1.1   What Do We Know: Qualitative and Quantitative Evidence?

The travelogues of Europeans in India in the sixteenth and seventeenth centuries often described the great wealth and opulence of the citizens, but this perspective reflected their narrow exposure to the ruling elites. The ruling elites enjoyed a luxurious lifestyle, enjoying high-quality food, clothing, and ornaments, and living in high-quality housing. This was a great contrast to the rudimentary lifestyle of the common men and women (Chandra 1982). Moreland, in his book *India at the Death of Akbar* (1923), described the luxurious lifestyles of the nobility, who were patrons of the arts and supported scholars, poets, physicians, painters, musicians, and dancers and employed many servants. The wealthier among the middle classes included merchants, money-lenders, and other professional groups who tried to imitate the lifestyles of the nobility. The middle class was small and the merchants that European travellers had contact with enjoyed a comfortable lifestyle (Moreland 1923).

At the same time, most travel accounts of the places outside the urban centres in Mughal India and the Deccan noted that the majority of Indians lived in poverty (Chandra 1982; Fukazawa 1982). The labouring classes lived in mud huts with thatched roofs, consumed inferior grains, had minimal clothing, and most did not use footwear. Wheat was not widely consumed, even in the wheat producing areas, and inferior grains such *as jowar and bajra* were grown everywhere (Moreland 1923, pp. 197–203). Pelsaert, a representative of the Dutch East India Company who was in Agra in the early seventeenth century, commented on the contrast between the extravagant luxury of the ruling classes and the poverty of the masses (Thatcher 1926). Francis Buchanan (1807), an employee of the East India Company, conducted surveys in the Bengal and Mysore regions and documented the economic conditions in the first decades of the nineteenth century. Buchanan claimed that, although weavers enjoyed a comfortable lifestyle, the majority of cultivators lived in poverty. Moreland (1923) confirms that the poverty of the majority was largely unchanged in the early twentieth century.

An assessment of Indian lifestyle by Europeans based on the type of clothing, footwear, and furniture used in their homes reflected the cultural values of the writers and is not an objective assessment. However, information on the type of food consumed and the quality of dwellings provides valuable information to make comparisons possible, despite the cultural prejudice that might have characterized the comments by European travellers. By distinguishing between the lifestyles of the elites and those of the common men and women, these accounts documented the inequality between the rich and the poor.

There exist other sources that come from local observers, but these are relatively rare. Abul Fazl, a member of Akbar's court who documented the economic conditions during Akbar's reign, commented on the basic lifestyle of the common people (Chandra 1982). Analysing temple records in Southern India, Ramaswamy (1985) confirms a similar picture. There was a prosperous nobility, a small middle class of weavers, and a populous group of rural poor and low-caste artisans. The rich and the middle social classes consumed rice, but others could only afford inferior grain, such as *ragi* (Ramaswamy 1985, pp. 99–100).

A different view comes from the work of Parthasarathi (1998, 2011) and Sivramkrishna (2009) using evidence from Southern India. Parthasarathi (1998) compares the living standard of weavers in South India with that of the British weavers in the mid-eighteenth century. Using wages of weavers documented by the East India Company, Parthasarathi finds that, in real terms, they were similar to that of British weavers. More recently, Sivramkrishna (2009) used evidence from Buchanan's survey of Mysore to calculate living standards in terms of the consumption of a cheaper grain, *ragi*, rather than rice. This comparison suggests that wages in many occupations reflect living standards well above subsistence at the beginning of the nineteenth century, although not at the level of parity with English weavers that Parthasarathi found.

Another indicator of economic development that historians can use in the absence of other systematic data is the relative price of factors of production. Wages as the price of labour indicate the relative abundance or scarcity of labour, and similarly rental cost of capital indicates its scarcity or abundance. Typically, low wages are correlated with lower indicators of economic development. Pelsaert (1925) and Bernier (1916) refer to the scarcity of capital and cheapness of labour (Habib 1969). In all sectors, from palaces and royal courts to services for the nobility, foreigners noted the excess employment relative to Europe, pointing to labour abundance. While European writers spoke of the high quality and skills of the craftsmen, they noted the rudimentary nature of the technology used and the sparing use of metal, indicating that the mining and engineering sectors were underdeveloped. Pelsaert noted with respect to crafts in Agra: 'For a job which one man would do in Holland, here it passes through four men's hands before it is finished' (Habib 1969).

Bayly's (1983) description of a thriving market economy in North India during the eighteenth century leaves an impression of a prosperous, mainly urban, commercial sector but says little about the living standards of the vast majority of the population, even in the urban centres. Bayly's rich account of the vibrancy of markets does not quantify the size of the commercial sector nor its share in GDP and therefore it cannot say much about the representativeness of this sector and how the average Indian lived. While cultural and climatic conditions can explain some of the consumption differences between India and Europe, most qualitative accounts suggest that the average Indian lived in poverty. The image of the prosperous weaver, or the rich nobility, or a vibrant commercial sector did not represent the living standard of the majority of Indians.

1.2   Quantitative Measures of Living Standards

The first accounts using quantitative indicators of living standards come from the work of Shireen Moosvi (1973, 1977, 2015) and Najaf Haider (2004) for North India, and Vijaya Ramaswamy (1985) and Brennig

(1986) for South India. In their research spanning decades, Irfan Habib and Shireen Moosvi methodically documented the economic markers in Mughal India, from wages, prices, and interest rates to agricultural productivity and fiscal capacity. The first step for building time series evidence can be found in Mukherjee's (1967) estimates of real wages from 1600. The book puts together data on wages and prices from different parts of the country, so that real wages can be calculated at the regional level. Broadberry and Gupta (2006) took a further step to construct silver and grain wages for North and South India, using systematic evidence of wages and prices from different sources for all regions of India. This made it possible to compare long-run development of the Indian economy with that of other countries.

The starting point is 1595, in India under Akbar. Wages from different occupations were documented in Abul Fazl (1595) *Ā' īn–i-Akbarī* and can be classified into skilled and unskilled wages. This is a reference point for real wage comparisons over the next centuries. Desai (1972) claimed that, at best, the average standard of living in 1961 was no higher than in 1595 in Mughal India. The average wage during Akbar's reign would buy fewer industrial goods, such as clothing, but it could buy more food, given the relative prices between agriculture and industry in the sixteenth century. The average wage in 1961 could buy less food but more cloth than the average wage in 1595. (Desai, 1972) while this comparison was useful in assessing Indian living standards soon after independence with pre-colonial Mughal India, it did not say anything about the intervening centuries. When did the decline begin? Did colonization contribute to the real wage decline and stagnation over the centuries or did the decline begin before the conquest of Bengal by the East India Company?

Mukherjee (1967) found a downward trend in real wages during the seventeenth and eighteenth centuries, before recovering during the twentieth century. Based on evidence from 1595 and other archival and secondary sources for the seventeenth, eighteenth, and nineteenth centuries, Broadberry and Gupta (2006) constructed a wage series over this period for northern, western, and southern India. Using prices of the staple foods, such as rice or wheat, depending on the region, and a representative selection of wages from different regions for unskilled and skilled workers, they constructed a series for money wages and grain wages. Money wages show the nominal value of wage and the grain wage computes the purchasing power of the wage in terms of food grains. This data can be used to establish not only the trend in living standards over the centuries, but also what Indian living standards might have looked like relative to the prosperous societies of Northwest Europe (Table 1.1).

1.3   Silver Wage and Grain Wage

The simplest way to think of grain wage is how much food the money wage of a typical unskilled worker would buy. A similar calculation can be made for a typical skilled worker. The grain wage of an unskilled worker proxies the lowest wages in the economy and is therefore a good measure of the average living standard. The difference between wages of skilled and unskilled workers is also indicative of the skill premia in the economy and the relative shortage of skilled workers and therefore the level of economic development measured in terms of human capital.

The established practice in the literature for measuring living standards in Europe across time and place has been to gather data on money wages of unskilled and skilled workers and convert these to a common unit of grams of silver. This gives us the silver wage. Converting money wages in various currencies to a silver standard makes international comparisons possible. The silver wage is then divided by the silver price of the common local grain. This would give us the grain wage, a crude but common measure of the standard of living. If prices of non-food items in consumption are not available, then measuring the purchasing power of wage in terms of grain price is a reasonable approximation of real wage in subsistence economies. The closer an economy is to subsistence, the more accurate is the grain wage as a measure of living standards, since a large part of the income is spent on basic foods for survival. The more industrial an economy, the more diversified is the consumption basket. It contains more processed foods and industrial products. If we do not consider a suitable consumption basket, this would bias the grain wage. However, during the period of the comparison in this chapter, most economies were close to subsistence and therefore grain wage is a good approximation of real wage. This method has been applied to India by Broadberry and Gupta (2006).

Part A of Table 1.1 shows silver wages and grain wages in northern and western India, drawing largely on sources for Agra and Surat. Note that these are urban wages and there is little information on rural wages. Grain wages in northern and western India are obtained by dividing the silver wages by the price of wheat, the main grain produced in the region, expressed in terms of silver. Although the silver wages rose between 1595 and 1874, grain wages declined in northern and western India as money wages failed to keep up with rising grain prices.

Data for southern India is in part B of Table 1.1. The wage and price data are largely from the area around Madras and in many cases are the wages of skilled and unskilled workers in textile weaving. Money wage

Table 1.1 *Indian silver and grain wages (1595–1874)*

(A) Northern and western India

	Silver wage (grams per day)		Wheat grain wage (kg per day)		Rice grain wage (kg per day)	
	Unskilled	Skilled	Unskilled	Skilled	Unskilled	Skilled
1595	0.67	1.62	5.2	12.6	3.1	7.5
1616	0.86		3.0		2.4	
1623	1.08		3.8		2.9	
1637	1.08	2.37	3.8	8.3	2.9	6.5
1640	1.29		4.5		3.5	
1690	1.40		4.3			
1874	1.79	5.27	2.5	7.5		

(B) Southern India

	Silver wage (grams per day)		Rice grain wage (kg per day)	
	Unskilled	Skilled	Unskilled	Skilled
1610–13	1.15		5.7	
1600–50	1.15		3.2	
1680	1.44	2.44	3.9	6.9
1741–50	1.49		2.1	
1750	(3.02)*	(7.56)*	(4.2)*	(10.5)*
1779	0.86		1.1	
1790	1.44		1.8	

Note: * These figures come from Parthasarathi (1998) and are outliers compared to the rest of the series. These wages may have been isolated cases of high-skilled weavers
Source: Broadberry and Gupta (2006, p. 14)

rates here are available in pagoda units, a gold coin, and are converted to silver rupees using East India Company's standard rates from Chaudhuri (1978). Silver wages for Southern India are then converted to grain wages using the price of rice, the main grain consumed in the region, as the deflator. Overall, the levels and trends of silver and grain wages in Southern India fit well with the levels and trends in the North, except in 1750. As explained in the note Figure 1.1, these particular wages are outliers.

To make any normative statement about the standard of living, we need to have a measure of the subsistence level. Brennig (1986) argues that subsistence consumption for a household of six was 3.1 kg of rice

Table 1.2 *An England–India comparison of the daily wages of unskilled labourers (1550–1849)*

(A) Silver wages (grams of silver per day)

Date	Southern England	India	Indian wage as a % of English wage
1550–99	3.4	0.7	21
1600–49	4.1	1.1	27
1650–99	5.6	1.4	25
1700–49	7.0	1.5	21
1750–99	8.3	1.2	14
1800–49	14.6	1.8	12

(B) Grain wages (kilograms of grain per day)

| | England | | India | |
Date	(wheat)	(wheat)	(rice, on wheat equivalent basis)	Indian wage as a % of English wage
1550–99	6.3	5.2		83
1600–49	4.0	3.8		95
1650–99	5.4	4.3		80
1700–49	8.0		3.2	40
1750–99	7.0		2.3	33
1800–49	8.6	2.5		29

Source: Broadberry and Gupta (2006, tables 5 and 6)

per day. The wheat/rice ratio of calories per lb gives the calorie equivalence of 4.7 kg of wheat per day for a family of six (Parthasarathi 1998, p. 83). On this basis, grain wages were always above subsistence for skilled workers but fell below the subsistence level for unskilled workers during the seventeenth century. This raises the question: how did the families of unskilled labourers survive? The evidence suggests that, although we use the price of rice and wheat as the deflator, poorer families tended to consume mainly cheaper grains such as *ragi*, as discussed by Sivramkrishna (2009). Rice and wheat prices are used because the market price of these goods is recorded more systematically. Therefore, the tables capture the declining trend in grain wage rather than suggesting that people lived below the subsistence level.

Table 1.2 provides a comparison of silver and grain wages for unskilled labourers in England and India. Part A shows that Indian silver wages for unskilled workers were little more than one-fifth of the English level in the late sixteenth century and fell to just over one-seventh of the English level during the eighteenth century. Part B of Table 1.2, the grain wage, shows that India remained closer to the English level until the end of the seventeenth century. The data indicates a sharp divergence during the eighteenth century, partly due to a rise in the English grain wage, and partly due to a decline in the Indian grain wage. Table 1.1 shows the decline in Indian living standards, from a high point in 1595 for northern India and in 1610 for Southern India. Table 1.2 illustrates the timing of the Great Divergence. The grain wage declined from 80 to 95 per cent of the British wage to less than 30 per cent by the middle of the nineteenth century. The table also shows that the decline began well before colonization.

I noted that grain wage is a crude approximation of living standards and therefore has two limitations. As stated before, it is more accurate at low levels of economic development when grain accounts for a very large share of consumption. Another concern is that grain wage is calculated mainly with urban wages and prices and gives a biased view for economies that are agricultural. In the following section I will discuss the refinements that have been introduced in estimating real wages.

1.4   Real Consumption Wages and Welfare Ratios

The first step towards a different measure of consumption is to introduce a cloth wage. The simplest consumption basket consists of grain and cloth. Historical prices of cloth and grain are more easily available than for many other goods. The cloth wage is constructed by systematically collecting evidence on the price of cotton cloth in India from the records of the East India Company for the period before 1833 and from Parliamentary Papers for subsequent years (Broadberry and Gupta 2015). The cloth wage represents the amount of cloth the silver wage would buy and indicates that changes in the relative price of cloth and grain that can affect consumption of cloth. A basic subsistence basket includes both grain and cloth and therefore a weighted average of the grain wage and the cloth wage would be a better measure of a real consumption wage. Consumers' budgets during this period (Allen 2007; Buchanan 1807) typically shows that consumers spent two-thirds on grain. The typical consumption basket is more diversified, but a consumption wage using basic shares of grain and cloth is a good approximation of the real wage when prices of all commodities are not available systematically.

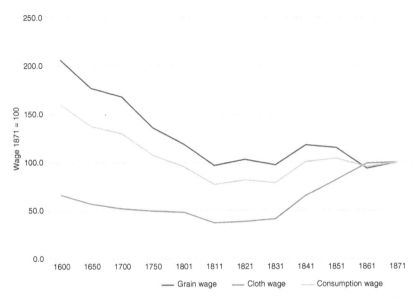

Figure 1.3 Grain wage, cloth wage, and consumption wage (1600–1871): 1871=100
Source: Broadberry and Gupta (2015, table 2.3)

Figure 1.3 presents these different measures of living standards: the grain wage, the cloth wage and the real consumption wage using a weighted average of grain and cloth. The cloth wage started at a lower level, did not change much during the seventeenth and eighteenth centuries, and increased substantially during the nineteenth century. This reflects the change in the price of cloth relative to the price of grain. The turning point came in 1851 with the arrival of cheaper, machine-made cloth from Britain. Cloth consumption per capita increased from the second half of the nineteenth century. This is in line with the evidence from Desai (1972) a century later that the average wage in 1961 could have bought less food but more cloth than the average wage in 1595. As Figure 1.3 shows, the grain wage in 1871 was half of what it was in 1595, the cloth wage rose, and the real consumption wage declined (although less than the grain wage) and rose in the nineteenth century.

What did the actual consumption basket of an unskilled worker in the seventeenth century look like? Allen (2007) constructed a consumption basket for northern India and Bengal that included a variety of food items such as the basic grain, usually rice or millet, and other comparable foods using the items that were common in a basic European basket of this period, and non-food, such as cloth.

Table 1.3 *Allen's bare-bones consumption basket for India*

	Rice-based consumption			Millet-based consumption		
	Quantity per year	Nutrition per person		Quantity per year	Nutrition per person	
The basket	Kilogram	Calories	Protein	Kilogram	Calories	Protein
Rice	164	1627	34			
Millet				209	1731	63
Beans	20	199	11	10	100	5
Meat	3	21	1	3	21	1
Ghi	3	72	0	3	72	0
Sugar	2	21	0	2	21	0
Cotton cloth	3 metres			3 metres		
Total		1940	46		1945	69

Source: Allen (2007)

Allen (2007) went on to construct welfare ratios, defined as the number of consumption baskets that can be purchased with the average annual earnings of a wage labourer using that country's typical subsistence consumption basket. A welfare ratio above one indicates that wages are sufficient for a society to feed itself. Allen (2007) compares living standards in England and India by introducing the concept of a European respectability consumption basket. This included grain, bread, beans, cheese, meat, eggs, butter, beer, linen, candles, lamp oil, and fuel. British workers enjoyed a welfare ratio of one or above. Using a basket that included equivalent consumption items in the Indian context, Allen found that the welfare ratio for India was always below one, except in 1600. Table 1.3 shows Allen's bare-bones subsistence consumption baskets for India based on rice, the superior grain, and millet, an inferior grain. The welfare ratios calculated using the bare-bones subsistence basket rarely fell below one.

Allen's (2007) international comparison of real consumption wages between England and India broadly confirms the grain wage findings of Broadberry and Gupta (2006). Real consumption wages in North India and Bengal were close to the English level in the early seventeenth century but fell substantially behind during the eighteenth century.

There is evidence on the actual consumption basket from Bengal and Mysore from Buchanan's survey of the 1810s. This basket gives us a glimpse into the lifestyle of the poorest people from a few districts in Bengal in the early nineteenth century. Eighty per cent of the consumer expenditure was

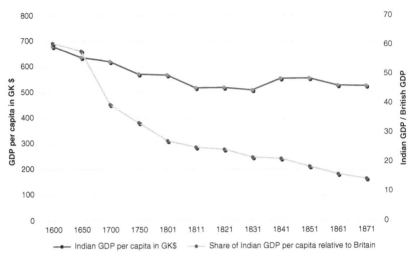

Figure 1.4 Absolute and relative decline of Indian GDP per capita (1600–1871)
Source: Broadberry et al. (2015)

on food, which included coarse rice, lentils, oil, and salt. All fish, meat, and fuel were gathered, not bought in the market (Buchanan's survey of Dinajpur, 1833, pp. 149–150). Other evidence from the survey shows that most of the expenditure was on food for labourers, with minimal expenditure on dwellings and clothing and some expenditure on religious ceremonies. A comparable expenditure pattern was observed in surveys of the consumption of Bombay cotton mill workers in the 1920s.

The unskilled workers were relatively better off in India under Akbar, according to the indicators of grain wage, consumption wage, and Allen's welfare ratio, than at the end of colonial rule. The decline in the grain wage during the seventeenth and eighteenth centuries was accompanied by an increase in population from 142 million in 1600 to 207 million in 1801 (Visaria and Visaria 1983, p. 466). Grain wage stagnated as the population rose further to 256 million in 1871, but the growth rate of population was not high. Periodic famines created spikes in grain prices, sometimes with devastating consequences for mortality, until the beginning of the twentieth century (Broadberry and Gupta 2015). The main decline in grain wage occurred in the seventeenth and eighteenth centuries. As Figure 1.4 shows, most of the nineteenth century saw stagnation. While Akbar's reign was the high point in living standards, the decline began well before colonization and coincided with the rising trade in textiles and the decline of the Mughal Empire.

1.5 From Wages to Per Capita Income: Historical National Accounting

So far, this is a picture of Indian economic performance before 1871 based on wages and prices. One limitation of wages is that most wages are from non-agricultural activities, while most of the population in India was engaged in agriculture. Therefore, a full assessment of living standard requires information on the population engaged in agriculture. This requires us to move from wages to GDP per capita, which is a challenging task going back in history.

To estimate GDP for India over several centuries, Broadberry, Custodis, and Gupta (2015) followed the historical national accounting methodology that has been used to estimate GDP for several European countries and increasingly for countries outside Europe. The method builds demand side estimates of sectoral output for a given population on the basis of what is needed for subsistence. The estimates are then revised based on income elasticity of demand using information on wages. The robustness of the demand side estimates come from cross-checks with supply side estimates of sectoral output at given points in time for which information is available. Broadberry et al. (2015) used this methodology to have demand side estimates with the currently available Indian data on population and consumption, and the series analysed earlier on wages, grain prices, and cloth prices. The estimation used data on agricultural and industrial exports, crop yields and cultivated acreage, cloth consumption per capita, urbanization rates, and government revenue to build up to aggregate output for agriculture, industry, and services from the supply side in benchmark years. This provides the first systematic long-run estimates of GDP per capita, challenging Angus Maddison's estimates that started in 1000 CE. Maddison assumed that most economies were at subsistence and therefore his estimates of Indian GDP per capita show no change until modern economic growth in the twentieth century. The new estimates are based on careful analysis of available statistical evidence and show changes over the centuries.

In Table 1.4, agricultural output is constructed from the demand side using data on population, wages, and prices to estimate domestic demand and data on exports for foreign demand. These demand-based estimates are then cross-checked with agricultural supply, estimated using data on crop yields and the cultivated land area. Industrial production for the domestic market can also be estimated from information on wages and prices and cross-checked against independent information on cloth consumption per capita. Output of the export industries is based

Table 1.4 *Changes in GDP by sector (1600–1871) (1871=100)*

Year	Agriculture	Industry and commerce	Rent and services	Government	Total output	Per capita GDP
1600	67.8	80.0	95.5	84.3	71.9	129.7
1650	63.8	75.3	95.5	48.2	67.3	121.2
1700	72.2	87.0	103.0	60.4	75.7	118.2
1750	76.8	97.0	110.8	46.9	81.3	109.6
1801	79.3	127.0	120.7	74.5	87.5	108.2
1811	76.0	104.6	125.3	77.3	82.9	98.8
1821	72.9	89.0	110.3	70.6	79.2	98.9
1831	77.5	82.4	116.2	71.3	81.8	97.0
1841	82.8	92.9	104.6	79.3	87.3	105.5
1851	91.5	99.6	114.4	87.8	95.9	105.8
1861	89.2	107.3	109.4	86.9	95.6	100.3
1871	100	100	100	100	100	100.0

Source: Broadberry et al. (2015, table 11)

on the export data collected by the European East India Companies. A weighted average of the output of home and export industries is used to estimate changes in industry and commerce. For services, the output of the government sector is measured using data on tax revenue, while the size of the private services and the rent sector is assumed to move in line with the urban population. The cross-checks, where possible, match estimated agricultural output from the supply and demand sides and the estimation of home industrial output matches with independent estimates of cloth consumption per head.

Table 1.4 shows that total industry and commerce grew rapidly between 1650 and 1801. This sector includes home industry and export industry. The latter grew faster in the seventeenth and eighteenth centuries as Figure 1.5 shows, driven by exports of cotton cloth. This industry grew rapidly as European trading companies traded in cotton cloth that dominated the international market. The decline of this industry in the nineteenth century, when British cotton textiles flooded the Indian market, is known as deindustrialization. The agricultural sector grew, but more slowly. Total output or GDP growth, although positive, failed to keep pace with a slow growth in population during this period. This is shown in the last column. The index of per capita GDP is then converted into 1990 International Geary-Khamis dollars to get comparable estimates to British GDP per capita. As Table 1.5 shows, in 1600 Indian GDP per capita was just over 60 per cent of the British level, but by 1871 it had declined to under 15 per cent.

Table 1.5 *Indian and British GDP per capita (1600–1871)*
(1990 International Geary-Khamis dollars)

Year	Indian GDP per capita	British GDP per capita	Indian GDP per capita/British GDP per capita (%)
1600	682	1,123	61
1650	638	1,100	58
1700	622	1,563	40
1750	576	1,710	36
1801	569	2,083	27
1811	519	2,065	25
1821	520	2,133	24
1831	510	2,349	22
1841	555	2,613	21
1851	556	2,997	19
1861	528	3,311	16
1871	526	3,657	14

Source: Broadberry et al. (2015, table 14)

The timeline of this decline is shown in Figure 1.5. As the blue line shows, India's per capita GDP declined from a high point in 1600, when it was well above Maddison's subsistence level per capita GDP of $550 (1990 International Geary-Khamis dollars). By the early nineteenth century, the level was close to that estimated by Maddison. India's relative decline with respect to Britain was in part due to the absolute decline of Indian living standards and in part due to Britain's growing prosperity. The new estimates of GDP per capita by Broadberry et al. (2015) confirm the findings based on the wage data that the gap in living standards between India and Britain was relatively small during Akbar's reign. The decline began during the next phase of the Mughal Empire and continued under the first decades of East India Company rule. The nineteenth century saw stagnation rather than decline with short periods of economic growth that were not sustained.

The phenomenal rise in industrial exports from India, as shown in Figure 1.5, had a small effect on GDP because industry was a small part of the economy. Indian economic growth was largely driven by agriculture, the largest sector. This is shown in Figure 1.6. The trend GDP per capita did not track the changes in exports per capita in industry and agriculture. While industrial exports per capita rose sharply, this was not reflected in GDP per capita. Instead GDP per capita tracked agricultural output per capita all the way up to 1871.

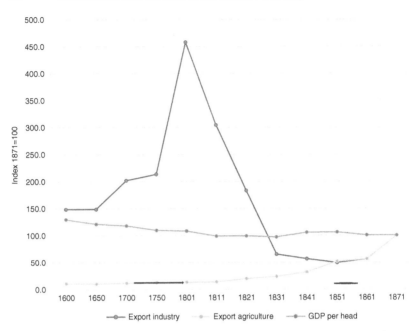

Figure 1.5 Industrial and agricultural exports per capita relative to GDP per capita (1871=100)
Source: Broadberry et al. (2015)

As Table 1.5 shows, the beginning of the Great Divergence can be traced back to the seventeenth century. Indian GDP per capita declined relative to Britain, but also relative to its high point in 1600. Contrary to the view that the golden age of textile exports from India to the rest of the world had made the country prosperous, this chapter has shown that there was economic decline in the seventeenth and eighteenth centuries. The political aspects of the decline in the seventeenth and eighteenth centuries have been explored, but more research is needed to understand the economic decline of this period. One possible explanation is that most of the fertile plains were already densely populated and as populations moved out of this area, the marginal land was less fertile and produced less output per head. Without more extensive irrigation and better technology, agricultural output could not keep pace with population growth. The declining trend in GDP per capita during the seventeenth and eighteenth centuries occurred in China as well as India. In both countries, this was driven mainly by trends in agriculture, as population growth outstripped the growth in cultivated land area and crop yields did not increase sufficiently to offset the decline in the land-labour ratio.

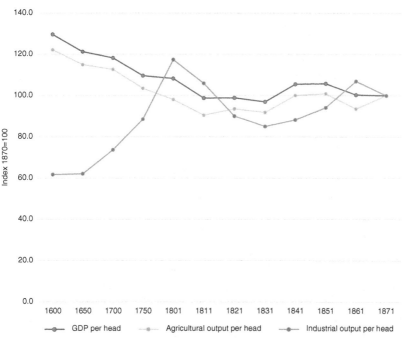

Figure 1.6 Agricultural and industrial output per capita relative to
GDP per capita (1871=100)
Source: Broadberry et al. (2015)

1.6   Globalization and Stagnation: Economic
Performance 1860 to 1947

From 1871 there are systematic annual estimates of GDP by Alan Heston
(1983) covering 1870–1900 and Sivasubramonian (2000) from 1900 to
2000. These studies have been conducted within a national accounting
framework, drawing on the wider availability of statistical information from
the beginning of Crown rule. From Table 1.6, we can observe short periods
of growth in GDP per capita during the late nineteenth century. From the
turn of the twentieth century GDP per capita stagnated and since 1950
it has grown, indicating a transition to sustained economic growth. The
Indian economy grew faster than the historical trend but has lagged behind
more successful East Asian countries. However, East Asia was an exception among countries emerging from colonization. I will return to this in
Chapter 6. The stagnation of Indian incomes and living standards over
100 years of Crown rule points to a failure of colonial policies to generate
modern economic growth. Although India became more integrated into

Table 1.6 *Economic growth in the long run (% per year)*

	Per capita income
1870–1885*	0.5
1885–1900*	0.8
1900–1947	0.1
1950–1980	1.4
1980–1990	3.0
1990–2000	4.1

Source: Gupta (2019, table 1) based on
*Heston (1983) and Sivasubramonian (2000)

the trading world of the British Empire and could have access to the British capital market, the stagnation was driven by stagnation in agriculture, as I will discuss in Chapter 2. The literature has emphasized the decline of the indigenous textile sector as a cause of economic decline in the nineteenth century. This impacted on communities engaged in this sector. Its effect on average living standards was small because the industrial sector was a small part of the economy, as I have argued in this chapter.

Why did a globalized economy fall into stagnation? Was the integration of India into the global network of the British Empire harmful to economic growth? By the middle of the nineteenth century, Britain had abolished the Corn Laws that imposed tariffs on grain imports and adopted the doctrine of free trade, a policy that suited Britain's industrial specialization and demand for imported raw materials for the industrial sector. Free trade was imposed on India and other colonies. It is not clear that free trade was the appropriate policy for India at this time, when most countries, including the USA and Germany, were using tariffs to industrialize and grow. The data points to some growth of the Indian economy between 1870 and 1900, when India integrated into the global trading network of the British Empire, but this was short-lived. (see Table 1.6).

The effect of trade on growth, and the differential effect of trade on producers of agricultural and producers of manufactured goods, are debated issues. Theories of trade based on comparative advantage can be applied to colonial trade. Both countries could gain by specializing in the production of goods that could be produced more efficiently. The colonies specialized in agricultural goods and the imperial countries specialized in industrial goods. The colonies gained from the growing demand for food and raw material in the industrial countries and saw rising incomes. The Prebisch–Singer thesis cautioned against

Table 1.7 *Share of trade in income: from colonial times to independent India (%)*

Year	Trade/GDP
1835*	1.1–2.4
1857*	3.6–4.8
1913*	>20
1950–1960	6.8
1960–1970	5.2
1970–1980	6.0
1980–1990	7.0
1990–2000	10.0

Source: Sivasubramonian (2004, table 5.7); *Roy (2006, table 2.1)

this by showing empirically that the terms of trade of agricultural products relative to industrial products declined from the middle of the nineteenth century to the middle of the twentieth century and argued that specialization in agricultural production was not beneficial for economic development (Singer 1989). In reality, the nineteenth century saw divergence in living standards between agricultural and industrial countries, with a few exceptions (Findlay and O'Rourke 2009, p. 415). Cross-country data from the second half of the twentieth century finds a positive effect of trade on per capita GDP (Frankel and Romer 1999). However, the evidence from the nineteenth century is mixed. Mitchener and Weidenmier (2008) show that being part of an empire increased the volume of trade compared to countries outside the empire. Pascali (2017) uses cross-country data to show that, for colonies, trade did not always have a positive effect on indicators of economic development. Countries with good institutions benefitted from trade, but others did not and trade may have contributed to the increasing divergence between developed and underdeveloped economies. Therefore, even without considering implications of terms of trade, trade did not necessarily lead to higher incomes in the nineteenth century.

As India integrated into the world economy, trade, investment, and migration rose. The trade–GDP ratio increased dramatically, from 2 to 3 per cent in the mid-1800s to 20 per cent on the eve of the First World War (see Table 1.7). India received 8 per cent of British overseas investment during 1865–1914 (Gupta 2021). This was not sufficient to raise the rate of gross capital formation above 7 per cent of GDP. Most of this investment went to the railways.

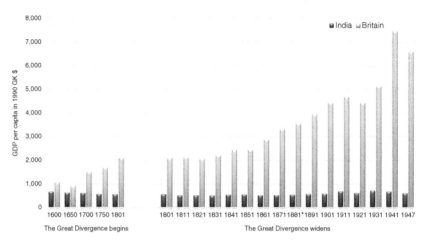

Figure 1.7 The Great Divergence between India and Britain (1600–1947)
Source: Gupta (2019)

The nationalist historians have argued that the railways integrated the agricultural hinterland and the ports, and paved the way for a rising volume of trade in agricultural goods that supported industrial Britain's demand for food and raw material. I have argued that, despite rising trade, the effect on economic growth was small. This is consistent with Pascali's (2017) argument that not all countries gained from trade in the first period of globalization. Britain enjoyed a positive trade balance with India. India imported more from Britain than from the rest of the world and exported less to Britain compared to the rest of the world. India's net exports were positive all through this period, but net exports to Britain turned negative from the 1870s (Gupta 2018). During the interwar years, India's trade with Britain became more concentrated with the policy of Imperial Preference. Differential tariffs benefitted Britain at the cost of other trading partners (Arthi et al. 2024).

Figure 1.7 shows an increasing divergence between Britain and Indian per capita GDP over the colonial period. The divergence increased during the first half of the twentieth century as British income increased and Indian income stagnated. As discussed in this section, integration into the global economy of the British Empire did not increase the investment rate or have a significant effect on growth. Stagnation in per capita GDP paralleled agricultural stagnation in the first half of the twentieth century. This will be discussed in Chapter 2.

1.7 Stagnation to Modern Economic Growth: From Free Trade to Regulation

In 1947, the newly independent state of India moved away from the colonial policies. The first step was to set out an agenda for industrialization and break with the global economy. Global integration and the specialization in agriculture was seen as a hindrance to economic development. This view was expressed in other parts of the under-developed world too. The Economic Commission of Latin America, under Raul Prebisch, raised similar concerns. The newly independent states of South Korea and Taiwan adopted industrialization as a goal. Newly independent states in Africa moved in a similar direction a decade later.

To the policymakers in the less developed countries, an open economy was a part of the imperial connection, and an international division of labour based on comparative advantage had adverse consequences on economic development. Industrialization was the way to change this division of labour. While national prestige and tariffs to protect an infant industry had motivated economic policy towards industrialization in nineteenth century Europe and the USA, the rhetoric in post-colonial countries was to break with their imperial connection and move away from specialization in agriculture. The policies for industrialization adopted in the twentieth century were far more interventionist. In the industrialization of Japan and the Soviet Union in the first half of the twentieth century, the state had played a more important role. After 1945, policy makers in Latin America adopted import-substituting industrialization as the goal. Countries gaining independence from colonial rule in Asia and Africa followed a similar path. Import-substituting industrialization was the path of economic development in the less developed world in the 1950s and 1960s. In the short term it raised the rate of growth in many countries. The outcome in the medium and long term, depended on how countries reoriented their policies to reintegrate into the global economy. Newly independent countries in East Asia, such as South Korea and Taiwan, initially followed policies of import-substituting industrialization and regulated international trade. East Asian countries embraced the Japanese model and moved quickly towards reintegration with the international market. Many import-substituting economies, including India, remained protectionist, with adverse consequences on growth.

The vision of Jawaharlal Nehru, India's first prime minister, was industrialization and self-sufficiency not global connections. Industrial development was at the core of this policy. India moved from being an open economy to one of the most regulated economies in the world. GDP per capita grew at less than 2 per cent per year, which was low in comparison to the fast-growing economies in East Asia. In comparison with other developing countries, India was not that different. Delong (2003) sees India's performance under planning as average rather than disastrous. Output per worker and the share of investment in GDP was comparable to the average developing country during the period 1960–1992.

The new government introduced Soviet-style five-year plans that set targets for different sectors, regulated international trade, restricted the entry of the private sector into certain industries, and put the public sector in control of the development of intermediate and capital goods industries. A full discussion of the successes and failures of this policy will be taken up in the next chapters. At this point, it is worth noting that the increase in economic growth was due to rising agricultural growth and rapid industrial growth in the early phase of import-substituting industrialization. The policies of state-directed development pulled India out of stagnation, but did not turn it into a high-growth economy.

The country faced several economic and political crises in the 1960s and 1970s. The monsoons failed in 1965 and 1966 with a consequent fall in grain output by 10–20 per cent and India turned to the USA for food aid, which undermined the policy of self-reliance. American food assistance came with the demand for a devaluation of the rupee to ensure greater integration with the global economy. The lack of adequate export earnings showed the vulnerability of inward-looking developmental policies and industrial growth based on import substitution began to slow down. The country did not have enough foreign exchange reserves to pay for food imports. The crisis saw a change in the direction of policies towards agriculture. Infrastructure and subsidized inputs to facilitate adoption of high yielding varieties of seeds paved the way towards the *Green Revolution*. Chapter 2 will discuss these changes and their implications in more detail.

The political crises that followed changed the nature of Indian politics. The Congress-led government under Nehru had commanded support in all parts of the country. With Nehru's death in 1964, the political leadership passed on to Lal Bahadur Shastri as prime minister. Shastri's untimely death in 1968 created a vacuum in leadership and Nehru's daughter, Indira Gandhi, became prime minister. She did not have the same support. The Congress Party split into two groups. Gandhi built her own brand of socialist developmental policies by nationalizing Indian banks in 1969 and removing the *privy purse* that the rulers of the princely states enjoyed as a compensation for giving up territorial sovereignty of the regions they had ruled at the time of independence. Gandhi invoked the rhetoric of 'get rid of poverty' and signalled redistribution from the privileged to the poor. In reality, Gandhi centralized political power and in 1975 suspended the carefully built democratic institutions of the country.

The 1970s brought further political crisis. The Green Revolution in agriculture had created a strong agricultural lobby whose interests were different to that of industry. New political parties representing agricultural interests demanded more subsidies towards agriculture and different economic policies. The new political groups fragmented the political space and weakened the dominant position of the Congress. When Gandhi called elections in 1977, she was defeated. Indian politics had changed forever from being dominated by the Congress to several regional political parties dominant in the provinces, creating more political competition on the national stage. A number of regional and group-based parties held the balance of power and short-lived coalitions were in government until Gandhi's re-election in 1980.

In the new regime, the focus of economic policy turned from redistribution to growth. The years leading to the assassination of Indira Gandhi in 1984 and the election of Rajiv Gandhi as prime minister saw a new direction in policy making. From state-directed development in the first three decades after independence, economic policy signalled a greater role to the private sector. The first step was the dismantling of industrial regulation and a gradual removal of industrial licensing. Second, the extensive quantitative controls of trade, such as import quotas, were replaced with price-based controls such as tariffs and subsidies. Both policies opened up opportunities for the private sector, that had previously faced barriers to entry in several industries.

Rodrik and Subramanian (2005) and Kohli (2006) distinguish between the 'pro-business' reforms of the 1980s, when the regulatory framework towards private investment was relaxed, and the 'pro-market' reforms that followed a large devaluation of the Indian rupee in 1991. Rodrik and Subramanian (2005) see the removal of industrial licenses and price controls as indicative of an 'attitudinal shift' towards the private sector. Private investment was given access to new sectors and faced a favourable environment. The 'pro-market' changes, on the other hand, were indicative of opening up the economy to international competition. Rodrik and Subramanian (2005) argue that, during the years of planned industrialization, the Indian economy was at some distance

Table 1.8 *Accounting for growth: a long view (1950/51=100)*

	GDP	Employment	Capital	TFP
1890/91	73.5	79.7	29.1	138.0
1900/01	76.7	81.3	38.7	127.0
1910/11	94.7	86.4	39.1	150.5
1920/21	87.4	85.2	41.6	136.5
1929/30	109.1	86.0	51.7	155.5
1935/36	110.4	88.7	64.3	141.4
1946/47	116.1	97.9	93.2	121.0
1950/51	100.0	100.0	100.0	100.0
1960/61	147.1	116.7	130.6	120.5
1970/71	211.2	143.3	218.3	124.6
1980/81	286.7	153.5	344.6	135.2
1990/91	494.0	196.1	556.1	166.0
1999/00	819.1	268.0	971.2	182.6

Source: Broadberry and Gupta (2010)

from its potential and the new environment created favourable conditions for existing firms in the private sector and led to a large increase in productivity.

Growth in output per worker increased from 1.3 per cent per year during 1960–1980 to 3.7 per cent per year during 1980–2004. Total factor productivity growth increased from 0.2 per cent to 2.0 per cent per year (Bosworth et al. 2007). The pro-market reforms of the 1990s lowered price-based controls and removed restrictions on international capital flows. The change from a low to a high-growth path followed the reforms of the 1980s. The small steps taken to reduce regulation in the 1980s generated a large response in terms of GDP growth (Delong 2003).

The growth rate in GDP per capita doubled from 1980 and rose above 4 per cent per year after 1990 (see Table 1.6). The 1980s marked a clear break with the past. Srinivasan and Tendulkar (2003) attribute the growth in the 1980s to an increasing fiscal deficit and argue that it was unsustainable. Panagariya (2004) claims that the upsurge in growth in the 1980s could not have been sustained without the reforms of the 1990s.

What can we learn by taking a historical perspective? Table 1.8 presents the trends in GDP, capital accumulation, employment, and total factor productivity growth from 1871 to 2000. Before 1950, GDP moved in line with changes in employment. After 1950, capital accumulation increased significantly and changes in GDP moved in line with changes in capital stock. The efficiency cost of the Nehruvian strategy shows up

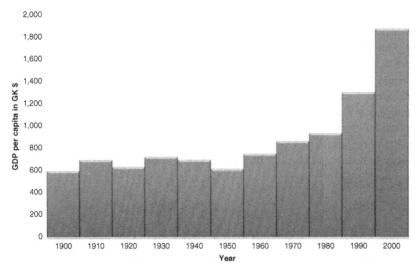

Figure 1.8 Reversal of fortune: Indian per capita GDP (1900–2000)
(1990 International Geary-Khamis dollars)
Source: Maddison Data Project

in the slow growth of total factor productivity before 1980. As Delong
(2003) has argued, despite the loss of efficiency, the increase in resource
mobilization had a positive effect on Indian growth. Gross domestic capital formation rose from 6–7 per cent of GDP before 1940 to 13 per cent
in 1951, climbing to 20 per cent in the 1970s. The independent republic of India saw a reversal of fortune with the end of colonization as the
economy moved from stagnation to growth.

The debate on the turning point in India's economic growth after 1950
has identified two years, 1980 and 1990. The former coincides with the
re-election of Indira Gandhi and her new approach to policy making
and the latter with the devaluation of the rupee in 1991. A standard
approach is to estimate a structural break in indicators of GDP to
identify a statistically significant change in the rate of growth. Most studies of Indian GDP look at the data from 1950. A consensus has emerged
in the literature that a structural break in India's economic growth
occurred in the early 1980s, brought on by the pro-business reforms
(Balakrishnan and Parameswaran (2007), Rodrik and Subramanian
(2005), Wallack (2003)).

Hatekar and Dongre (2005) take a long view from 1900 and test for a
statistical structural break. The structural break in GDP growth was in
1952 following Indian independence. They argue that this is not because

growth under the Nehruvian planning was exceptionally high, but because growth in the colonial period was dismally low. The Nehruvian regime was a response to the inadequacies of the colonial period and the transition from stagnation to growth coincided with the regulatory policies of the Nehruvian plan. Figure 1.8 charts the reversal of fortune in Indian per capita GDP from 1950. Per capita GDP grew slowly in the first thirty years and the rate of growth accelerated after 1980. India's so-called growth failure after independence is relative to the East Asian miracle. A long-run view is a better way to assess the economic outcomes of the first thirty years after independence and the transition from a colonial economy.

1.8   Conclusion

In this chapter I have covered four centuries of Indian economic performance and living standards. Using data on real wages and GDP per capita, I have shown that the Great Divergence began before colonization. In 1600, the living standard in India was lower than that in Britain, but the difference was small. The gap widened during the seventeenth and eighteenth centuries as real wages and GDP per capita declined in India and rose in Britain. By the early nineteenth century, Indian real wages and GDP per capita stabilized at a low level. There were short periods of growth in the late nineteenth century, but Indian income stagnated during most of the colonial period, particularly in the first half of the twentieth century. Colonial policies of one of the richest countries in the world did not put India on the path of modern economic growth.

The Indian economy moved out of stagnation into growth after independence and 1950 was a turning point in India's long-run economic growth. Another turning point came around 1980 with the adoption of a more liberal economic environment. Although Indian growth was low compared to East Asian economies, it was similar to most other countries in the developing world. The policies of regulation and state-directed industrialization under Nehru brought about a reversal of fortune in a decolonizing economy. The efficiency cost of an import-substituting industrialization policy was in part compensated by a rapid increase in capital accumulation.

2   Agriculture as the Engine of Growth

At the time of independence in 1947, agriculture was the dominant sector in the Indian economy. It produced half of the nation's output and employed two-thirds of the country's workforce. Most Indians lived in the countryside. Two hundred years earlier, at the time of British conquest in 1757, revenue generated from agriculture was the main source of the fiscal capacity of the state. It was in this sector that the East India Company introduced the first institutional change in order to maximize revenue collection. The colonial interventions were to have long run effects on India's economic development. I have argued in Chapter 1 that the decline and stagnation of Indian incomes from the middle of the seventeenth century were driven by agriculture rather than the fortunes of traditional industries. In 1947, agriculture had low output per worker compared to the non-agricultural sectors.

In this chapter, I will explore the factors that held back growth in agriculture, the changes in land tenure, and taxation that impacted on various aspects of cultivation and markets in land and labour. I explore the role of investment in infrastructure: railways and irrigation and the commercialization of agriculture. I will emphasize that the failure to increase land productivity was the most significant economic consequence of colonial policy. The stagnation in agriculture was reversed only after independence with investment in agricultural infrastructure and the onset of the Green Revolution.

Producing an agricultural surplus that would support an industrial population has been at the heart of the development experience in many countries. An agricultural revolution in Britain that increased land productivity preceded the industrial revolution. Britain's comparative advantage in industry led to specialization in industrial activity and trade in industrial goods for agricultural goods (Crafts 1989). Regional specialization in agriculture and industry in nineteenth-century USA paved the way for inter-regional trade in agricultural goods consumed in the industrial towns and cities. Primitive accumulation of capital that squeezed the surplus from the peasantry was a slogan of Soviet industrialization. In the age of empires, agriculture played the role of supplying the industrial centres in Europe with food and raw material. However, the magnitude of this trade was not that large for all colonies.

Food grains were less important in India's colonial trade compared to raw materials such as raw cotton and jute and strategic goods such as opium that was exported to China in the nineteenth century to pay for British imports of Chinese tea. The latter were the main exports in colonial India. The absence of a policy to increase yields in food production pushed much of this sector towards an ecological crisis. The colonial government set up experimental centres to develop better quality agricultural seeds, but this was limited.

Most Indians lived on the fertile plains. As the population expanded, cultivation moved to less fertile land. The traditional methods of the regeneration of soil, such as leaving land fallow, became increasingly infeasible as the population grew. Infrastructural investment in irrigation by building canals and wells began in the late nineteenth century and was available only in some parts of the country. As land productivity reached its limits, the colonial economy could only move into stagnation. Brij Narain, writing in 1929, claimed that the British did more for Indian agriculture than any other ruler by building canals and conducting research into new varieties of seeds. While this was true of parts of northwestern India, many regions faced a decline in yield per acre. Surprisingly, productivity in the drier regions increased more than in the rain-fed fertile plains (Ludden 1999, p. 24). What caused these differential changes in productivity? Why did productivity of less fertile land improve more than in the flood plains of northern and eastern India?

The colonial government had intervened on three fronts. First, it introduced new land tenure systems from the late eighteenth century. The system of land tenure determined the way tax was collected. The premise was that well-defined property rights would increase the productivity of land and generate more surplus. Second, the colonial government opened up an export market for agricultural commodities from the middle of the nineteenth century. It constructed railways and roads to link the hinterland to the ports, but also regional markets, reducing costs of trade. Third, it built irrigation canals in some parts of the country and invested in research to develop high-yielding varieties of seeds, mainly in sugarcane, jute, and cotton, but also in rice and wheat. Irrigation would mitigate water scarcity in monsoon-dependent agriculture and better-quality seeds would increase yields. However, investment in both was inadequate. Pray (1984) argues that even if more resources had been devoted to agricultural research, the investment in irrigation was inadequate and the fertilizer required for the new types of seeds too expensive to lead to wider adoption. In the following sections, I assess the impact of these interventions. I start with a description of agriculture before colonization and the changes over the next three centuries.

2.1   Pre-colonial Agricultural Landscape

'*India's agrarian history is a history of regions*' (Ludden 1999, p. 17). The diversity of climate, landscape, and soil led to differences in agricultural output, landholding, taxation, and other institutions. Broadly speaking the subcontinent can be divided by rainfall patterns into two agricultural regions: the more humid regions of eastern India and the coastal regions of the peninsula, and the drier regions of the north and the west and the rain shadow areas of the peninsula. The humid regions produced rice and the drier regions grew wheat, sorghum, and millet. Soil quality also determined what could be planted. The Gangetic plain in northern and eastern India has rich alluvial soil. This is where rice, sugarcane, and indigo were grown. Wheat was cultivated in the northwestern regions. The tracts of black soil in central and western regions are rich in nutrients and suitable for cultivation of raw cotton. In the rest of the dry regions of the peninsula, sorghum and millet were cultivated. Figure 2.1 shows the regions where main food crops like rice and wheat and a major cash crop like cotton were grown. The reliance on monsoon rains led to large fluctuations in output and famines were common, with significant localized effects and population decline. Consequently, population growth remained low until the twentieth century.

Marx had viewed Indian villages as self-sufficient economies, but the Indian villages in the seventeenth and eighteenth centuries were shown to be more connected and dependent on surrounding regions. There was trade in agricultural products on the caravan routes of central, southern, and western India and along waterways in the riverine delta of the east and north. Crops that were used as raw materials for industrial activity, such as raw cotton, were traded across regions. The magnitude of this trade was small, as indicated by the price dispersion across markets.

The earliest estimate of the share of agriculture in Indian GDP goes back to 1600 (Moosvi 2008, pp. 2–3). The share of the primary sector, including agriculture, animal husbandry, fisheries, and forest, was estimated to be 64 per cent; industry and mining was 11 per cent and the remainder was services. The fertile regions of rain-fed agriculture and the Gangetic plain of the north were densely populated. Areas under cultivation increased only by expanding into new, less fertile regions. Moosvi's estimates also give us an idea of the magnitude of the extensive margin in agriculture in northern India (Punjab, United Provinces, and Gujarat).

Figure 2.1 Agricultural map of India (1911)

Between 1595 and 1665, the annual rate of growth in total cropped area was 0.23 per cent, rising to 0.37 per cent from 1665 to 1909–1910 (Moosvi 2008, p. 6). Agriculture expanded into marginal land in western India from the middle of the nineteenth century and growth in agricultural output lagged behind population growth (Guha 1985, p. 83). Extension of arable agriculture into pastoral land came at the cost of a decline in cattle numbers per unit of land and soil erosion (Kaiwar 1994). The increase at the extensive margin was not matched by an increase in yield per acre in most regions. The productive capacity of land had not changed in the seventeenth and eighteenth centuries, as shown by Moreland and Moosvi for North India and by Chaudhuri for Bengal (Roy 2010). Even under new policies of land tenure, productive capacity did not change significantly in the nineteenth and early twentieth centuries.

Table 2.1 *Yield per acre (1600–1960)*

	Ratio 1910/1600	Ratio 1960/1600	
		Punjab average Highest yield	India average Middle yield
Wheat	0.75	0.64	0.66
Barley	0.88	0.60	0.74
Rice	0.69	0.51	0.66
Cotton	0.24	0.26	0.14
Sugarcane	2.21		
Average yield	0.91		
Acreage	1.89		
Output	1.57		

Source: Moosvi for 1600, 1910 (2015); Desai for 1960 (1972)

By 1900, the extensive margin was largely exhausted as cultivable 'wasteland' became scarce (Roy 2002). The only change was at the intensive margin. This was limited to regions that had irrigation or could switch to higher-value crops (Kurosaki 2003). Crop yield declined in most regions as the country faced an ecological crisis. Irrigated land under cotton and wheat saw increases in yield per acre, but in areas of rain-fed agriculture, lack of complimentary inputs such as fertilizer and irrigation led to stagnation that lasted until independence. Yield per acre in rice declined on the fertile plains of Bengal. Table 2.1 shows that land under cultivation nearly doubled between 1600 and 1910, but the increase in output was lower. Yield per acre was substantially lower in 1910 compared to 1600, for all crops except sugarcane. Desai (1972) divides regions according to high yield and middle yield, with reference to the median yields in the country, and compares yields in 1600 and 1960. He finds that yield per acre was lower in 1960 when comparing the most productive areas in 1600, with the most productive agricultural region of Punjab in 1960, and when comparing the median-yield regions of 1600 with the Indian average in 1960 (see Table 2.1). The data suggests that agriculture expanded to poorer quality land and that little was done to increase land productivity until the Green Revolution in independent India.

2.2 Land Tenure and Land Revenue Systems

Land revenue collection in colonial India was undertaken under three systems of land tenure. the *zamindari* or the landlord system, where the land was owned by a landlord and the cultivators were the tenants. The obligation to pay taxes was with the landlord. There were two different non-landlord systems: *ryotwari* and *mahalwari*. The *ryotwari* system of land tenure gave occupancy rights to the cultivators, who were then responsible for the payment of taxes to the colonial authorities. Under *mahalwari*, a village or a community of cultivators owned the land and paid the taxes collectively, although an individual's share was assigned by the community. The system adopted the norms and practices of many village communities in northern India.

The East India Company's win at Plassey gave it control of the fiscal system. Before British occupation, land was owned by the state and a local ruling elite of tax collectors were appointed as the fiscal intermediaries. Under the customary rights, the right to cultivate a piece of land could pass on from the cultivator to the next generation together with the tax liability. This did not confer legal ownership of land to the cultivator. To the British, this did not constitute 'well-defined property rights'. In the customary system, land could not be bought or sold. Arbitrary evictions were rare, although non-payment of taxes could lead to dispossession or forced labour on land (Kumar 1998, p. 181). To the British rulers, the definition of property rights came from their own system of legal ownership and the consequent ability to buy and sell. Without these, they did not see a scope to incentivize the cultivators to invest in land and increase productivity. The East India Company introduced European norms of legal ownership to land. As the ruler of Bengal, the Company relinquished state ownership of land and gave property rights to the local landlords or *zamindars* (Baden-Powell 1896). The customary landlords became the legal owners and could lease their land to the cultivators. The landlords collected rent from the cultivators and were responsible for the payment of taxes. They could also use the land as collateral or sell it at a market price. Under this system, land tax was fixed at a share of output that was to prevail in perpetuity. Hence the *zamindari* system is also known as the system of permanent settlement. As the Company extended its political control to the rest of India, the *zamindari* system of permanent settlement was adopted in the newly conquered areas initially, but from the 1820s two different systems of non-landlord tenure were introduced, which made the cultivator responsible for paying taxes. The tax rate could be revised periodically and, therefore, differed from the earlier system of permanent settlement.

Why was the introduction of legal property rights important to the East India Company? The main concern was revenue and land was the main source. The agricultural revolution in Britain had relied on the enclosure movement that demarcated each piece of land to an owner instead of un-enclosed plots across open fields (McCloskey 1972). This was seen as a necessary condition for farmers undertaking improvements in agriculture and the consequent technological change. From the point of view of the East India Company, it was necessary to clearly define ownership of land in India in order to increase agricultural productivity. This would generate more revenue. The Company also assumed that in the landlord system, fixing the tax rate would encourage landlords to improve land productivity.

The expectation that the landlord system would produce an entrepreneurial class of landlords did not materialize (Barber 1975, p. 161). The landlords lived off the rent and became absentee urban dwellers. Yields dropped on the fertile plains of Bengal because of intensive land use without investment in regeneration. After 1818, influenced by utilitarians such as James Mill and the Ricardian theory of rent, the net produce or the surplus over basic costs of production was considered to be a more efficient way to tax land in India (McAlpin 1974). Therefore, the cultivator rather than the landlord became the tax payer. Figure 2.2 shows where the systems prevailed.

In the fertile tracts where population density was high and land was scarce, there was scope to extract rent and landlords became a dominant social group (Stokes 1959). In the dry agricultural regions, where pastoral communities eked out a living, land was abundant and labour was in short supply. Granting ownership to the cultivators was intended to strengthen ties to land, establish settled cultivation, and move the labour force away from their pastoral lifestyle (Ludden 1999, pp. 23–24). The difference between the landlord and the non-landlord systems, as the British rulers saw, was in the incentives it created for technological improvements. It was a direct transposition of the British experience of the enclosure movement and agricultural revolution to India. The Indian context turned out to be different. Where surplus could be extracted as rent, the landlords did not undertake investment in land. In the non-landlord regions, the constraint was the availability of an investible surplus for the cultivators. Land tax was half of total revenue in the nineteenth century (see Table 2.2). While the returns on investment in agricultural infrastructure by the state was low in landlord regions because land tax rate could not be raised, in non-landlord regions the state could gain substantial increases in revenue by improving land productivity. I will come back to this point in the section on investment in irrigation and an evaluation of colonial policy.

The two systems created different institutions of labour and credit. They also created different paths to inheritance. Unequal land ownership

Table 2.2 *Composition of revenue (1858–1940)*

	1858–1859	1870–1871	1900–1901	1921–1922	1930–1931	1940–1941
Land revenue	50	40	53	27	23	19
Customs	8	5	9	30	36	
Excise	4	6	10	14	13	16
Income tax	0.3	4	3	15	12	19
Salt	7	16	16	5	5	5
Opium	17	12				
Others	13	18	9	10	11	13

Source: CEHI (tables 12.4 and 12.7)

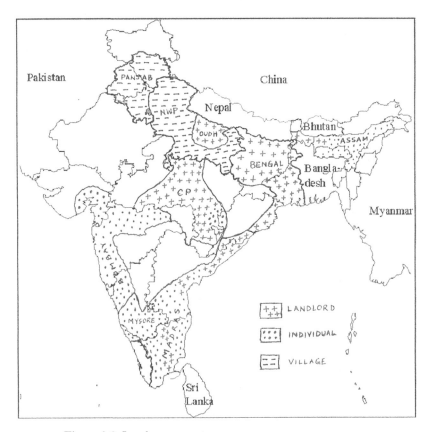

Figure 2.2 Land tenure systems
Source: Banerjee and Iyer (2005). Copyright American Economic Association; reproduced with permission of the *American Economic Review*

remained a feature of landlord regions, where land ownership was concentrated from generation to generation. In the non-landlord regions, inheritance created grounds for subdivision of plots cultivated by households and the fragmentation of land had implications for technological change. Kaiwar (1994) suggests that fragmentation of land in the *ryotwari* system in western India led to dispersed land holdings for a given household, creating very little incentive to increase output beyond subsistence. Ironically, the colonial attempts to create incentives through well-defined property rights resulted in a structure of landholding that minimized incentives for improving the quality of land. The property rights in land created a market in land. Land could be used as collateral for loans, paving the way for transfer of land through indebtedness. Land could be sold by choice or because of economic distress. The latter led to a rise in landless workers, such as sharecroppers or seasonal workers. In *ryotwari* areas, famines resulted in increased indentured migration (Aggarwal 2022, chap. 1). It also allowed land ownership to pass on to non-cultivating groups. The role of moneylenders assumed a new importance. Overall, the land tenure and land revenue systems had lasting effects on the Indian economy and society.

2.3   Commercialization of Agriculture

From the middle of the nineteenth century, two major changes in transportation technology contributed to the rapid expansion in trade in agriculture. A new railway network connected the interior to the ports and, over time, it connected different parts of the interior, reducing transport costs. Before the construction of a rail network, trade in agricultural products relied on pack bullocks, country river boats, and coastal routes. Commodities were transported by pack bullock in most parts of the country and volumes were limited. Moreland (1923, p. 226) estimated that each ox could carry 336 pounds and travel six to eight miles a day. The railways revolutionized transport. It reduced travel time and massively increased the volume of bulky agricultural goods that could be shifted within regional markets, and to the ports for export. Railways increased trade in cash crops and in food grains.

The second major change was in shipping technology. The switch from sail to steam and the opening of the Suez Canal in 1869 increased the speed of travel and reduced the cost of shipping between Europe and Asia. Trade between Europe and Asia used to take a long route along the coast of Africa and the Suez Canal made it profitable for Europeans to import agricultural goods from India and export industrial products. The changing composition of trade is shown in Table 2.3.

Table 2.3 *Changing composition of Indian exports (1811–1935)*

	Raw cotton	Cotton goods	Indigo	Raw silk	Food grains	Raw jute	Jute goods	Opium	Sugar	Tea
1811	4.9	33.0	18.5	8.3				23.8	1.5	
1828	15.0	11.0	27.0	10.0				17.0	4.0	
1850	19.1	3.7	10.9	3.8	4.1	1.1	0.9	30.1	10.0	0.2
1870	33.2	2.5	5.8		8.1	4.7	0.6			2.1
1890	16.5	9.5	3.1		19.5	7.6	2.5			5.3
1910	17.2	6.0	0.2		18.4	7.4	8.1			5.9
1935	21.0	1.3			13.5	8.5	14.5			12.3

Source: CEHI, *Volume 2:* Tables 10.10 and 10.11

India became a source of raw material for British industry and played an important role in trade in the British Empire. The export of large quantities of opium to China balanced the triangular trade of selling opium to the Chinese people and buying tea in China for the British market. In 1811 opium was the second largest component of India's exports, after textiles (see Table 2.3). After the Opium Wars, the unoccupied land in Assam and Bengal was developed for tea cultivation by British companies and the importance of opium in trade declined. Tea had been discovered growing wild in Assam and British companies set up plantations to grow tea as a commercial crop for export. Tea plantations were established in large areas of eastern India and the hills of southern India and by the end of the nineteenth century India was the main supplier of tea to the British market.

During the American Civil War, raw cotton from India temporarily replaced American cotton in the British textile industry. In the black soil regions of western and central India there was a big expansion in cotton cultivation. Even after American cotton exports resumed, Indian cotton acreage did not decline. Raw cotton was sold to the emerging modern cotton textile industry and cotton became a major cash crop. In 1810, cotton cloth had been one-third of total exports. Over the nineteenth century, indigo, opium, and raw cotton displaced cotton textiles as the main traded good, reflecting India's integration into the global network of the British Empire. Food grains such as wheat and rice were exported too, but in small quantities until 1870 and did not ever become the largest single item.

The integration of regional markets and access to the world market changed the world of the Indian cultivator. It opened up opportunities for cultivation of new crops and increased the response to changing prices. It created the possibility for trade within a region as well as across regions. The literature on commercialization of agriculture often sees self-sufficiency as necessary for survival and cultivation of cash crops as the road to destitution. An alternative view is that trade creates opportunities for gains from specialization.

Crop suitability depends on soil type, gradient, and climate. Regions specialized in basic food grains: rice grew in the rain-abundant areas of the east and wheat and millet in drylands in the south. The black soil of the Deccan was suitable for growing cotton, and tea had grown naturally in Assam. Sugarcane requires water-intensive cultivation and therefore can be grown in places with abundant water. Specialization opened opportunities for gains from trade in interconnected markets. The modern transportation network paved the way for rising interregional trade.

It has been argued that specializing in cash crops makes cultivators vulnerable to harvest failures (Dutt 1952, pp. 348–50, 536, 662). This is a valid concern if markets are not integrated and, in such contexts, harvest failures could also lead to food shortages. Before the railways, prices diverged across markets in response to weather shocks. Price data from Coromandel in the eighteenth century shows large differences in prices between places within 100 kilometres of each other. The Enquiry into Wages and Prices in 1914 also points to large differences in the price of grain across districts in 1838 (Datta 1914). When the railway network expanded, market integration enabled specialization due to reduced vulnerability to rainfall shocks.

McAlpin (1974) has argued against the view that the cultivators had no agency in the process of commercialization and became victims of the market. Instead she shows that cultivators took rational decisions to grow food or cash crops by responding to longer term changes in the relative prices of food and cash crops. In the absence of a reliable transportation network and irrigation, cultivators could mitigate the risk of harvest failure by investing in storage and responding to market prices in a limited way. Irrigation, where available, reduced the risk of harvest failure. Railways reduced the risk of starvation due to harvest failure because grain could be transported from other regions. Therefore, as the transportation and irrigation networks expanded, the cultivators could respond to prices. The context of McAlpin's analysis is the cotton producing tracts and the extent to which cultivators switched from food to cotton during the international shortage in raw cotton during the American Civil War of the 1860s. As McAlpin (1974) argues and Dharam Narain (1965) confirms, the supply response to price changes in cotton was bigger in the irrigated areas of Punjab and the Deccan, supporting the idea of rationality in the crop choice made by the peasants when irrigation reduced the risk of harvest failures.

If railways improved the speed and volume of transport of grain from regions of surplus to regions of shortage, this would be reflected in declining price dispersion and fewer famines. Hurd (1975) has shown that the coefficient of variation in prices, which captures price difference across markets, declined with the construction of the railways. Donaldson's (2018) recent careful statistical analysis also finds greater integration of markets with the construction of the railway network. This increased specialization into cash crops and food crops, depending

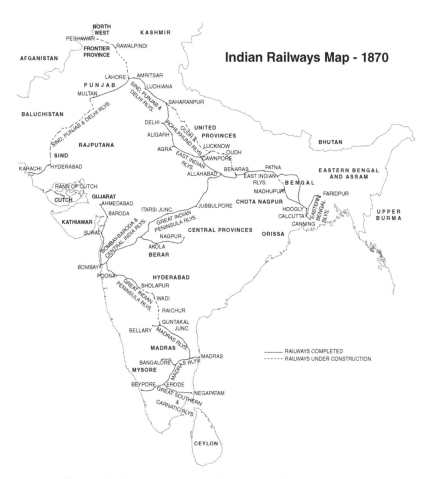

Figure 2.3 Expansion of the railway network
Source: Bogart and Chaudhuri (2015b, Figures 9.1, 9.3)

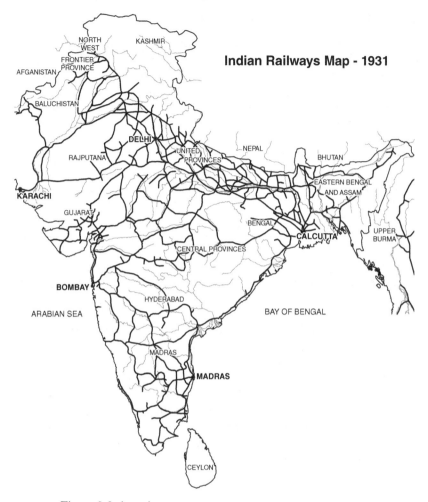

Figure 2.3 (cont.)

on soil and climate suitability of crops. Regions that could produce cotton, jute, or sugarcane increased their acreage under these crops and bought food from other regions. It increased the volume of food traded within the country. Figure 2.3 shows the expansion of the railway network. The first railway lines connected ports to the hinterland, but over time the network became denser and connected the interior. By 1930 the railways had connected large parts of the country and there were few districts that did not have a railway line.

2.4   Property Rights and Investment in Land

The colonial administration created property rights based on the British experience, but the two environments were not comparable. By the middle of the eighteenth century most of the agricultural population lived at subsistence level in India (see Chapter 1). British income in 1600, on the cusp of the agricultural revolution, was twice as high as Indian income in 1750 (Broadberry et al. 2015). Who could be the entrepreneurial farmers in India?

In the landlord regions, rents increased due to population pressure and made it possible to extract a surplus without improving the quality of land. In the non-landlord regions, the cultivators did not have the resources to invest in irrigation or other improvements or even to buy inputs such as fertilizers. Individual cultivators had small holdings and made decisions to invest in implements and cattle if resources were available, but investment in irrigation was costly. The lack of formal channels of credit and the failure of the landlords to undertake improvements were institutional failures. The state could have filled in this gap, but did not undertake large investments in agriculture in all parts of the country. This is in contrast with East Asia and will be discussed in Chapter 6.

There are two measures of investment in land: availability of water and availability of capital stock. Irrigation was mainly canals and wells. Capital stock comprised of agricultural implements such as carts, ploughs, bullocks, and cattle. Households required a plough to prepare land for cultivation. Bullocks increased the efficiency of ploughing land and were the most valuable capital asset. At least one pair was needed for ploughing and bullocks pulled carts and provided manure as fertilizer (Chaudhary and Swamy 2017). In times of distress or credit constraint the cultivator would sell these assets.

Traditional techniques of keeping land fallow to regenerate soil ran into constraints as population pressure intensified. There were some changes in cultivation, such as double cropping or cultivation of different crops in the same plot from one season to the next, in particular from wet to dry season, which increased after 1920. But the share of double-cropped land was small and varied across provinces. It was less than 5 per cent in Bombay and Sind, 10 per cent in Central Provinces, 15 per cent in Punjab and Madras, 20 per cent in Bengal, and 25 per cent in United Provinces (Blyn 1966, p. 190).

Manure was the most common fertilizer. Use of chemical fertilizers was low and was applied mainly for the cultivation of cash crops. Tea was the largest user. Pray (1984) found that the cost of fertilizers was too high in India relative to East Asia and, in the absence of irrigation, it was not viable in most regions. The main technological change was introduction of new varieties of higher productivity seeds in the cultivation of cotton, jute, sugarcane, and wheat. In 1922, the share of land under better seeds was less than 2 per cent. In 1938, this had increased to 11 per cent (Blyn 1966, p. 200). The crops that benefitted most from new varieties of seeds were cash crops and 76 per cent of the sugarcane acreage, 63 per cent of jute acreage. Thirty-five per cent of acres under cotton used new varieties of seeds in 1938. For food crops, the share was 7 per cent, with wheat being the main beneficiary (Pray 1984). There were regional variations in this too. A large proportion of land in Punjab and Sind adopted new varieties of seeds. The special position of these provinces in agricultural production arose from the availability of irrigation, which will be discussed in the following section. Irrigation was to prove a key investment that led to productivity gains.

2.5 Irrigation: A Policy Failure?

Most regions of Asia, from South Asia to Japan, relied on seasonal rains and therefore experienced periodic water shortage. Irrigation was important to deal with water scarcity. In 1952, South, South-East, and East Asia had 68 per cent of the world's irrigated areas, of which 34 per cent was in China and 17 per cent was in India (Sengupta 1985). The colonial government built one of the largest irrigation networks, but this was available in only 20 per cent of the total cultivated land. Irrigation canals were built in some regions, but not in others. The expansion of land under cultivation came from increasing provision of water. The areas in northwestern India, that were brought under cultivation with the building of canals, became fertile land.

In pre-colonial India, irrigation was available in some regions. This was mainly in the form of anicuts to divert water from the rivers and tanks to store water. Sengupta (1985) refers to the irrigation tanks discussed in Kautilya's *Arthashastra*, written in third century BCE, and the Grand Anicut built on the river Kaveri in the second century CE. Habib (1982b, p. 49) mentions the Jamuna canal built by Feroz Shah Tughlak. A few canals had been constructed or expanded in the Mughal period from the Kaveri, Yamuna, and Indus rivers, but these facilities were localized and did not cover much of the land that needed irrigation. The population pressure on land was not comparable to the situation in the nineteenth century, when rainfall shocks affected more

58   Agriculture as the Engine of Growth

Table 2.4 *Land under irrigation (% share)*

	Area irrigated / Total area sown	Govt canals	Private canals	Tanks	Wells	Other sources
		Percentage of area irrigated in 1936 by:				
British India – 1886	16.5	29.9	4.0	19.0	37.8	9.3
British India – 1904	14.3	41.3	6.2	16.7	31.4	4.3
British India – 1913	17.8	39.0	5.5	15.0	27.1	13.4
British India – 1920	19.2	42.0	5.4	15.0	25.9	11.7
British India – 1936	19.7	46.1	7.5	11.7	24.8	9.9
Madras	24.2	43.2	1.7	36.0	16.2	2.9
Bombay	3.6	20.0	8.2	10.7	58.6	2.4
Bengal	5.8	12.9	12.9	44.5	3.7	26.0
UP	24.7	32.6	0.3	0.6	49.2	17.3
Punjab	47.2	67.5	2.8	0.2	28.6	0.9
Bihar	18.8	16.0	18.1	32.9	12.9	20.2
CP & Berar	4.9	0.0	82.7	0.0	12.3	4.9
Assam	9.0	0.1	53.1	0.2	0.0	46.6
Sind	78.7	90.0	0.3	0.0	0.5	9.3
Orissa	15.2	28.0	4.6	30.4	7.5	29.5

Source: Chaudhary et al. (2015, chap. 7)

people at a given time, increasing the possibility of famines. Therefore, the pressure to expand irrigation was more compelling for the rulers in the nineteenth century.

Under the colonial government, the five main irrigation zones were: Punjab, Sind, Western United Provinces, Narmada Valley, and Coastal Andhra. There were state and private initiatives to construct perennial and inundation canals. Government canals were funded out of revenue or from the capital account. Private canals could be financed mainly by loans from the state government, but this accounted for a small share of irrigation. Table 2.4 shows that state-built canals dominated. By 1936 government canals were the main source of irrigation, servicing 46 per cent of the total irrigated area. Other irrigation facilities included storage tanks and wells. Wells serviced 25 per cent of irrigated land in 1936 and they were mostly private. Tanks were 12 per cent of the capacity. Private canals covered only 8 per cent of cultivated land. While in Punjab the share of irrigated land was close to 50 per cent and in Sind nearly 80 per cent, in provinces such as the Central Provinces and Bengal it was around 5 per cent; it was even lower in Bombay. The large variation in acreage under irrigation across states is shown in Table 2.4. Large tracts of land could be brought under cultivation in Punjab and Sind because of irrigation. Nine perennial canal projects were set up in the sparsely populated arid region of Punjab. Land grants were made available and the canal colonies relied on migration from other areas to expand cultivation (Ali 1987).

The Nationalist critique was, first, that too little was spent on irrigation relative to the railways, as the railways served the strategic interests of the Raj, and second, that the government invested in irrigation to promote the cultivation of cash crops. Sweeney (2011) has argued that the colonial emphasis on railways was socially inefficient because of the link between irrigation and agricultural development. Others, such as Whitcombe (1972) and Agnihotri (1996), emphasize the adverse ecological effect of canal irrigation in northwestern India. Ali (1987) points to the social and economic advantages gained by the land-owning peasantry who acquired occupancy rights and the Punjabi military veterans who were rewarded with land allocation in the canal colonies. The canal colonies did not address the socioeconomic inequalities of the region and did not make land available to the landless agricultural workers. The canals strengthened the caste and class hierarchies. While recognizing the unequal access to irrigated land and the negative effect on ecology, Stone (1984) has argued that irrigation canals raised yields. Stone compares villages in the United Provinces that had canal or well irrigation and finds that access to a canal increased crop intensity and diversification and resulted in more continuous employment throughout the year (pp. 111–123).

The Famine Commission of 1880 made a case for providing access to water to increase the productivity of existing agriculture and to bring new areas under cultivation in order to reduce the impact of droughts and famines. However, rainfall and soil quality would determine where irrigation would be useful and what type of irrigation was suitable. The British built two types of canals: perennial canals in northern India and inundation canals elsewhere, which filled when water overflowed from the main rivers. In Punjab and Sind, where rainfall was uncertain, inundation canals were filled by underground streams from the Indus, Sutlej, and Chenab rivers during the monsoons.

The Famine Commission argued that estimated returns to irrigation should include returns from higher crop output due to protection from drought, the number of lives saved through famine prevention, and also insurance against lost revenue and costly relief measures. Irrigation provided greater security against fluctuations in rainfall, increased output per acre, and was conducive to a greater variety of crops to be planted.

Table 2.5 *Comparative yields per acre (lbs per acre)*

Europe 1910		India 1911		
Wheat yields		Wheat yields	Irrigated	Non-irrigated
Spain	839	Punjab	898	555
Italy	856	Sind	1,340	
France	1,178	North-West Frontier Province	874	559
Germany	1,651	United Provinces	1,250	850
Sweden	1,891	Bombay	1,340	510
UK	1,909			
Netherlands	2,132	India (weighted average)	1,037	679
Rice yields 1900				
Japan	1,702	India	944	
Indonesia	1,076			

Note: European data is not disaggregated by irrigated and non-irrigated land
Source: Wheat: Agricultural Statistics of British India 1911 Europe: Bairoch (1997); rice: Roy (2007)

The canals increased returns as cultivators could shift to higher-value crops (Kurosaki 2003). The returns to irrigation were estimated to be around 7 per cent, a decade after completion of the infrastructure. The revenue stream in a year from capital outlay in irrigation in 1900 was estimated at 12 per cent in Punjab, 26 per cent in Sind, 5 per cent in United Provinces and Madras, with an average of 6 per cent for India (Irrigation Commission Report 1901–03, p. 22). Thus, the expected returns were higher than those from railways.

There was a large variation in expenditure at the province level. These numbers do not consider the rainfall deficit in a province. However, there is overwhelming evidence across regions that yield per acre was higher on irrigated land. For food crops, such as wheat, yields on irrigated land were higher and comparable to that in some European countries. The average yield on irrigated rice fields in India in 1900, on the other hand, was lower than in Japan and Indonesia (see Table 2.5). Most of the land under rice cultivation was not irrigated.

At the same time, it is difficult to argue that irrigation served only the interests of the colonial government and was motivated only by imperialist concerns. Higher yields meant there were large private returns on irrigated land. There is no evidence that irrigated land cultivated mainly cash crops. Figure 2.4 shows that food crops and non-food

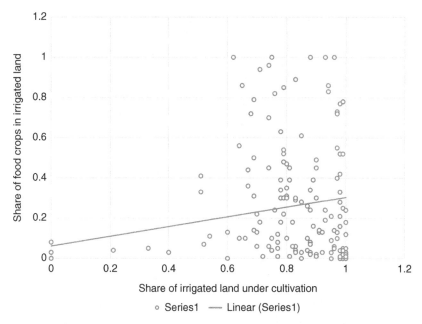

Figure 2.4 Share of food crops on irrigated land (1920)
Source: Agricultural Statistics of British India

crops were cultivated on irrigated land and do not support claims that only cash crops benefitted from irrigation. Irrigation increased yield per acre in the first half of the twentieth century, but the constraint was that it did not cover enough land and not enough was spent on it. Therefore, irrigation did not raise output per acre for the country as a whole.

Why did the colonial state not invest in agriculture? Investment rate in colonial India was very low. The share of agriculture in gross capital formation was higher in colonial India than after independence, but gross capital formation was only 6–7 per cent of GDP, compared to 13 per cent in 1951 and 24 per cent in 1991 (see Table 2.6). Therefore the total outlay on agriculture was inadequate for building an agricultural infrastructure for development. Investment in irrigation was low compared to the railways (see Table 2.7). About 90 per cent of capital outlay was spent on the railways and irrigation received less than 10 per cent. From revenue, irrigation received 3–4 per cent of total spending. The economic stagnation in colonial India was largely due to the failure to build an adequate agricultural infrastructure.

Table 2.6 *Gross domestic capital formation*

Colonial period	Gross fixed capital formation in GDP	Share of agriculture in gross fixed capital formation	Post independence*	Gross fixed capital formation in GDP	Share of agriculture in gross fixed capital formation
1850–51	5.0	41.6	1950–51	13.1	19.06
1860–61	4.8	38.2	1960–61	17.7	11.1
1870–71	5.1	35.0	1970–71	19.7	11.6
1880–81	4.8	40.4	1980–81	20.8	11.5
1890–91	6.2	30.2	1990–91	23.7	6.1
1900–01	7.0	25.6			
1910–11	6.6	23.3			
1920–21	6.2	26.0			
1930–31	6.3	22.1			
1940–41	6.7	22.2			

Source: Roy (1996, table 55, p. 347), *Dhawan and Yadav (1997), Nagaraj (1990)

Table 2.7 *Government spending on infrastructure: irrigation and railways*

	Proportion of expenditure charged against revenue (%)		Proportion of gross expenditure charged against capital	
	Railways	Irrigation	Railways	Irrigation
1894–95	23.4	3.1	87.2	12.8
1900–01	24.4	3.2	93.7	6.3
1910–11	15.5	4.1	90.3	9.7
1919–20	10.2	2.9	94.4	5.6
1935–36	15.2	3.2		

Source: Chaudhary et al. (2015)

2.6   Commercialization and Prosperity

Did commercialization improve living standards for cultivators? I showed in Chapter 1 (Figure 1.6) that from the middle of the nineteenth century per capita growth was low but positive. The value of agricultural exports increased at 4 per cent per year between 1876 and 1913. With increasing commercialization and trade in agricultural products, in the last quarter of the nineteenth century and the first decade of the twentieth century, GDP growth was higher than population growth for a short period of time. Most of the growth in the nineteenth century came from bringing more land into cultivation and very little from changes in yield per acre in existing land under cultivation. From 1910, agricultural output and GDP per capita stagnated and this did not change until independence.

Evidence on yield per acre comes from the work of George Blyn (1966), who documented changes in acreage and output at the district level from 1891. Blyn's data shows overall stagnation, but big regional differences. While there was an increase in productivity in dryland regions, in the fertile, rain-fed areas, output stagnated or declined. More generally, yield per acre in cash crops increased and declined in food crop. In wheat, however, there was an increase in some regions as a result of irrigation (see Table 2.8). Punjab, with an extensive irrigation system, saw an increase in land productivity. In rain-abundant, eastern regions, where investment in irrigation was low, land productivity declined. Recent work by Kurosaki (2017) confirms this pattern for the colonial regions of India, Pakistan, and Bangladesh. The irrigated regions of northwestern India grew faster than other parts of the country (Kurosaki 2017, pp. 29–31).

Table 2.9 shows the differences in growth in yield per acre across provinces and by crop. Bengal shows a decline and Punjab and Madras, where the share of irrigated land was higher, show some growth. Yield per acre in rice declined. Yields grew in cash crops, such as cotton, sugarcane, oilseeds, and tea. The increase matched the rising demand from processing industries, which developed rapidly after the First World War. However, cash crops took up only a small proportion of cultivated land. In the 1940s, cotton had the largest share at just over 5 per cent, sugarcane less than 2 per cent, and oilseeds less than 5 per cent. Most of the cultivated land was used for food crops. Therefore, growth in agricultural productivity depended on productivity of food production. There was a decline in yield per acre in rice. The decline and stagnation in output of food grains had

Table 2.8 *Changes in yield per acre, before and after independence (% per year)*

	Colonial period			Post 1950	
	1891–1916	1916–1921	1921–1946	1950/51–1989/90	1989/90–2004/05
All crops	0.47	−0.36	−0.02	1.37	1.29
All food	0.29	−0.63	−0.44	1.60	1.27
All non-food	0.81	0.34	1.16	1.08	1.39

Source: Roy (2012) and Jha (2007)

Table 2.9 *Differences in growth in yield per acre by region and by crop (1891–1946)*

Regional variation in growth in yield per acre (% per year)		Crop-level growth in yield per acre (% per year)	
Bengal	−0.34	Rice	−0.10
United Provinces	0.15	Wheat	0.36
Central Provinces	0.01	Ragi	0.12
Bombay and Sind	0.28	Cotton	0.95
Madras	0.65	Sugarcane	0.73
Punjab	0.63	Groundnut	0.23
		Tea	1.45

Source: Blyn, G. (1966). *Agricultural Trends in India 1891–1947: Output, Availability and Production*, Philadelphia, University of Pennsylvania Press, Appendix 5A and 5B

serious consequences at a time when population growth began to increase. Per capita food availability declined in the first half of the twentieth century (Roy 2006, p. 82).

2.7   Railways and Famines

Access to railways could mitigate output shortfall in response to rainfall shocks. The variation in prices of food grains across markets declined, as discussed in a previous section. If output declined in a region connected by a railway line then food grain could be transported from a region of plenty. There was a decline in the number of famines in the first half of the twentieth century.

For centuries, India experienced periodic famines when the monsoon failed. Droughts led to crop failures and floods destroyed crops, which led to cholera outbreaks. Wars also lead to famines. Many famines were localized, but there were several years when famines were more widespread. The first major famine under Company rule was in Bengal in the 1770s. Lack of rain caused crop failure on the fertile plain and famine: one-third of Bengal's population is estimated to have perished. High taxation and other policy failures also played a role in this disaster (Datta 2019; Damodaran et al. 2019).

Bengal also experienced the last major famine of the British Empire in 1943. The Bengal Famine is a symbol of the negligence of the colonial government. Despite the concerns expressed in the deliberations of the Famine Commissions set up by the colonial government, military interests

Table 2.10 *Frequency of famines (1759–1947)*

	Number of years of famine	Provinces affected
1759–1800	11	Bengal, Madras, Sind, Hyderabad, Bombay, Gujarat, Rajasthan, Orissa, central India, Kutch, NW Provinces
1801–1850	19	Bombay, central India, Rajasthan, Mysore, Bombay, NW Provinces, Sind, Madras, Punjab
1851–1900	21	Madras, Rajasthan, NW Provinces, Punjab, Kutch, Orissa, Hyderabad, Mysore, Gujarat, Bombay, Madras, Bengal, Bihar, Central Provinces, Kashmir
1901–1947	5	Bombay, Madras, Bengal, Bihar, Central Provinces

Source: CEHI Visaria and Visaria (1983)

dominated humanitarian concerns in 1943. Four million people died in what was seen as a man-made famine (Sen 1977). More recent work has shown that there was a harvest failure that year (O'Grada 2008b). The debate about whether the famine was a result of a shortfall in output rather than diversion of food for the war effort when there was a plentiful harvest is somewhat redundant in the context of public policy. In her book *Churchill's Private War*, Mukerjee (2011) documents the diversion of food from a region of food shortage to meet the military needs of the eastern front of the Second World War. Public policy not only failed to move food from regions of plenty to regions of scarcity, it aggravated the shortfall and bears responsibility for the last famine of the British Empire.

Famines, however, were less frequent in the twentieth century (see Table 2.10). Recent work by Burgess and Donaldson (2010) shows that when districts were connected to a railway line, it reduced the risk of a famine when rains failed. Therefore, the Bengal Famine of 1943 stands out as an example of a massive failure of public policy.

2.8 Credit Institutions: The Interlinked Factor Markets in Agriculture

Credit, land, and labour markets became interconnected as land could be used as collateral to borrow. Most cultivators relied on the informal credit market for loans. In the event of a failure to repay the debt, the cultivator could lose the land and become an agricultural labourer or migrate to a new agricultural area or an urban centre. The caste-based occupational structure interacted with the development of a market for land. It opened the door to transfer of land from the debtors to the creditors and led to the growth of landless wage labour. Cultivators, landlords and moneylenders belonged to different castes. Indebtedness was not uncommon in the pre-colonial times as peasants borrowed against contingencies, but land as collateral added a new dimension to indebtedness.

Cultivators borrowed at the start of the sowing season when food prices were high, and paid back after the harvest when food prices were low. Interest rates in this informal market for credit were high. Loans against crops to cultivators started at 9 per cent, but could be as high as 50 per cent on informal short-term loans, known as hand loans (Baker 1984, p. 285). The increasing commercialization of agriculture changed the magnitudes of borrowing and repayments. Cultivators in western and central India switched from barley and millet to higher value crops, cotton, and wheat. When more arable land became available for cultivating cash crops in western India, urban moneylenders were often the source of credit. When the cultivators could not repay loans, land was transferred from the cultivators to the moneylenders.

The nature of the credit market varied across regions. In Punjab, indebtedness among the peasantry was high. Darling (1925) argued that the prosperity of the Punjabi peasant also increased their credit worthiness and the capacity to borrow. In 1929–30, the debt burden of an average cultivating family in Punjab was at least three times that of a similar household in Bengal, Bihar, and Eastern United Provinces (Bhattacharya 1985). The capacity of repayment of the Punjabi peasant was also greater.

The conflict between cultivators and moneylenders took on a caste dimension. The Deccan riots of the 1870s involved Kunbis as cultivators and Marwaris as moneylenders. The cultivators involved in the riots against the moneylenders targeted mortgage documents. It raised some concern among the British policymakers about social unrest, and the colonial government introduced laws to regulate usury. The Deccan Agriculturist Relief Act was legislated in 1879. The Act restricted the punishments that borrowers could face in case of failure to repay and limited the amount of interest that could accumulate (Chaudhary and Swamy 2017). Similar inventions followed in the Central Provinces and at the turn of the nineteenth century the Punjab Land Alienation Act of 1901 prevented non-agricultural castes from owning cultivable land in Punjab. Conflicts between cultivators and moneylenders following the Great Depression led to further legislation in Bengal and Madras in the 1930s. Banking enquiry committees in various provinces discussed the high interest rates charged by the moneylenders, which they found to vary between 12 per cent and 40 per cent.

In the *zamindari* areas, class conflict took a specific form. The cultivating tenants did not have secure land rights and landlords could increase rents arbitrarily. The tenants had the option to sublet to other cultivators or sharecroppers. The British administration reacted to the possibility of social unrest between the landlords and the cultivators in Bengal by enacting the Bengal Rent Act of 1859, which gave tenants occupancy rights after twelve years. There were loopholes in the Act that could be exploited by landlords to evict the cultivator. For example, the tenant did not necessarily cultivate the same plot of land over the twelve-year period. The Tenancy Act of 1885, which gave occupancy rights to the tenants even when they had cultivated different plots under the same landlord, closed this loophole and put limits on increases in rent (Swamy 2011).

In Bengal, there were two types of lenders: the trader–moneylenders, who came from the trading castes, and the upper caste landlords themselves. When landlords became moneylenders, it created a debt–bondage relationship in interlinked credit and labour markets. The tenant could become a bonded labourer. As the capacity of the cultivators to repay loans collapsed with the Great Depression, the threat of peasant revolts led to a series of legislations that were modelled on the British Moneylenders Acts and attempted to provide a mechanism for debt settlement and regulation of interest rates (Bose 1994, pp. 269–270). This culminated in the Bengal Agricultural Debtors Act of 1935, which provided a regulatory framework for debt repayment.

In the Madras Presidency both landlord and non-landlord settlements existed. Here too, the creditors could be the landlords or the merchants (Baker 1984, pp. 238–240). Nath (2022) argues that moneylenders rationed credit and charged higher interests in drylands compared to the regions of rain-fed agriculture. Communities like the Chettiars were the financiers of the rice trade. The Great Depression brought regulation of moneylending in this region. Although the initial version of the bill sought to regulate the interest rate, the law that passed, the Madras Debtor's Protection Act of 1937, only provided a mechanism for debt conciliation (Baker 1984, pp. 302–303).

Colonial laws had paved the way for a market in land. The consequences of introducing transferable property rights in land had far-reaching effects and resulted in various legal interventions as well as a growing class of landless agricultural labourers. The volatility in agricultural incomes caused large migration flows, not only within the country but also to distant parts of the British Empire as indentured workers

(Persaud 2019). This was more prevalent in the non-landlord districts (Aggarwal 2022, chap. 1). The primary objective of the land revenue system had been to maximize revenue and create an enterprising class of cultivators. As the economy changed, the importance of land revenue declined and the growth in agricultural productivity remained an illusion, except in some parts of the country.

2.9   Independence and a Change in Policy

Underinvestment in agriculture has continued to be a cause for concern in independent India. However, there are some qualitative differences. From 1950 growth in agriculture turned positive for the first time in half a century. This coincided with a change in policy. The first plan, covering 1951/2–1955/56, explicitly targeted agriculture and emphasized investing in irrigation to raise agricultural growth. Twenty per cent of the planned outlay went to irrigation and 26 per cent to transport and communication (Chakravarty 1987, table 2.9). This was intended to rebalance the colonial spending pattern. Inaugurating the construction of the Bhakra Nagal dam Jawaharlal Nehru, the first prime minister, hailed it as a 'temple of modern India'. The results of the emphasis on agricultural infrastructure could be seen in a 30 per cent increase in agricultural output over the plan period. However, the second plan shifted the emphasis to industry and took attention away from the deeper problems of Indian agriculture and its ability to provide food security for a growing population. The focus of policy returned to agriculture from the late 1960s.

There were several significant policy inventions in agriculture. The first was to reform the colonial institutions and the second was to bring about technological change. I start with a discussion of the institutional changes in agriculture and then discuss the interventions to raise agricultural productivity.

Land reforms took three forms: the first was the abolition of the *zamindari* system, the second was to provide secure rights to cultivators, and the third was to impose land ceilings to break down concentration of agricultural land (Besley and Burgess 2000). The objectives of land reforms had been set out in the plans, but the specific interventions were implemented by the provincial governments. The reforms were legislated by the provinces at different points in time and the types of reform varied. Besley and Burgess (2000) document the reforms enacted by sixteen provinces between 1958 and 1992 and find a significant variation in intensity of reforms. Most provinces had abolished the *zamindari* system before 1958. In the landlord regions, the reforms aimed to strengthen the rights of the tenants and subtenants as the cultivators. The reforms imposed land ceilings in order to break up the large *zamindari* estates. There is a consensus in the literature that the land ceiling was not effective. It has been argued that the reforms allowed the *zamindars* to retain a substantial amount of land for their 'personal cultivation', resulting in millions of tenants and subtenants being evicted. Further, the joint family system was used to divide the property into smaller units, but still kept these within the family (Besley and Burgess 2000). Besley and Burgess (2000) show that the higher the intensity of land reform, the greater was the decline in poverty. This was mainly a result of the removal of intermediaries and tenancy reforms rather than land redistribution.

The tenancy reforms were more widespread. Among them, Operation Barga in West Bengal provided cultivation rights to share croppers. The tenancy system in colonial Bengal had led to subrentals and widespread sharecropping. These groups did not have secure rights to the land they cultivated. Operation Barga, introduced by a left-wing government in the state of West Bengal, aimed to give permanent and inheritable tenure rights to the sharecroppers. The landlord could impose a maximum of 25 per cent of output as rent. The take up was widespread and the reform led to a rise in agricultural productivity in West Bengal (Banerjee et al. 2002).

A second major intervention, and the source of the biggest shift in agricultural productivity, was the Green Revolution of the late sixties. It was a widespread introduction of high yielding varieties of seeds, starting with wheat but expanding to other crops. After the severe droughts and harvest failures of 1965/66, the Indian government had to turn to the USA for food aid. This was a failure of the strategy of self-reliance and seen as a national humiliation. The policymakers turned their attention to raising agricultural productivity. The scientist who had led the search for new technology in agriculture, Dr M. S. Swaminathan, got approval to bring to India the high yielding varieties (HYV) of wheat and rice that had been successful in Mexico and the Philippines. The first success of the Green Revolution was visible in wheat cultivation and later on spread to rice. The HYV of wheat and rice required more intensive use of fertilizer and water. The Green Revolution increased agricultural productivity and agricultural incomes, and had consequences for living standards in rural India.

The success of this experiment in staple food crops was essential to the policy of self-sufficiency in food. Its adoption was most effective in areas with irrigation. Two supplementary policies encouraged adoption of HYV of seeds – the minimum purchase price for food grains and the subsidies on fertilizers and water use. The Green Revolution increased investment in agricultural infrastructure and subsidies towards inputs (Fan et al. 2000). The irrigation canals of the colonial years and the extension of irrigation in the first plan made northwestern regions of India more conducive to the adoption of the new technology. Literacy also mattered in the adoption of new technology. Take-up of HYV of seeds was higher among households where members had primary schooling, either due to the greater ease of adoption of the new technology or better access to information (Foster and Rosenzweig 1996). The share of cultivated area planted with HYV of wheat in northern India went up from an average of 10 per cent to 81 per cent between 1965–1969 and 1975–1979 and from 11 per cent to 82 per cent in rice (Barker et al. 1985, p. 218).

Table 2.11 shows gains were made between 1950 and 1997 in different crops. The largest increase came from the adoption of HYV of seeds in wheat. Coarser cereals like *jowar* and *bajra* did not see big increases initially. This was also true for cash crops like cotton and sugarcane. All crops saw increases in yield per acre over time (see Figure 2.5). However, despite the rise in yields, India still lagged behind the world average yield per acre in rice, coarse food grains, and oilseeds (Renuka 2003).

The crop mix varied across regions and agricultural growth exhibited big differences across regions and over time. Average annual growth in agricultural output was over 2 per cent per year but varied by crop, as shown in Table 2.12. From 1966 to 1981, the fastest growth in value of output was in wheat, and in the 1980s in rice, but growth in both food grains slowed in the 1990s when high value products such as spices, fruits, and vegetables saw the largest increase (see Table 2.11). From the mid 1960s to the early 1980s, the fastest growth was in the northwestern states, the first region to experience the Green Revolution, followed by the west and south, while growth in the east was slower (Bhalla and Tyagi 1989). In the following decade as the Green Revolution spread, provinces in the east saw a big increase in growth, particularly in West Bengal.

Kurosaki (2017) divides the districts of colonial India into these three regions, India, Bangladesh, and Pakistan, and measures output growth. He finds that all three countries grew faster after independence, but Pakistan had the fastest growth. Dar (2019), using evidence from the Green Revolution in India, shows that districts with colonial investments in irrigation in 1931 adopted the new varieties more successfully and saw rising yields. On the other hand, districts where canals were proposed in 1857 but never built continue to have worse agricultural outcomes more than a century later, despite being similar in dimensions of soil suitability.

Table 2.11 *Average annual growth in the value of agricultural output*

	1950/51–1965/66	1966/67–1980/81	1981/82–1990/91	1991/92–2006/07
Rice	3.6	2.6	4.0	0.9
Wheat	3.4	6.4	3.2	1.4
Coarse grains	1.6	0.9	0.7	0.5
Oil seeds	2.5	1.4	5.4	0.7
Sugarcane	4.4	2.5	2.6	4.1
Spices	2.5	3.2	4.5	4.9
Fruits/vegetables	1.8	4.3	2.1	4.3

Source: Tripathi and Prasad (2009)

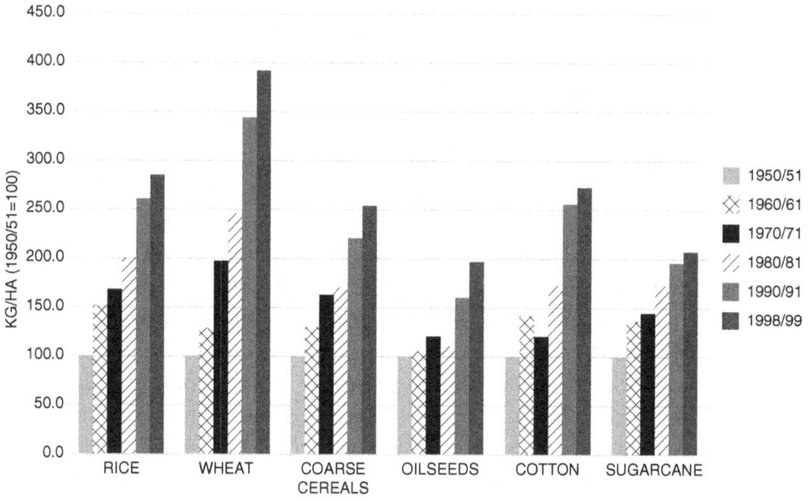

Figure 2.5 Changes in yield per acre by crop: KG/HA (1950/51=100)
Source: Renuka (2003)

The Green Revolution needed a reliable supply of water. With the Partition, a large proportion of the canal-irrigated land in Punjab and Sind was in Pakistan. In 1950/51, the share of irrigated land in India was 17.6 per cent.[1] This increased to 19.3 per cent in 1965/66, 39 per cent in 2000/01, and 47 per cent in 2012/13. The average annual rate

---

[1] This is lower than the share of irrigated area in colonial India. A large share of irrigated land was on the Pakistan side of the border.

Table 2.12 *Expansion in irrigation as a share of total cultivated land*

Colonial Provinces 1936	Share of irrigated land	Indian Provinces 2000	Share of gross irrigated land
Madras	24.2	Tamil Nadu	54.8
Bombay	3.6	Maharashtra	17.8
Bengal	5.8	West Bengal	55.5
United Provinces	24.7	Uttar Pradesh	71.6
Punjab	47.2	Punjab	96.5
Bihar	18.8	Bihar	68.5
Central Provinces & Berar	4.9	Madhya Pradesh	25.7
Assam	9.0	Assam	4.4
Orissa	15.2	Odisha	28.9

Source: Table 2.4 of this chapter and Dutta (2017, table 7)

of growth of land under irrigation between 1965/66 and 2012/13 has been 2.45 per cent in gross irrigated land and 2 per cent in net irrigated land (Dutta 2017, pp. 97–98). The difference between gross and net irrigation reflects the spread of multiple and double cropping. Well irrigation gained as a share of total irrigation, and the importance of canals declined. In 1965, canals covered 42 per cent of irrigated land. From the 1970s, private investment in tube-wells increased. In 2012/13, wells accounted for 62 per cent of all irrigation, canals 24 per cent, and tube-wells were over 80 per cent of well irrigation (Dutta 2017, pp. 98–100). Table 2.12 shows the expansion in irrigation after independence. Bengal had seen a decline in land productivity in the colonial period. This was also a region with less than 6 per cent of land under irrigation. The share of irrigated land was over 55 per cent in 2000 (see Table 2.12). West Bengal's Green Revolution followed the institutional change in the rights of the sharecroppers, but the initiative of the local government in making available new seeds, fertilizers, and other inputs also had a significant impact on the adoption of new technology and increasing yields (Bardhan and Mookherjee 2011). The institutional change was followed by public and private investment in irrigation (Bardhan et al. 2012).

    After decades of stagnation in colonial India, the eastern region of West Bengal benefitted from land reform and investment in agricultural infrastructure. In 2000, there was still some regional variation, but Table 2.12 shows evidence of convergence. Provinces like West Bengal and Bihar have seen significant changes. At the same time, the increase in well irrigation has led to over-exploitation of ground water that has contributed to the lowering of the water table.

There have been major changes in access to credit. Most agricultural credit in the colonial period came from private moneylenders. After independence, there was an expansion in lending by cooperatives, commercial banks, and regional rural banks and the share of agricultural credit from the formal sector in agricultural GDP increased significantly from 0.5 per cent in 1950/51 to 3 per cent in the 1960s, 5 per cent in the 1970s, 8 per cent in the 1980s, and 10 per cent in 1999/2000. In 2003/04 it was 15 per cent (Mohan 2006). The change in the share of borrowing from moneylenders by agricultural households broadly reflects this change. Informal sector credit to agricultural households declined from 70 per cent in 1951 to 16 per cent in 1981 but increased to 27 per cent in 2002 (Mohan 2006).

2.10   Developmental Outcomes of the Green Revolution

The Green Revolution directly increased agricultural growth and productivity and raised incomes. It also increased inequality due to unequal access to land and technology. The landed households benefitted more. Cultivators with large and medium landholdings enjoyed a larger share of the investment and subsidy. There could also be an indirect effect on growth through an increase in non-farm rural activity. Foster and Rosenzweig (2004a) found that growth in agricultural productivity did not lead to more non-farm activity locally: this occurred mainly in areas where the effect of the Green Revolution was weak. In these areas, the landless unskilled workers benefitted from the expansion in non-farm employment (Foster and Rosenzweig 2004b). Recent work by Asher et al. (2022) find that the Green Revolution villages have not seen an increasing share of non-farm activities, but the regional towns have seen growth in non-farm industry.

There was a decline in the number of people living below the poverty line from around 60 per cent before 1965 to 37 per cent in 1994. Fan et al. (2000) consider different types of investment in the rural economy, such as research into agricultural technology, road building, education, irrigation provision, and community development. They find that, between 1970 and 1993, all categories of investment in rural communities contributed to higher agricultural productivity and lowered poverty, and that the most significant poverty reduction came from agricultural research and construction of rural roads.

The Green Revolution had a favourable impact on health outcomes. Infant mortality declined in areas where a large share of land was devoted to HYV of seeds between 1966 and 1998 (Bharadwaj et al. 2020). The return to schooling increased significantly in areas of rapid technological change and resulted in greater private investment in schools in areas of high adoption (Foster and Rosenzweig 1996). At the same time, it increased inequality in education between households that owned land and the landless (Foster and Rosenzweig 2004b). Children from landed households withdrew from the market for child labour and were replaced with children from landless households.

2.11   The Slowdown

Growth in land productivity began to peter out from the 1990s. Agricultural growth in all regions slowed as yields declined. The factors that had held back agriculture in colonial India continue to hamper progress in recent years: low public investment in irrigation and water management, and underinvestment in scientific research. The ecological crises of lowering the water table and soil degradation had serious consequences for the sector (Bhalla and Singh 2010). In 1950, agriculture contributed to half of GDP but employed over two-thirds of the workforce. In 1999, the contribution of agriculture to GDP was less than a quarter, but it employed over half of the workforce.

The share of agriculture in gross capital formation was 20 per cent in 1950/51, but declined sharply from the 1980s (see Table 2.6). Although total public spending in agriculture was much larger than in the colonial period, it was only 15 per cent of total public investment at its peak (Balakrishnan 2010, p. 117). By the 1990s, it had declined to 6 per cent (Dhawan and Yadav 1997). Agricultural policy after the Green Revolution has focused on subsidies on water, electricity, and fertilizer. Since two-thirds of the land is owned by large- and middle-sized farmers, the policies to raise productivity have mainly benefitted these groups. Large groups of the agricultural workforce did not gain from the Green Revolution.

2.12   Conclusion

Colonial policies did not lead to prosperity in agriculture, although India became a part of the international division of labour with Britain and exported agricultural goods. Land under cultivation expanded over the nineteenth century and there were increases in land under cotton and sugarcane. For most crops, yield per acre was lower in 1910 than in 1600 (see Table 2.2), although we do not know precisely when the decline began. Table 2.9 shows the growth rate in yield per acre in different periods from 1891, when reliable agricultural statistics became available (Blyn 1966). The stagnation after 1916 was driven by a decline in land productivity in food crops. Productivity declined in eastern India but increased in the canal-irrigated regions of the north-west. The declining yield per acre in food grains also meant that there was less food available per head of the population.

Declining land productivity was due to a lack of investment in irrigation, availability of better quality seeds, and fertilizers.[2] Roy (2007) sees this as an ecological crisis arising from various types of market failures to improve quality of land. The new systems of land ownership and taxation, introduced by the British, did not lead to the expected investment in land. The landlord system of taxation that sought to incentivize landowners to carry out improvements in land failed to deliver. Yields fell in the rice-growing areas under the landlord system. Cultivators in both landlord and non-landlord systems were too poor to make large investments and needed some mechanism to ease the credit constraints faced by small cultivators. Colonial India did not have the institutions to provide credit to cultivators, who were dependent on local moneylenders with high interest rates for any type of credit. Lack of access to affordable credit meant there was no local private investment in land improvement.

The colonial state built irrigation canals. This was one of the largest networks in the world, but only 20 per cent of land under cultivation was irrigated in 1935. There was large variation across regions and the regions with a high share of irrigated land had higher yields (see Table 2.5). Irrigation canals made it possible to increase land under cultivation, but also increased output per acre through a shift to higher-value crops (Kurosaki 2003). Yield per acre for food crops, such as wheat on irrigated land, was higher across different regions and comparable to European levels. The average yield on rice fields in India in 1900 was lower than in Japan and Indonesia (see Table 2.5).

Although the lack of investment in agriculture had consequences for growth, the contribution of the railways in connecting markets and allowing movement of food to regions of scarcity cannot be underestimated. By the end of the nineteenth century, India had a large railway network and the literature shows unequivocally that the railways integrated markets. Not only did price gaps across markets decline (Hurd 1975; Donaldson 2019), the railways also reduced the incidence of famine (Burgess and Donaldson 2010) and increased agricultural incomes in districts with access to a railway line (Donaldson 2018). There were large social savings too as railway transport was more efficient compared to the alternatives (Bogart and Chaudhary 2015b). But the railways had little impact on agricultural productivity and the lack of investment in

[2] The contrast with East Asia is discussed in Chapter 6.

agricultural infrastructure had far more serious consequences for the economy in the early twentieth century than deindustrialization did in the nineteenth century. Agricultural stagnation in colonial India was only reversed with new policies in independent India (see Table 2.3).

The reversal of agricultural stagnation was one of the main achievements of the first decades after independence. It started with the policies of extending irrigation and was boosted by the Green Revolution. Both public and private investment in infrastructure increased in absolute terms as the share of investment in GDP increased. However, with market-based economic reforms, the emphasis has shifted away from productivity-enhancing investments in agriculture and many of the problems that agriculture faced in the colonial period have resurfaced. The water crisis and environmental degradation in India today echo the ecological crisis that Roy (2007) discussed in the context of the early twentieth century.

3   From Handlooms to Modern Industry and the Emergence of a Planned Economy

An important debate in Indian economic history is the decline of the traditional textile industry in the nineteenth century. It is viewed by many as a consequence of India's integration into the British Empire and the imposition of free trade, contributing to India's economic decline. From being a dominant producer and exporter of cotton cloth in the seventeenth and eighteenth centuries, India became a net importer of British-manufactured cotton cloth in the nineteenth century. As industrial employment declined, India integrated into the international economy of the British Empire as a supplier of food and raw material. The nineteenth century is characterized by deindustrialization as the handloom-based cotton textile industry declined. The term 'deindustrialization' was coined by historians in the context of the decline of this traditional cotton textile industry, well before the term was used to describe the declining share of manufacturing in industrialized economies of the twentieth century as industrial jobs disappeared and the service sector became more important in employment and GDP. In the Indian context of the nineteenth century, this was a decline in the share of industrial employment as people lost their livelihoods and moved back to agriculture.

Several changes occurred simultaneously in nineteenth-century India. Handmade textiles lost their position in the world market, agricultural exports increased, and the contribution of industry to the GDP and employment declined. However, at the same time as the jobs in the traditional industry disappeared, new industrial jobs became available. These jobs were in the newly emerging modern industries that used new types of technology, borrowed from Europe.

In this chapter I ask the following questions: Did colonial policy lead to deindustrialization? How did the new industries develop in a colonial economy? Who were the investors and who were the entrepreneurs? What was the role of colonial policy? How did Indian industrialization during the colonial period impact on developments after independence? Was there continuity or change? I will focus on policies towards industries in

India before and after independence and their impact on the industrial sector. I start with the nineteenth-century deindustrialization and go on to discuss a unique pattern of industrial development in the second half of the century that occurred in the absence of a supportive state and was led by the social networks of Indian trading communities.

3.1   Deindustrialization

Traditional technology was used in India to produce good quality cotton fabrics: muslin and calico. The former was sold in the luxury end of the market and the latter was for regular use. These products experienced a big rise in demand in the international market with the arrival of European trading companies in India–British, Dutch, French, and Danish in the seventeenth century. The companies contracted with the weavers, typically through middlemen, to produce cloth of a given size and design within a period of eight to ten months. The weavers were given a cash advance to buy raw material and food and deliver the finished textile products to the agents of the European trading companies. The textiles were exported to Europe and the rest of the world and dominated these markets. The English East India Company (EIC) became a key player in this market along with the Dutch East India Company. The companies established settlements and production centres, first in the western parts of India, then in the south, and finally in Bengal in the east, to buy textiles for export.

In return, India imported bullion. To raise the cash advance paid to the weavers, the companies, including the EIC, borrowed heavily from Indian merchants and bankers. The house of the merchant Jagat Seth was one of the main lenders to the EIC and assisted them in the conquest of Bengal. In 1757, the ruler of Bengal was defeated by the EIC and Bengal came under Company rule. The purchase of textiles was now funded by land revenue from Bengal. This opened up a new phase in the Company's commercial enterprise in India: the EIC set its goal to colonize other regions and by the middle of the nineteenth century, a large part of the country had come under its rule. The EIC continued to trade in textiles during this time, but the textile trade had begun to lose its importance well before the Company's trading monopoly in India ended.

The external environment of the textile trade had changed in the decades following the conquest of Bengal. The industrial revolution in England dramatically transformed international trade in textiles. Machine-made British goods were cheaper than handloom-based Indian cloth and British yarn and cloth flooded the world market. It is arguable that the technological revolution in spinning and weaving in cotton textiles did not happen without assistance from the British state. Faced with protests from the local producers of woollen and silk textiles against the entry of Indian textiles in the British market, the British government raised tariffs on these imports from the 1690s. In 1700, the first Calico Act banned import of printed calico for sale in the British market. White calico could still be imported for printing locally and printed calico could be imported for re-export to other markets by the EIC. In 1721, the second Calico Act banned sale of all calicos in the British market (O'Brien et al. 1991). Thus, the British state that implemented free trade in the nineteenth century used tariffs and import bans to create conditions for the development of an import-substituting industry.

The high demand for imported cotton textiles has created conditions for import substitution in Britain, but the conditions of developing an import-substituting cotton textile industry in Britain borrowing labour intensive technology from India did not exit. British wages were five times the Indian wages (see Chapter 1) and the labour intensive technology used in India would not have given the British industry an advantage in early eighteenth century. High wages (Allen 2009) and useful technical knowledge among the workforce (Mokyr 2009) provided conditions for developing a new labour-saving technology. Once labour-saving spinning and weaving processes were developed, the new technology of the industrial revolution gave Britain an advantage over India in the cost of production. The weaving technology in India had changed little over centuries (Habib 1976). Innovation tended to take the form of new weaving designs and new types of dyeing (Ramaswamy 1985). The spinning technology in India was the *charkha,* an equipment for hand-spinning that was operated mainly by women as a part-time activity. The invention of the flying shuttle in Britain changed the technology of spinning in a major way, giving British spinners a big advantage.

Tables 3.1 and 3.2 show the emergence of British advantage in textile production. Table 3.1 compares the advantage of a spinning machine in Britain over the hand-spinning equipment used in India and Table 3.2 illustrates the reversal of the competitive advantage in the textile market from India to Britain. Table 3.1 shows that, in 1780, Crompton's mules required one-fifth of the working hours to process the same quantity of raw cotton into yarn. By the end of the century, this had declined to one-tenth of the working hours in India. The rapid decline in the time to process cotton into yarn continued with successive new inventions.

India had another advantage over Britain. Raw cotton was produced locally in India. Initially input costs were higher in Britain, as wages were high and raw cotton was expensive. The Napoleonic Wars drove cotton

Table 3.1 *Best-practice labour productivity in spinning 80s yarn in England (1780–1825) (operative hours to process 100 lb) in comparison to traditional technology in India in the eighteenth century*

India eighteenth century	Hand-spinning	10,000
Britain 1780	Crompton's mule	2,000
Britain 1790	100 spindle mule	1,000
Britain 1795	Power-assisted mule	300
Britain 1825	Roberts' automatic mule	135

Source: Broadberry and Gupta (2009)

Table 3.2 *Emergence of British comparative advantage: relative total factor input cost, price, and total factor productivity*

	Total factor input cost $(TFIC_{Br}/TFIC_{In})$	FOB price (P_{Br}/P_{In})	Total factor productivity (TFP_{Br}/TFP_{In})
1680	206	200	203
1770	289	209	144
1790	357	150	238
1820	150	43	349

Source: Broadberry and Gupta (2009)

prices even higher, but when they ended, the cost of importing raw cotton declined. Cotton was imported from the American South and use of slave labour on the American plantations allowed British industry to narrow the price disadvantage. The new literature revisiting the role of slavery in providing a plentiful supply of raw cotton to Britain has revived the thesis of Eric Williams on the importance of slavery in the industrial revolution (Beckert 2015). This discussion remains outside the scope of this book.

As the quality of machines improved, British producers gained an advantage in total factor productivity. With labour-saving technology, the British firms produced a larger output per worker and newer machines enhanced this advantage. By 1820, the efficiency gains and the declining raw cotton prices reduced the manufacturing cost of textiles in Britain well below the Indian price.[1] As Table 3.2 shows, British prices of textiles were twice as high as Indian prices in 1770, one and a half times in

---

[1] This calculation does not factor in the role of slave labour on cotton plantations in keeping prices low.

1790 and, by 1820, 35 per cent of Indian prices (Broadberry and Gupta 2009). Table 3.2 shows the relative decline in total factor input cost in British industry and the relative increase in total factor productivity. This advantage, by 1820, was large enough for British goods to make inroads into the Indian market.

Bengal was the main production centre for the textile trade in the middle of the eighteenth century, but only 9–11 per cent of the total industrial workers in textile production in Bengal produced for the textile trade (Prakash 1976). The decline in textile production resulted in the loss of the international market and also the loss of market share in the home market to British goods. Ray (2009) explores the decline of the industry in Bengal and argues that 28 per cent of textile workers lost their jobs between 1830 and 1859. This is large for the sector, but the share of the sector in total employment was small. Ray (2011) suggests that, if Britain had not imposed tariffs on Indian products between 1795 and 1826 in response to the demand from British textile interests, the price disadvantage faced by Indian goods in the British market might have been delayed. However, by 1826 tariffs no longer protected the British industry. Instead the machines of the industrial revolution enhanced the comparative advantage of British goods in the international market. Broadberry and Gupta (2009) find a similar timeline in the decline of Indian traditional industry in terms of the shift in competitive advantage from India to Britain.

The deindustrialization of Bengal has been documented by Bagchi (1976) based on evidence of industrial employment in Bengal in 1811 and in 1901. The decline in the share of the workforce in industrial occupations was large. Twomey (1983) shows that, during the period of 1850 to 1880, there was an absolute decline in industrial employment. Over 50 per cent of the full-time equivalent jobs in textiles had disappeared. Whatever the estimate of unemployment in this sector, economic historians agree that the traditional textile industry lost its place in the globalized economy and that there was a significant decline in industrial jobs and thousands of industrial workers moved to agricultural occupations. The impact was particularly large in areas where the textile industry had a significant share in employment. However, measuring societal gains and losses does not suggest that all groups lost out.

As a colony, India did not have tariff autonomy. A back-of-the-envelope calculation based on Table 3.2 would suggest that a tariff rate of 133 per cent on yarn might have stopped imports from flooding the Indian market for some time. However, Indian consumers gained from lower prices of imported cloth. Cloth consumption per capita increased from 5.2–6.7 sq. yards in 1795 to 8.2 in 1880 and 13.5 in

1920 (Roy 2012). The rising cloth consumption coincided with deindustrialization and was mainly due to cheaper imports rather than rising income. Handloom weavers benefitted too. The first segment of
the traditional industry to decline was spinning, as handloom weavers
switched to imported yarn. The Indian handloom industry lost out to
British imports initially, but, after 1880, also faced competition from
products of the newly developing modern textile industry that used
imported British machinery.

The emerging modern industries added some dynamism to the industrial sector. The traditional industries survived in niche markets and
reinvented their technological skills (Roy 2006, pp. 192–195). The share
of British cotton cloth in the Indian market declined from 60 per cent
in 1880 to 51 per cent in 1900 but by 1930 British goods supplied only
one-third of the market (Twomey 1983). The share of the large-scale
sector rose from 8 per cent to 15 per cent between 1880 and 1900 and
continued to rise at the expense of the handloom sector (Tomlinson
2013, p. 90). It has been estimated to account for 44 per cent of the market in cotton cloth in 1920, rising to 62 per cent in 1940. The handloom
sector continued to contract and stabilized at a market share of 25 per
cent (Roy 2006, p. 195).

3.2   Rise of Modern Industry

From 1850, machinery was imported from Britain to set up a modern
cotton textile industry in western India and a modern jute textile industry in eastern India. The location of the two industries was partly determined by proximity to raw material and partly by the social composition
of commercial interests in the regions. The main cotton growing region
was in the hinterland of Bombay and the jute was mainly cultivated in
the hinterland of Calcutta. Calcutta was the hub for British businesses.
Bombay, on the other hand, had a strong representation of Indian trading communities in the commercial sector.

British investment in and around Calcutta was in three sectors: tea,
jute, and coal. All three sectors served colonial interests in the export
market or supplied to the railways. Britain was the main market for Indian
tea and it was a common item in the British consumption basket. Jute
products were used as packaging for transport and sandbags in wars and
floods. An industrial or commercial firm could be registered in Britain as
a Sterling company or in India as a Rupee company. Sterling and Rupee
companies were defined by the place of registration rather than ownership. A large share of the tea companies were set up as Sterling companies in London and the investors were British, but a sizeable group of

firms were British owned and registered in India and were run by British management companies. Jute firms were set up mainly in India as Rupee companies, with a few set up as Sterling companies in Britain. Coal mining firms were mainly registered in India. Investors in the Rupee companies came from both Britain and India and many expatriate British men and women in India owned shares in these companies. Systematic information on the social background of the shareholders is difficult to get. Information from one jute firm in Calcutta shows that, of the 119 shareholders in the jute firm in 1874, 105 were 'Christian'[2] and the rest from Indian communities of Bengali, Marwari, Muslim, and Parsi (Rungta 1985). A similar pattern was also true for a British-owned cotton textile firm. Where the firms were registered did not matter. British firms in tea, jute, and coal were managed by a few British managing agents, an institutional innovation in several Asian countries that were colonized by Britain.

Managing agents were typically British firms that owned shares in several companies, both Sterling and Rupee, and were responsible for their management. They provided the initial capital and their reputation was useful for selling shares to potential investors. Contrary to an earlier literature, Nomura (2014) shows, on the basis of archival evidence, that the managing agents had majority shareholding. The managing agents contributed to the concentration of economic power in the hands of a few companies across several industries. The Investors India Year Book of 1911, which published information about companies registered in India, shows that eight managing agents controlled 55 per cent of the jute companies, 61 per cent of the tea companies, and 46 per cent of the coal companies (Bagchi 1972, p. 176).

The cotton textile firms were set up as Rupee companies in India. There were a few British firms in this industry, but an overwhelming majority of entrepreneurs were Indians, as were the investors. This casts doubt on claims by Max Weber (1967) and Vera Anstey (1929) about the cultural disadvantage of Indians in entrepreneurship. Max Weber wrote in *The Religion of India: The Sociology of Hinduism and Buddhism* (1916):

Capitalism would remain weak in India because the ancient religions of India have no element of the Protestant ethic, a necessary element for the growth and development of capitalistic thoughts. (Mishra S.K., Kamal K.K. (2014) Capitalism in the Indian Social Environment: An Ethnic Perspective. Palgrave Macmillan, London)

---

[2] British in this context.

Table 3.3 *Sterling and Rupee investment (1914–15) (£m)*

Sectors	Sterling	Rupee	Total
Tea	19.7	2.9	22.6
Cotton	0.4	13.0	13.9
Jute	2.7	7.8	10.5
Gold	2.3	0.3	2.4
Cotton and jute press	1.2	1.2	2.4
Total	27.4	29.0	56.9

Source: Chapman (1992)

Table 3.3 shows such claims do not have empirical validity. By 1914, there was significant Indian investment in cotton textiles, second only to tea plantations set up with British investment. British investment was concentrated in the export industries like tea and jute, while Indian investment dominated the import substituting industry of cotton textiles (Morris 1983; Gupta 2014). The commercial world of Bombay and Calcutta was segregated by industry and social networks.

How did Indian entrepreneurs develop a local cotton textile industry that could compete with Lancashire? The industry developed without supportive government policies that were available in many other countries in Europe and North America. Even attempts to put tariffs on British imports of cotton goods for revenue purposes were met with resistance from the textile interests in Lancashire, the centre of the British industry. These interests successfully lobbied for countervailing excise duties to be imposed on cotton textile goods produced in Indian factories. The United Cotton Manufacturers' Association of the North and North-East and Lancashire Cotton Spinners' and Manufacturers' Association lobbied Parliament in 1895, confident that they could sway policy in their favour:

We do not ask, nor do we require any favourable consideration, but we do ask that if for purposes of revenue, either now or at any other time, the imposition of import duties is essential, that they shall be imposed equally on the products of India with those of Lancashire. Justice to India must not mean injustice to Lancashire. Their interests are identical, and an injustice cannot be imposed on one without being reflected on the other. The cry of 'Perish India!' meets with no response in Lancashire, for with the prosperity of India our interest is bound up; but as the custodians of the welfare of the cotton trade, on which the prosperity of Lancashire depends, we cannot allow its interests to be sacrificed to the Indian mill-owners ...

We believe that our interests can be safely entrusted to you, and we look with confidence to your decision, which we feel will be such as will assist in renewing prosperity to our industry by restoring to us the right of free and equitable trading.[3]

The cost of establishing a cotton mill in India was three times that of an equivalent mill in England and the cost of borrowing was five times higher (Oonk 2001).[4] The entrepreneurs came from community-based trading networks that had accumulated wealth in pre-industrial activities, such as trade and informal banking, and the community became the source of capital for the industry. The commercial sector in India had comprised of caste and religious subgroup-based networks of traders and indigenous bankers. These communities were defined by occupational specialization, where skills and jobs passed from father to son. Endogamous marriage cemented the social and economic interactions. The trading communities in the Bombay region were the Parsis, the Hindu communities of Vanias and Bhatia, Jain Vanias, Khoja and Bohra Muslims, and the Baghdadi Jews. These groups had amassed wealth from various commercial activities, such as selling opium to China and raw cotton to Britain, shipping in the Indian Ocean, trade with West Asia and East Africa, and moneylending. Profits from the opium trade had declined after the Opium Wars in China. The American Civil War of the 1860s increased demand for Indian cotton and trading groups in western India invested heavily in trade in raw cotton. Raw cotton was purchased from the cultivators and baled for export. When the civil war ended and profits from the cotton trade declined, many of the traders turned to industry.

Gupta et al. (2022) studied the pattern of entry into the cotton textile industry in the aftermath of the American Civil War, using data on individual entrepreneurs. They found a strong concentration of members from the same community as directors in a firm. Figures 3.1A and 3.1B show the concentration of directors in firms by community in the regions of Bombay and Ahmedabad, where the early cotton mills were set up. When an entrepreneur joined a firm as a director, an overwhelming majority of the other directors of the firm were fellow community members, indicating that an entering director was more likely to trust a member of his community with his investment. The timing of entry also indicates the presence of strong community connections. In the trading world of the Indian merchants in the nineteenth century, social connections had been the main source of information and contract

---

[3] Papers relating to the Indian Tariff Act 1896 and the Cotton Duties Act 1896.
[4] Based on the annual report of the Bombay Millowners' Association (1879, p. 44).

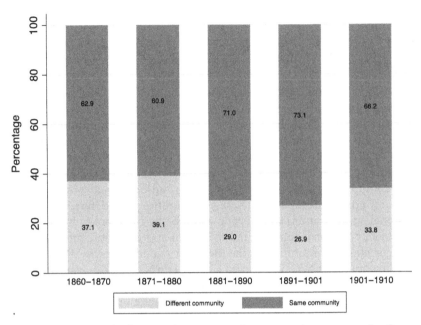

Figure 3.1A Community concentration at entry in cotton textiles firms in the Bombay region (1860–1910)

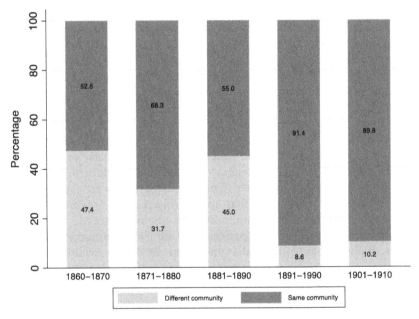

Figure 3.1B Community concentration at entry in cotton textiles firms in the Ahmedabad region (1860–1910)
Source: Gupta et al. (2022)

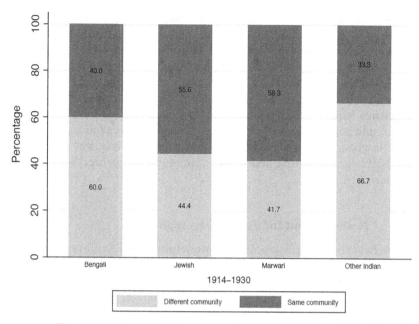

Figure 3.2 Community concentration at entry in jute textiles firms in the Calcutta region (1914–1930)

enforcement. When industrial firms were set up, community networks played a role in mitigating problems of contract enforcement and drawing resources for investment in the absence of well-functioning legal and credit institutions and a supportive state. Community connections were the means of capital accumulation and growth in the domestic cotton textile industry.

Similarly, when Marwari traders entered the British-dominated jute industry in Calcutta after the First World War, community connections were important. During the war, profits rose in export industries such as jute, used for gunny bags at the frontline. Share prices rose in jute firms and many shareholders of the Rupee companies sold their shares to the Marwaris. The Marwari traders in Bengal controlled the trade in raw jute and had close connections with British firms. A few firms were also set up by the Marwaris during and after the war. Among the Indian entrants, the Marwaris dominated. The concentration of community ownership in firms was lower than in cotton textile firms as entry was via share transfers in British firms (Figure 3.2). Looking at these two major industries, the role of community networks in early industrialization in India is of particular interest.

The First World War changed the external environment for industries catering to the domestic market. The natural protection provided by the war allowed the import substituting industries to prosper. The first successful iron and steel factory had been set up before the war by Parsi entrepreneurs from the Tata family, and went into production during the war. The war was also advantageous for other large-scale factory industries, such as breweries, paper manufacturers, cement manufacturers, and sugar refineries. When the war ended, these industries could form interest groups to lobby for protection. The interwar years saw the establishment of the first tariff commission and protection of local industries.

3.3   Railways and Industrial Development

At the heart of the British policy for modernization of India was the railway network. From the middle of the nineteenth century, the British government in India guaranteed a rate of return on investment in British railway companies that entered the Indian market. Shares and bonds were mainly sold in the British market with a guaranteed rate of return of 5 per cent per year. In contrast to 51,519 British shareholders, there were only 368 Indians (Morris 1967). The rate of return on railway investment, though attractive to a British investor, was much lower than returns for the commercial activities of Indian traders. The private railway companies had a twenty-five-year window of private ownership and could be nationalized thereafter. Indeed, this happened from the middle of the 1880s, with the government taking over both ownership and operation of the railway lines or having public–private partnerships (Bogart and Chaudhary 2015a).

Although the railway lines initially developed in response to pressure from British business to connect ports to the hinterland, the lines spread rapidly across the country, creating a dense network, and 52 per cent of British Indian districts were connected to a railroad by 1881. By 1901 this had increased to 87 per cent and by 1921, 96 per cent were connected (Chaudhary and Fenske 2020).

Being connected to a railway line had several positive consequences: it integrated markets across India and reduced price dispersion (Hurd 1975); increased trade and income in districts connected to the railway network (Donaldson 2018); and the connected districts were less vulnerable to weather shocks (Burgess and Donaldson 2010), as pointed out in Chapter 2. However, railway construction in India did not have the same effect on industrialization as in Germany and the USA, where backward and forward linkages led to the development of other industries. The backward linkages developed local production of iron and steel and rolling stock. In the Indian case, most of the rolling stock was imported from Britain. Between 1865 and 1940, local industry manufactured 700 locomotives and imported 12,000 (Hurd, 1983). The coal industry was a linkage sector and sold 30 per cent of output to the railways (Hurd, 1983). Railway workshops trained local workers, who became skilled at repairing rail stock, but the railways did not lead to widespread development of related industries.

3.4   Interwar Years: Tariffs and Industrial Development

The First World War brought changes in colonial policy towards local industries. Industrial activities increased during the war and domestic firms engaged in import substituting activities strengthened their position. The connection between Indian businesses and the Nationalist movement concerned the British government in India. It generated support for policies that would protect the industrial sector (Lockwood 2012). The Industrial Commission of 1916–1918, an inquiry into the viability of local industry, made a case for protecting nascent industry. The Fiscal Commission of 1923 recommended setting up a tariff board that would look at individual industries on a case by case basis for protection rather than a general tariff. Industries that had developed during the war, such as iron and steel, found it hard to compete with imports once the war ended and demanded tariffs. Tariffs were imposed on imported cotton goods from 1921, for revenue purposes. Other new industries also received some tariff protection, but the industrial interest groups wanted more (Tomlinson 2013, pp. 111–112). The tariff board reviewed individual cases by industry and raised tariffs on eleven sectors, including cotton textiles, iron and steel, paper, sugar, matches, and chemicals. In the 1930s, several industries benefitted from new tariffs or an increase in the tariff rate.

Changes were introduced in stores' purchase policy of the government of India, that decided where equipment for public projects would be purchased. Before the war all machinery and equipment for public projects was bought in Britain, and the contracts for purchases were coordinated in Britain. The office relocated to India to coordinate the procurement for public investment and contracted with local vendors of chemicals, metals, and construction materials (Roy 2018, pp. 127–128).

Protection of the iron and steel industry was at the core of tariff policy in the interwar years. A few engineering industries that used iron and steel became eligible for tariffs, but this was not a systematic policy for developing manufacturing capability in capital goods. Wagon building was protected, but locomotive production was not. These decisions were made by the tariff board on the basis of the difference in the cost, insurance, and freight inclusive (c.i.f) price of imported products and the locally manufactured goods (Bagchi 1972, pp. 338–351).

Britain's position in international markets was undermined by the war and Japan had emerged as a competitor in the Asian markets. To regain its market share in the colonies, Britain gradually moved towards a policy of discriminating protection, that would allow British goods preferential access in the colonial markets. This would impose a disadvantage on Japanese textiles in the Indian market. The policy was implemented as the Imperial Preference Agreement in 1932 and countries outside the Empire paid higher tariffs to export to the colonies. In India, tariff on textiles from outside the Empire was 50 per cent, while British goods paid 25 per cent (Markovits 2002, pp. 51–52). Sugar that was imported from Java had supplied 85 per cent of the Indian market until 1932. The local industry saw a massive expansion as prohibitive tariffs were applied to sugar imports from outside the Empire (Markovits 2002, p. 58). TISCO, the iron and steel producing firm, increased its market share from 25 per cent to 75 per cent between 1929 and 1939 (Markovits 2002, p. 59). Arthi et al. (2024) found that, although tariffs lowered imports over all, Britain gained at the expense of other countries from the trade diversion effect of discriminating protection.

The increase in textile production in India during the First World War had been based on existing capacity. When the war ended, there was a large increase in imports of textile machinery (Bagchi 1972, p. 258). The cotton textile industry began to expand in locations outside the main centres in Bombay and Ahmedabad, where wages were lower. In the new locations new entrepreneurs came from different trading communities. The industrial base began to spread beyond the Presidencies of Bengal and Bombay, although the two remained dominant.

The entry of new firms and the increase in industrial output was driven mainly by Indian entrepreneurs. The profitability in trade and moneylending had declined during the Great Depression and regulation of the informal credit market gained legal legitimacy in several provinces, as discussed in Chapter 2. Investment in industry became attractive to members of trading networks. New groups of entrepreneurs outside Bombay and Calcutta gained visibility in industry: the Chettiars in the South; the Punjabi Hindu Bania, Lala Shri Ram in the North; and the Marathi Brahmin, Kirloskar in the West. Much of the initial investment by Indians had been in textiles but the new entrepreneurs diversified into other sectors too. Although no specific support for industries producing machinery was available, a few individual entrepreneurs took up the challenge. Kirloskar was among the few. Diversification became the route to technological upgrading for Indian business interests.

The Kirloskar brothers offer an unusual case of a family firm that moved early into machinery production. Unlike most other industrial entrepreneurs, the Kirloskars did not come from a trading background and members of the second generation had formal engineering degrees (Tripathi and Mehta 1990). The other new business group, Shri Ram, came from a trading community in Punjab and was initially involved in cotton textiles. The group diversified into sugar and light engineering in the 1930s (Tripathi 1987, p. 8). There were a few British firms that manufactured white sugar before the First World War but of the new firms in the interwar period were founded by Indians. Names familiar in Indian industry after independence – Singhania, Dalmia, and Thapar – started with sugar mills, but diversified to other sectors (Tripathi 2004, pp. 194–197; Roy 2015, pp. 135–140). The coal companies, which were mainly British owned, saw Indian capital enter in the 1930s. The import-substituting industries made gains in the interwar years and consolidated their position during the Second World War.

The Chettiars are a good example of the shift from banking to industry. Although they had some presence in the industrial sector, their main entry into industry was in the 1930s, when their business of providing credit for rice cultivation in Burma was adversely affected. As the indebted Burmese peasantry could not repay their loans and faced losing their land, the Chettiars faced hostility from the agricultural producers (Kudaisya 2010) and looked for alternative opportunities. A large part of their new investment was in the Madras Presidency and in textiles, but they invested in other sectors too, such as rice and oil mills, chemical manufacture, potteries, and sugar refining (Mahadevan 1978; Rudner 1994). This was also the time when the Birlas, one of the dominant industrial groups after independence, diversified from trade to industry. The family moved into textiles, sugar, and paper, and less successfully into textile machinery just before the Second World War (Tripathi 1987).

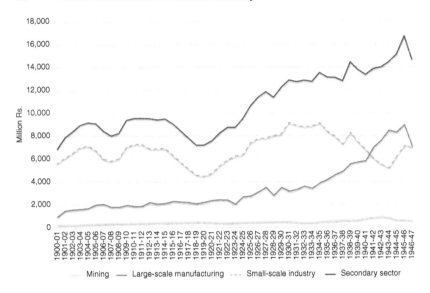

Mining —— Large-scale manufacturing --- Small-scale industry —— Secondary sector

Figure 3.3 Growth in industry (1900–1947) in million Rupees in 1938/39 prices
Source: Sivasubramonian (2000)

The balance between large and small industries began to change. Figure 3.3 illustrates that, by 1946, they had equal shares in industrial output. Large-scale manufacturing drove industrial productivity growth over this period. Manufacturing output increased two and a half times in India between 1913 and 1939, well above the world average but behind Japan, where manufacturing output increased by a factor of five (CEHI 1983, p. 609). Although both India and Japan had set up a modern cotton textile industry during the last decades of the nineteenth century, by the 1930s India did not compare favourably with Japan, not only in terms of rate of industrial growth, but also in terms of diversification of the industrial sector. Japan developed intermediate goods and machinery industries, while India lagged behind. Productivity in the Japanese cotton textile industry had been comparable to the Indian industry in 1890, but by 1910 Japan had an advantage and it widened in the interwar years. But Japan's industrialization was exceptional.

In the interwar years, there was growth and diversification of India's industrial sector. Figure 3.4 shows the fast rise of new industries such as sugar, cement, matches, and iron and steel, while growth in textiles plateaued. The jute industry faced a major crisis when the wartime

Table 3.4 *Shares of subsectors in net output in modern manufacturing*

	1913/14	1938/39	1939/40 to 1946/47
Cotton textiles	36.2	29.9	23.2
Jute manufactures	15.0	8.0	5.3
Refined sugar	1.6	3.4	4.1
Paper products	0.4	0.5	0.6
Cement	–	1.0	1.1
Woollen cloth	0.3	0.3	0.5
Iron and steel	0.8	4.4	3.6
Matches	–	1.2	0.8
Other	45.7	52.2	60.8
Net value of large-scale manufacturing output in 1938/39 prices (Rs million)	635	1701	2258.5

Source: Morris (1983) (CEHI) table 7.22

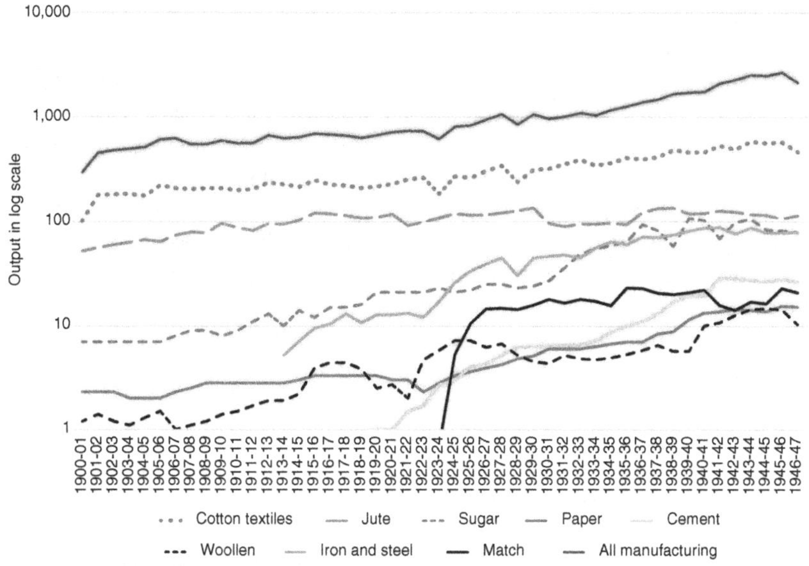

Figure 3.4 Growth of subsectors in the modern manufacturing industry
Source: Sivasubramonian (2000)

demand for hessian disappeared. The changing shares of the subsectors and an increase in the share of new industries is shown in Table 3.4. The net value of large-scale manufacturing increased rapidly.

3.5   British Firms in the Interwar Years

Firms in the old export industries that were owned by managing agencies did not adjust to the new environment. The managing agents who controlled and managed these did not diversify into new industries, a path that was taken by Indian business groups. The new form of British investment at this time was foreign direct investment. British multinational corporations entered the Indian market in the changing economic situation and in response to tariffs. Their involvement was in new import substituting industries such as machinery, food, tobacco, and chemicals (Tomlinson 1981).

The two major British-owned export industries faced excess capacity after the First World War in a situation of declining demand. Their response was to organize cartels that would reduce production. The cartels in tea and jute sought governmental support to legislate in favour of the cartel. The outcomes of the two cartels were very different. In tea, output had increased during the war and there was excess supply in the 1920s. The Indian Tea Association made a big push to develop a market in India. However, with the onset of the Great Depression, the international tea prices declined sharply. An international tea cartel formed in 1930 involving the producers in India, Ceylon, and the Netherland Indies, the three main producers, to stabilize prices. The cartel was successful in reducing output and preventing further decline in prices (Gupta 1997, 2001). The cartel fell apart in 1931/32 and was reconstituted in 1933. The governments of the three countries were lobbied to bring in export quotas that reduced exports by the existing companies and deterred new entry. The Indian Tea Association was a powerful lobby and successfully influenced policy in favour of the cartel. Tea prices recovered. The older and more established tea companies were the beneficiaries. The cartel was also successful in preventing new production in countries outside the cartel with a ban on the export of seeds.

The jute industry similarly faced an excess capacity as the war ended: demand for jute in the international markets had collapsed after 1929 and did not recover until the onset of the Second World War. The value of exports was 40 per cent of its 1929 level in 1934 (Bagchi 1972, p. 280). The industry responded by forming a cartel that reduced working hours all through the 1920s. However, this cartel faced a significant challenge from a group of new entrants, who remained outside the cartel (Goswami 1982; Gupta 2005). They were new Indian firms. The entry of the Marwari traders into the boardrooms of the British-owned jute companies during and after the First World War, as discussed in a previous section, signalled a major change in the ownership and development of the industry. The Indian firms increased production, leading to acrimony between British and Indian firms (Goswami 1982). The jute interests did not get the same support from the government in Delhi. The Montagu–Chelmsford reforms in 1919 had increased provincial autonomy, and political representation through elections made the provincial political groups mindful of the interests of the cultivators, traders, and emerging Indian industrial groups, and not just of British business.

The managing agents of the British firms had enjoyed social and political privileges, and had lobbied the colonial state for favourable policies. They had excluded Indian business from the industrial associations, such as the Bengal Chamber of Commerce. In a more competitive environment they were unable reinvent themselves and move into the new sectors. Influential managing agents such as Bird and Company, dominant in jute and coal, found it difficult to enter in the new industries as the business environment changed (Tomlinson 1981). British business groups like Parry's and Binnys in the south were connected to import-substituting sectors, such as sugar and textiles, (Tripathi 2004, pp. 211–213).

A new type of British firm succeeded and established their positions in the growing industrial sector. British multinational companies like Unilever, Guest Keen Williams, Metal Box, Philips, and Dunlop, took advantage of the protected environment and entered the Indian market. So too did multinational companies from other countries, such as Bata Shoes, Siemens, and General Electric (Tripathi 2004, pp. 219–220). The Indian firms that took advantage of the new environment were more willing to cooperate with the new foreign companies. Collaboration between Indian and British entrepreneurs emerged in consumer goods, such as Britannia Biscuits, and intermediate and capital goods produced by Martin Burn and Indian Standard Wagon (Roy 2015, p. 142).

The Second World War consolidated the position of Indian industrial groups. The Tatas emerged as the largest business group, operating in sectors as diverse as textiles, iron and steel, and chemicals, and the new entrants began to spread across the new industries. The Indian Nationalist movement's connection with industrial interests grew stronger through the different phases of resistance to British rule. On the eve of Indian independence, the Indian-owned modern industrial firms had a significant presence and there were a number of industrial groups that provided effective industrial entrepreneurship. The traditional and small-scale industry did not disappear. It catered to niche markets and adapted to the changing technological environment (Haynes 2012).

3.6   Planning and Industrialization

As India moved from colonial rule to independence, regulation rather than global connections became a tool for industrialization, with the public sector playing the leading role. Jawaharlal Nehru, the first prime minister in independent India, put industry at the heart of the development strategy. India was among other countries in the developing world, including Brazil in Latin America and South Korea and Taiwan in East Asia, that saw state intervention to support industrialization as a pathway to development. Imposing controls on trade was at the centre of this policy. Trade, often described as a 'handmaiden of colonialism', was associated with the lack of industrial development. Regulation in post-independence India went further and adopted the Soviet model of planning industrial development in order to develop a capital goods sector, which had been missing in the colonial period. This was laid out in the Second Plan (1956–1961). The Mahalanobis model, named after its architect, the statistician Prasanta Chandra Mahalanobis, divided the economy into two sectors: capital and consumer goods. To raise the investment rate, the economy had to increase its production of capital and intermediate goods that would affect the rate of growth of all sectors. Therefore, capital goods production had to be prioritized.

The framework of the Mahalanobis Model is one of *unbalanced growth*, where the capital goods sector was to generate linkages with other sectors and pull the economy out of a low growth equilibrium (Ray 1998, pp. 142–143). Balakrishnan (2010, p. 42) argues that the strategy to raise public investment followed Rosenstein–Rodan's theory of *big push* to move an economy out of stagnation. Gross domestic capital formation as a share of GDP during the colonial period had been 6–7 per cent. Following the Second Plan, gross domestic capital formation as a share of GDP rose to 19 per cent by the late 1960s. The public sector stepped in as a producer and its share rose dramatically from 25 per cent in 1950 to 50 per cent in 1980 (see Table 3.5) The share of manufacturing in gross fixed capital formation rose over this period. Capital formation in manufacturing rose faster than in other comparable countries initially, but this advantage was short lived as South Korea and Taiwan raised their investment rate and India began to fall behind (see Table 3.6).

Why did the government not rely on the private sector? In colonial India, there were a few private entrepreneurs producing iron and steel, and engineering. Several did not survive. Balakrishnan (2010) discusses the coordination problem for private entrepreneurs, who were

Table 3.5 *Capital formation and the public sector*

	Gross domestic capital formation as share of GDP	Share of the public sector
1850/51	5.0*	2.24*
1880/81	4.8*	25.21*
1900/01	7.0*	21.59*
1920/21	6.2*	32.68*
1940/41	6.7*	19.81*
1951–1955	13.1 (11.6*)	25.0*
1956–1960	17.3	–
1961–1965	17.7	43.2
1966–1970	19.3	39.2
1971–1975	19.7	40.2
1976–1980	21.2	45.2
1981–1985	20.8	51.4
1990–1995	23.7	38.4
1995–2000	24.8	29.2

Note: * Refers to the ratio to Gross National Income in 1980/81 prices
Source: * Roy (1996) (tables 46, 52, 55) Post 1951: Nagaraj (1990), Kohli (2004, 2006)

Table 3.6 *Share of manufacturing in gross fixed capital formation (%) in a comparative perspective*

	Share in gross fixed capital formation				
	1950	1960	1970	1980	1990
Brazil	13.0	8.1	19.7	13.8	13.5
South Korea	13.6	15.0	17.0	28.3	32.3
Taiwan	19.5	23.5	36.1	29.0	25.7
India	11.6	27.8	27.5	12.5	10.4

Source: Amsden (2001, tables 6.3)

not certain about the future rates of return (pp. 64–65).[5] The emerging capitalist class in 1950 was shaped by the social networks of trading communities that had ventured into industry. Many sections of the business community had supported Congress in the struggle for

[5] Rodrik (1995) discussed the coordination problem for South Korean entrepreneurs in the 1960s and 1960s and the role of government intervention. The particular policies differed in the context of South Korea.

independence and were involved in the drawing up of the Bombay Plan of 1944, a plan for economic development after independence. The plan was drawn up by the Congress party in consultation with Indian entrepreneurs, and put investment in industry as the driver of growth (Rothermund 1993, pp. 123–124).[6] The signatories included J. R. D. Tata, Ghanashyam Das Birla, Lala Sri Ram, Kasturbhai Lalbhai, and Purushottamdas Thakurdas, the founder of the industrial association representing Indians, the Federation of Indian Chamber of Commerce and Industry (FICCI). Even when the Indian business interests were not in complete agreement on specific policies, there was no disagreement on protecting the market for Indian producers and controlling foreign investment (Roy 2018, p. 148).

The Second Plan introduced regulation of industrial investment by demarcating the areas of public and private investment. Private entrepreneurs had to apply for licenses to invest in an industry. Several industries of strategic interest, as well those producing capital and intermediate goods, were out of bounds for the private sector. The emphasis was on reducing dependence on imports and self-sufficiency in industrial output. The plan used quantitative controls, such as import licences and quotas, rather than tariffs to regulate foreign trade. Unlike in many other newly industrializing economies, such as Brazil and in East Asia, multiple exchange rates were not used to protect some sectors and allow easy imports in others. The Rupee remained overvalued and built in an anti-export bias. The competitiveness of Indian traditional exports declined and the products of the new industries could not compete in the world market. Exports grew at 2.3 per cent between 1950 and 1973, well below the growth in world exports at 7.9 per cent per year. Exports/GDP ratio declined from 7.1 per cent in 1951 to less than 3 per cent in 1965.

The motivation to industrialize was not unusual. Alexander Hamilton in the USA and Fredrich List in Germany had made a case for tariffs to support industrialization in the nineteenth century. They had argued that economic prosperity and national prestige depended on industrialization. Colonial India had been dependent on Britain for industrial goods, particularly on capital goods. The Second Plan transformed the industrial sector away from this dependence. The production of basic, intermediate, and capital goods grew faster than the production of consumer goods until 1965. The picture was to change after 1980 when intermediate and consumer goods industries, in particular durable consumer goods, became the fastest growing sectors (see Table 3.7).

---

[6] Chibber (2003) has a different view and argues that the Indian business interests were opposed to the level of state intervention that was inherent in the Bombay Plan.

Table 3.7 *Annual industrial growth by sectors (1951–2004) (%)*

	Basic	Capital goods	Intermediate goods	Consumer goods	Durable consumer	Total output
1951–1955	4.7	9.8	7.8	4.8		5.7
1955–1960	12.1	13.1	6.3	4.4		7.2
1960–1965	10.4	19.6	6.9	4.9		9.0
1965–1976	6.5	2.6	3.0	3.4	6.2	4.1
1981–1991	8.0	5.3	11.2	8.9	12.0	6.5
1981–1998	8.0	6.7	10.7	9.1	12.5	5.8

Note: Basic goods refer to basic materials used in production and are intermediate goods
Source: Kelkar and Kumar (1990) and Nagaraj (2003b)

As in the case of import substituting industrialization, the initial growth spurt petered out once substitution of imports had progressed. Without a strategy to break into the world market, the high levels of protection made the industrial sector uncompetitive and dependent on the domestic market (Bhagwati and Desai 1970). Total factor productivity growth in manufacturing was negative over the period 1959/60 to 1979/8 (Ahluwalia 1991). The processing of licenses created rent-seeking activities as industrial interests lobbied for licenses. Despite the problems associated with the regime of regulation, a critique of the economic policy in the first decades of independence must also consider the colonial legacy and the environment in which these policies were made.

The slowing down of economic growth after 1965 brought about a change in the direction of economic policy. Trade policy switched from relying on quantitative controls to price based controls and import quotas were replaced by tariffs in the 1980s. There were significant changes in industrial policies. Industrial licensing that had created barriers to entry for the private sector was removed, opening up most sectors to private investment. The reforms of the 1980s are seen as 'pro-business' (Rodrik and Subramanian 2005; Kohli 2006). Rodrik and Subramanian (2005) argue that the removal of the constraints on the private sector made it more dynamic and in a position to take advantage of the new opportunities. Manufacturing became the fastest growing sector in the 1980s and there was an increase in productivity growth in manufacturing (Ahluwalia 1991). Wallack (2003) found that the increase in GDP growth was due to a changing composition of GDP, as resources moved away from slow-growing towards faster-growing sectors of the economy. However, the industrial sector did not emerge as the largest sector, either in GDP or employment, and was overtaken by the service sector by the 1990s as the driver of economic growth, as I will discuss in Chapter 4.

3.7   From Business Communities to Business Groups

In 1947, several communities dominated the industrial space. The roles of the Parsis, the Bhatias, and the Bohras in cotton textiles and the Marwaris in jute have been discussed earlier in the chapter. A few among them, such as the Tatas and Birlas, went on to build large business conglomerates. These groups had been involved in different segments of the industrial sector in the interwar years. After 1947, a few of these family firms developed into industrial houses.

The family-based business groups have been at the centre of Indian industrialization. Their entry into industries in the nineteenth century used community connections, as individuals belonging to the same community made an occupational transition from trade to industry as a group. For the family-based business groups that emerged as industry leaders, diversification after the First World War may have been the key to their success. They typically owned shares across industries and had financial and entrepreneurial control. Sarkar (2010) defines a business group in India as 'an agglomeration of privately held and publicly traded firms operating in different lines of business'. Most of them first entered into cotton textiles, jute textiles, or sugar and gradually diversified into more technologically sophisticated industries. The family firm of the Birlas is illustrative of this diversification. The group moved from jute and cotton textiles to the production of textile machinery and automobiles before 1947 and to aluminium, cement, and chemicals thereafter (Roy 2018, pp. 135, 174).

Michael Kidron (1965) documented the entry of Indians on the well-guarded boards of British firms. From a share of 5 per cent of directors on boards of jute companies in 1911, the figure rose to 51 per cent in 1950, in coal firms it went from 5 per cent to 54 per cent, and in tea companies from 5 per cent to 32 per cent. In 1920, 85 per cent of the tea companies had no Indian directors on their board. By 1950, 40 per cent had at least one. In other industries, Indian entry was even more dramatic, with 88 per cent of the coal companies having no Indian directors on their board in 1911. In 1950, this was the case for only 10 per cent of the firms. For jute companies the share of companies with no Indian directors declined from 84 per cent to just 2 per cent (Kidron 1965, p. 40).

Under the new policies after independence, British firms were required to register in India and gradually hand over majority shareholdings to Indians. The firms most affected were controlled by British managing agents and were in the export industries. Many of them sold shares to the Indian business groups, others were nationalized (Roy 2018, pp. 190–191). The tea companies, as a major export earner,

Table 3.8 *Top ten business groups by assets (1939, 1958, 1981, 2000)*

1939	1958	1981	2000
Tata	Tata	Tata	Reliance
Inchcape	Birla	Birla	Tata
Andrew Yule	Martin Burn	Mafatlal	Essar Ruia
Finlay	Dalmia Sahoo Jain	Singhania	Birla
E D Sassoon	Bird Heigler	Thapar	Larson and Toubro
Martin Burn	Andrew Yule	ICI	Jindal
Bird	Bangur	Sarabhai	PRPG Enterprises
Associated Cement	Thapar	Associated Cement	Bajaj
Killick	Singhania	Bangur	Thapar
Gillanders	Sri Ram	Sri Ram	Mahindra & Mahindra

Source: Markovits (2002, p. 192); Roy (2018, p. 171); Sarkar (2010)

retained a special position. The multinational foreign firms that catered to the domestic market were less affected by the changed economic environment. Within two decades of independence, the industrial sector came to be dominated by Indian business groups and public sector corporations.

Table 3.8 shows the changes in the top ten business groups. In 1939, these groups were mainly British managing agency houses that controlled companies in tea, jute, coal, and other industries. There were two Indian firms on this list, Tata and Sassoon, both of which originated in the cotton textile industry in Bombay in the nineteenth century. By 1958, the list was dominated by Indian family firms, although managing agents Bird and Company and Andrew Yule were still dominant in industry. By 1980, the top ten business groups were Indian with the exception of the multinational corporation Imperial Chemical Industries (ICI). Table 3.8 also shows some churn over the next twenty years and the emergence of new names. Among them, the success of the Reliance group stands out. However, Tata has remained in the top ten since the colonial period and a few of the business groups, such as Birla and Thapar, which came to prominence in the 1950s, have also maintained their position. Caste-based community networks have continued to play a role and certain communities dominate in specific industries, for example the Gounders in the garment industry in Tirupur (Banerjee and Munshi 2004). The transition of Kathiawaris from agriculture to the export-oriented diamond industry used the community network for occupational mobility (Munshi 2011).

Did the special position of the business communities give them an advantage under the policies of regulated industrialization? I have discussed at the beginning of this chapter the importance of social networks in industrialization when state intervention was missing. In the context of regulation, the business groups used the regulatory system to their advantage. During the period of 1956–1966, the top twenty business groups were able to take advantage of their organization to secure 41 per cent of the industrial licenses (Chibber 2003, p. 191).

The role of the multinational corporations (MNC) in India has never been as important as in some other parts of the world. The successive governments have put more restrictions on the functioning of MNCs than domestic firms. The economic reforms of the 1980s were more advantageous for the domestic firms. Collaboration with foreign firms was permitted in joint ventures or under technology transfer agreements, and the Foreign Exchange and Regulations Act of 1974 capped foreign equity holdings at 40 per cent (Nagaraj 2003a). The 'pro-market' reforms after 1991 opened the door to foreign direct investment in industry and consumer durables and communications were major beneficiaries. India's share of world foreign direct investment went up from 0.5 per cent to just over 2 per cent in the 1990s, but has remained small compared to that of China (Nagaraj 2003a).

3.8   Management Practices

The management structure that emerged in colonial India was the managing agency system. It was first adopted in British firms, but Indian firms used it too. A British managing agent was a British firm that owned shares in firms across industries and had administrative control. The industries were mainly tea, jute, and coal. The managing agents reduced risk by diversifying across industries. They transferred funds across firms as and when required. The managing agent also enjoyed a reputational advantage in selling shares of new companies. This institution fits in with the ideas in the recent literature, which suggests that new ventures rely on the brand name of a business group to signal reliability when institutions are weak (Maurer and Sharma 2001). However, the economic power of the managing agents led to an oligopolistic market structure in several industries. A handful of agents such as Andrew Yule, Bird and Company, and Shaw Wallace owned or managed the major export industries, and this made cartelization possible (Gupta 1997, 2001, 2005). Managing agents dominated industrial associations and operated as a political interest group to lobby for various privileges. The import-substituting Indian firms, based on community connections, evolved as community-based business groups. They too adopted a variant of the managing agency system and diversified risk by having ownership and control of several firms across sectors.

The management structure in colonial firms was a source of inefficiency. The management structure in British firms differed from that in Indian firms in one important aspect. Most directors in Indian firms came from trade and had little technical knowledge regarding industrial activities. The management of textile firms consisted of three tiers. The first tier were entrepreneurs, who typically came from trading communities, many of whom did not have technical training or formal higher education. The second tier was made up of technicians, who, initially, were mainly British or Parsi (Rutnagur 1927; Oonk 2001). The third tier were labour recruiters. The labour recruiters came from rural areas and used their community connections to recruit workers. Kiyokawa (1983) suggests that the lack of technical knowledge among Indian entrepreneurs and managers led to poor managerial decisions on choice of technology. The adoption of British technology rather than the more efficient American technology is one example. The failure to introduce double shifts, as in Japan, is another (Gupta 2011). The British and Indian firms across different sectors used labour recruiters, and most of the workers were recruited in the rural areas through community connections. Linguistic barriers between managers, technicians, and workers may also have played a role in generating inefficiencies in communication and transmission of knowledge.

The managerial inefficiency of family-based business groups has been discussed in the context of more recent developments in Indian industry. Khanna and Yafeh (2007) show that, between 1990 and 1997, one-third of Indian firms were affiliated to a business group. This share is lower than that in Indonesia, South Korea, and Taiwan in the 1990s and Japan in the 1930s. The recent literature on comparative management practices shows that, although in emerging economies such as India and Brazil there are many well managed firms, their average rank in terms of managerial practices is lower than that of most industrialized countries. Family firms with a family chief executive officer have low management scores. Three-quarters of Indian firms fall in this category, a much higher proportion than in advanced economies (Bloom et al. 2010). A related view comes from Caselli and Gennaioli (2013). They argue that dynastic management may reduce a firm's total factor productivity due to less talented managers. The literature on the measurement of total factor productivity in industrial firms in India during the regulatory regime is not able to distinguish between the adverse effect that can be attributed to dynastic firms and group-affiliated firms, and the part arising from inefficiency under regulation.

3.9   Industrial Labour

In the early stages, the workers for the emerging industries in the nineteenth century were recruited from the rural communities. Even though labour was abundant, finding workers for the modern industries was not easy. All industries employed labour recruiters or '*sirdars*' to use community connections to find workers. First-generation industrial workers travelled from the rural hinterland to the cities. Nearly 90 per cent of the textile workers in Bombay in 1911 were born elsewhere. Even in 1931 the share of workers born outside the city remained as high at 74 per cent (Morris 1965, p. 63). The first-generation workers in the cotton textile industry came from the hinterland of Bombay city and, over time, they were recruited from more distant regions. Workers in the jute industry were recruited from the hinterland of Calcutta and came from Bihar, Orissa, and Eastern United Provinces. The recruitment of indentured workers in the tea industry saw large-scale migration to tea plantations in Assam and northern Bengal. This too relied initially on community ties and later switched to professional recruiters as demand increased (Gupta and Swamy 2017). Caste and community-based networks led to fragmented urban labour markets (Morris 1965; Chandavarkar 1994; Rudner 1994 and Chakrabarty 1989). Even in the early 1960s, a survey of 500 mill workers in Bombay found that 81 per cent had relatives or members of their caste in the textile industry (Patel 1963).

Most of the migrant workers were men who came to the cities in search of higher wages. Their families continued to live in the village. The women who migrated were widowed and single women who had fallen into difficult times (Sen 1999). They worked in specific jobs and their social status was low. There was a certain non-permanence in this workforce. The urban world of the industrial worker remained closely connected to the village and community. Historians have emphasized the persistence of rural identity of the industrial workers, to whom the towns were places of work and the village was where the family lived. (Chakrabarty 1989; Chandavarkar 1994). The interconnection between the two disrupted the annual routine of the industrial workers.

Chandavarkar (1994, pp. 159–167) builds a rich narrative of the rural connections of the cotton textile workers in Bombay. Industrial workers returned to the village, especially during the planting and harvesting season. This was particularly true of workers from the surrounding districts. The railways made it easier to move between the village and the city. The workers went back to the village for festivals, when they were ill, when they were unemployed, and when they retired. Over a quarter of the average industrial earnings were remitted to the village in the 1920s.

The jute industry also developed with migrant workers. In 1921, only 24 per cent were Bengalis; the rest came from Bihar, Orissa, and beyond (Das Gupta 1976). As in the Bombay cotton mills, the rural and family connections of the jute workers in Calcutta endured. Few had families in the city (Chakrabarty 1989, p. 206). The migrant workers maintained their rural connections and this hindered the formation of a working class identity and adaptation to industrial discipline.

At the same time, trade unions emerged and workers joined unions to defend their rights. The textile workers in Bombay were more organized than industrial workers in other parts of India and wildcat strikes had been common in Bombay mills. These became more organized in the 1920s. Wages in the cotton mills had risen during the First World War and there was widespread industrial action to defend the higher wages when the war ended. Wolcott (1994) and Wolcott and Clark (1999) see India's lack of competitive advantage against Japan and the low productivity of Bombay mills as a consequence of unionization. Gupta (2011), on the other hand, argues that unionization resulted in higher wages in Bombay mills in the 1920s compared to other locations and was an impetus for increasing efficiency. In this competitive industry, the survival of cotton mills in Bombay depended on increasing output per worker by reducing the number of workers per machine. This happened in Bombay mills over the course of the 1920s. Bombay firms had fewer workers per machine, compared to other locations of the industry (Gupta 2011).

Over the twentieth century, the strong rural connections of the industrial workers weakened. Between 1901 and 1961 the share of urban population increased. Although there was continued migration from rural to urban centres in search of work, the unorganized sector absorbed an increasing number of migrants. As the industrial structure changed, skills and training became important and the urban labour market became the place to recruit industrial workers. As the world of the *sirdar* disappeared, workers' organizations and unions appeared in most industries. The rural connection of the industrial worker survived through the family economy as many workers had their families in the village (Ram 1984, p. 182).

From the Second Plan, the public sector employed thousands of workers in the manufacturing sectors and the employment conditions were formalized. The industrial workers in the public sector represented a different type of workforce from the traditional industries. Industrial workers in publicly-owned enterprises had greater representation from different social groups, job security, and benefits. This was also the sector that adopted affirmative action following the legislation to reserve a certain share of jobs for the disadvantaged caste groups and tribes

Table 3.9 *Economic reform and growth in manufacturing industry: organized versus unorganized sectors (% per year)*

	1984/85–1994/5	1989/90–1994/95	1994/95–1999/00
Value added			
Organized	7.2	8.3	6.9
Unorganized	1.0	−1.0	6.9
Employment			
Organized	0.6	2.1	0.7
Unorganized	−1.0	−1.7	2.2
Labour productivity			
Organized	6.6	6.1	6.2
Unorganized	1.9	0.8	4.8
Capital intensity			
Organized	5.3	11.4	11.4
Unorganized	−19.4	7.0	0.5

Source: Rani and Unni (2004)

(Breman 1999).[7] Real wages in the manufacturing industry rose faster than per capita income, with the wage growth reflecting growth in labour productivity (Tulpule and Datta 1988).

Labour legislation in the factory industry during colonial rule regulated hours of work and employment of women and children and was modelled on British labour laws. Often this was implemented under pressure from the industrial interests in Britain, who feared 'unfair' competition from the import substituting industries. The Trade Union Act of 1926 formalized the formation and recognition of trade unions. The first post-independence labour legislation in India was the Industrial Disputes Act of 1947. It provided for institutions of wage setting and dispute settlement, but also for protection against factory closures and redundancies.

The workers in the unorganized sector and in small-scale industries remained largely outside the scope of employment security and unionization. In 1983, 75 per cent of the workers in manufacturing were in the unorganized sector, rising to 84 per cent in 2003. The main increase in employment in the unorganized sector took place in the 1990s as a result of the increase in subcontracting and use of contract labour (Kotwal et al. 2011). The wage gap in the organized and unorganized sectors widened over time.

The economic reforms of the 1980s introduced competition in the manufacturing sector and the organized sector was better equipped to deal with it, as shown in the growth in value added (see Table 3.9).

[7] The nature of this affirmative action will be discussed again in Chapter 5.

The unorganized sector, on the other hand, was adversely affected both in terms of value added and employment. Labour productivity and capital intensity rose in the organized sector. However, after 1994, there was growth in value added and in labour productivity in the unorganized sector. This sector has been the main source of employment growth in manufacturing.

3.10 Conclusion

Although the traditional cotton textile industry declined in the nineteenth century, modern industries began to develop from the middle of the nineteenth century. Both British and Indian entrepreneurs invested in industrial enterprises. Initially British capital was in the export industries and Indian capital in the main import substituting industries. After the First World War, new industries developed that were import substituting. Industrial development in colonial India had a certain dynamism and performed better than agriculture. In 1947 industry was still a small part of the economy and relied on imports for machinery and intermediate goods.

The first government in independent India under Nehru changed the direction of industrial development. A planned development of 'heavy' industry with public sector involvement and extensive restrictions on the role of the market, changed the composition of the economy. When the Indian economy began to dismantle the regulatory system, the private sector made major gains and the role of public investment declined over time. The community-based structure of Indian industrial development has had an enduring legacy. Family-based industrial conglomerates have dominated Indian industrialization.

The growth and changes in the industrial sector did not lead the process of structural change that was experienced in most developed economies. The growth in manufacturing did not pull out workers from agriculture to industry as in the case of most industrialized countries. Nor did it absorb the surplus labour in agriculture. While the share of non-agricultural activities in GDP increased, their share in employment remained much lower. In Chapter 4, I will say more on structural change and how India has followed a different path from the countries that industrialized in the nineteenth and early twentieth century.

4   Origins of India's Service Sector Advantage

Economies transform from being dependent on agriculture to having a large industrial sector and eventually become service sector dominated as in most developed countries today. The transition for a low-growth, subsistence-based agricultural economy to a high-growth, modern economy with a large non-agricultural sector represents structural change. One of the six ways to characterize modern economic growth that was put forward by Kuznets is the rising share of the non-agricultural sector (Nobel Lecture of 1971). Syrquin, in the Handbook of Development Economics (Volume 1 1988), described structural change as the relative importance of sectors in the economy in terms of production and factor use. Industrialization is then the central process of structural change.

Economic growth in modern developed countries was driven by industrialization. In these economies, agriculture was the largest sector in employment and output in the Malthusian or subsistence phase. Modern economic growth began with a decline in the share of agriculture and a rise in the share of non-agricultural sectors, industry, and services in employment and GDP. The change was driven by industry as it emerged as the largest sector. This was followed by a decline in the share of industry and a rise in the share of the service sector. The structural change from underdevelopment to development therefore put industry at the centre of modern economic growth. This was the experience of most developed countries in Europe and North America and also in Asia's first industrializing economy, Japan.

In the developing countries today, industry has not always played the same role in structural change. Brazil and Mexico in Latin America, South Korea, Indonesia, Thailand, and Malaysia in Asia from the 1960s, and China from the 1980s have seen a big increase in the share of industry in GDP. However, in several Asian economies that industrialized after the Second World War, the share of the industrial sector in employment has not risen in line with the share in GDP and the share of agriculture in employment has not declined in line with its share in GDP.

Table 4.1 *Sectoral shares of value added in GDP in comparable developing countries and in employment (%)*

Sectoral shares of value added in GDP

	Agriculture			Industry			Services		
	1960*	1980	2000	1960*	1980	2000	1960*	1980	2000
India	50	38.9	24.6	20	24.5	26.6	30	36.6	48.8
S Korea	37	15.1	4.3	20	40.5	36.2	43	44.4	59.5
Indonesia	50	24	17.2	25	41.7	46.1	25	34.3	36.7
Thailand	40	23.2	9.0	19	28.7	42.0	41	48.1	49.0
Malaysia	36	22.6	8.8	18	41.0	50.7	46	36.3	40.5
China		30.1	16.4		48.5	50.2		21.4	33.4
Brazil	16	11.0	7.3	35	34	28.0	49	53	64.7
Mexico	16	9.0	4.2	29	33.6	28.0	55	57.4	67.8

Sectoral share in employment

	Agriculture			Industry			Services		
	1960*	1980	2000	1960	1980	2000	1960*	1980	2000
India	74	68.1	59.3	11	13.9	18.2	15	18.6	22.4
S Korea	66	34.0	10.9	9	29.0	28.0	25	37.0	61.0
Indonesia	75	55.9	45.3	8	13.3	17.3	17	30.2	37.2
Thailand	84	70.8	48.8	4	10.3	19.0	12	18.9	32.2
Malaysia	63	37.2	18.4	12	24.1	32.2	25	38.7	49.5
China		68.7	46.9		18.2	23.0		11.7	29.9
Brazil	52	29.3	24.2	15	24.7	19.3	33	46.1	56.5
Mexico	55	23.5	17.5	20	26.5	26.9	25	49.0	55.2

Source: Kochhar et al. (2006), based on World Development Report 2005,
* Bhattacharya and Mitra (1990), based on World Development Report of 1983

India is an outlier both in terms of the share of industry in output and in employment. The share of industry is smaller in both GDP and employment compared to similar developing countries (see Table 4.1). In 2000, nearly 50 per cent of GDP originated in the service sector. Although industry had been the focus of planned development in independent India, its contribution to the economy did not exceed 30 per cent of GDP at any time.

In 1960, India had a relatively high share of GDP and employment in agriculture, compared to several other countries in Asia emerging from colonization, and this was slow to change. India was an outlier in 2000, in the high share of services in GDP relative to employment. The service sector produced the largest share of national output, but was not the largest sector in employment. The comparison in Table 4.1 does not consider the differences in GDP per capita and land area of countries. Taking these into consideration, Kochhar et al. (2006) found that the share of industry in India was not significantly lower in 1980 as the data in Table 4.1 suggests. On the other hand, the service sector in 1980 was an outlier, accounting for less than what would be predicted by GDP per capita (Kochhar et al. 2006).

Economic reforms since the 1980s that led to faster GDP growth have been discussed in Chapters 1 and 3. This changed the relative contribution of the sectors to economic growth. As Table 4.1 shows, in 2000, the service sector accounted for the largest share of GDP, although agriculture still employed the largest share of workers. Services have grown faster than industry both in terms of output and productivity. What accounts for the rapid growth of the service sector?

This chapter takes a historical perspective to explore if the service sector had an inherent advantage that is specific to India. Does India's colonial history have a role? I begin with a description of caste-based service sector occupations and explore if they created an advantage for the service sector in a modernizing economy. I discuss what implications occupational inequalities had for productivity growth in the three sectors and offer an explanation of India's service sector advantage.

4.1   Caste and Occupation

In traditional societies most of the workforce is engaged in agriculture and the non-agricultural activities are mainly artisanal. Within the village community, there is exchange between agricultural and non-agricultural goods, but village communities are rarely self-sufficient and inter-village exchange and interregional trade have characterized societies even before the present millennium. In Indian villages, agricultural households divided time between agriculture and industrial production. For example, for women, spinning was a part-time activity. Other household production included basket weaving and *bidi* making. Specialization in industrial activities was mainly for the local market, and many products were traded in a larger market outside the local community and region. In early modern India regional specialization in textiles and artisanal products generated trade across regions. An urban artisanal sector, though small, flourished in Mughal India.

For those in the village economy who were not involved in agriculture and artisanal jobs, employment was available in a variety of services. In the nineteenth century in Madras Presidency, a large number of services were performed by specialists outside the household and there was occupational segregation by caste and religious subgroups. Village communities in India had greater specialization by occupation compared to other societies at a similar level of development (Kumar 1987). With the rise of modern, large-scale industries and access to larger markets, industry began to recruit from a national market. Industrial workers came from different castes and learned new skills. Many services remained specialized by caste and others saw more mingling of groups.

The occupational structure in India has been defined by caste since ancient times. Within the broad rules of the caste system there are four hierarchical *varnas*: Brahmans (the priests), Kshatriyas (the warriors), Vaishyas (the commercial interests), and Shudras (performing menial tasks). Within the *varnas* there are numerous subcastes or *jatis*. These were historically occupation-related categories. *Jatis* or subcastes had some fluidity. Occupation of a *jati* could vary across regions, but within a region members of a particular *jati* typically followed the same occupation. The term caste in the censuses and other enumerations is used to refer to *jatis*. Some castes had an advantage in literacy and wealth, arising from the needs of their occupation, and I discuss the consequences of this advantage for productivity and for the evolution of different sectors in the economy.

Dirks (2001) claimed that the census enumeration by the colonial government made caste identity salient, solidifying the link between caste and occupation. Munshi (2019) points out that the first enumeration of caste dates back to Mughal India.[1] Although colonial censuses might have enhanced caste identity in certain types of jobs, it did not create them. Subrahmanyam (1990) studied the occupational structure of two villages in Southern India in 1692, where the Dutch East India Company enumerated households by occupation. The composition of households from one of the villages is classified by occupational groups listed in Table 4.2. The weavers belonged to three different castes. Among other occupational groups enumerated by caste were Komattis, a trading caste, Brahmins, the priests, and Pariahs, low castes engaged as labourers. The rest of the households were enumerated by occupation, most of which were linked to particular castes. The left-hand and right-hand castes in Southern India were segregated into specific occupations within each group. The left-hand castes were in agricultural activities and trade in agricultural commodities, while right-hand castes were in artisanal production and trade in non-agricultural goods (Stein 1982). The weavers

[1] Munshi's claim is based on Appadurai 1993.

Table 4.2 *Classification of households by occupational groups in Golepa (1692)*

Weavers	Cultivators	Coppersmiths
Kaikkolas	Toddy-tappers	Brahmins
Salis	Oilmen	Embroiderers
Devangas	Milkmen	Carvers
Komattis	Painters	Barbers
Goldsmiths	Washers	Smiths
Betel sellers	Cobblers	Potters
Tobacco Sellers	Pariah	Textile-beaters

Source: Subrahmanyam (1990)

in the Coromandel were represented by various castes, each specializing in a particular type of cloth (Brennig 1990). Long before the colonial censuses, castes determined occupations.

The importance of trading castes in the commercial life of towns and villages is well documented. Maritime trade also involved caste-based networks. High-caste Hindus faced religious restrictions on overseas travel. The term *kalapani*, or black water, was a symbol of impurity associated with crossing seas to distant lands and was a hindrance to Hindu traders in participating in maritime trade. Consequently, the high seas were dominated by Muslim traders from Bohra and Khoja communities from the fifteenth century in western India, Bengali Muslim traders in the east, and Jewish and Christian merchants in Malabar (Bouchon and Lombard 1987, pp. 62–67). The *Parsis* became important in the trade with China. The bankers and financiers for this trade came from the Hindu trading communities, the Hindu Bania, the Chettiars, and the Jains (Arasaratnam 1987, p. 106; Rudner 1994).

Given the importance of caste in the occupational structure, skill formation in pre-colonial India was also caste specific. The skills of the weavers and metal workers of silver, copper, and other alloys were world renowned. The skills passed from generation to generation within castes, but there was little dissemination of these artisanal skills outside the group. While there were gains from specialization within the group, the caste-based occupation may have been a hindrance to diffusion of technology and technological change. Evidence suggests that the technology in various industrial sectors in India, such as textiles, changed little over the centuries (Habib 1976).

Kremer (1993) has argued that the likelihood of new technology increases with population size. A system that limits the spread of knowledge within a restricted group limits itself to a smaller population and fewer inventions, and hinders better dissemination of useful knowledge.[2] Useful knowledge was passed on by migrant artisans and industrial workers in Europe. The European institution of guild, apprenticeship, and journeymen employees might have allowed wider dissemination of knowledge and skills compared to kinship-based institutions of knowledge and skill transmission (De la Croix et al. 2018). The path of knowledge transmission through family and caste increased the cost of knowledge acquisition in India relative to Europe (Roy 2008).

At the same time, being in an occupation-based caste group might have conferred advantages on individuals within certain groups. For example, when an occupation required skills such as literacy and numeracy,[3] individuals belonging to these castes became literate. This would have encouraged human capital accumulation within certain castes and given these groups an advantage when economic development opened up new opportunities for individuals with valuable human capital. The Brahmans, for example, were required to read the religious texts and as a group had high literacy. When reading the Torah was made compulsory for boys in Judaism, it gave the Jewish community in a mainly agricultural Palestine an advantage in urban occupations (Botticini and Eckstein 2005, 2006). Human capital accumulation among Protestants due to the necessity to read the bible had given them an advantage in urban occupations in Prussia and led to industrial development (Becker and Woessman 2009).

The trading castes in all regions were more literate than most other groups, although traders belonged to different castes in different regions (Broadberry and Gupta 2010). Not all caste and religion based groups that were involved in trade had the same literacy level. Table 4.3 shows the differences in literacy by trading communities in Bombay Presidency in 1901 and 1911. These groups were Parsis, Jains, and the Baghdadi Jews. Parsis were the most literate community. The Hindu trading groups, such as Vanis and Bhatias, also enjoyed a higher literacy, as did the Muslim trading groups of Bohras, Khojas, and Memons. Timberg (1978) shows that literacy among the male members of the trading community of the Marwaris in Bengal was high. In caste and religion-based groups that mainly engaged in trade and banking, literacy was higher than the average for the larger communities of Hindus and the Muslims.

---

[2] Useful knowledge was a term coined in the context of the industrial revolution in Europe (Mokyr 2015).
[3] Trading communities in ancient Minoan, Phoenician, and Etruscan civilizations also enjoyed higher literacy and numeracy (Captivating History 2020).

Table 4.3 *Literacy among trading communities in Bombay Presidency*

	Literacy in 1901		Male literacy in 1911
Hindu	11	Vani	60
Muslim	7	Bhatia	56
Jain	50	Khoja, Bhora, Memon	41
Parsi	75		
Baghdadi Jew	54		

Note: Vani and Bhatia are Hindu trading castes. Khoja, Bohra and Memon are Muslim trading groups
Source: Censuses of India 1901 and 1911

4.2   New Occupations

The economic changes in India from the middle of the nineteenth century saw a decline in some traditional occupations and emergence of new occupations in new sectors. Castes that were literate could benefit in the new environment. This changed the connection between caste and occupation for some social groups and opened the door to upward mobility for certain castes. Upper castes began to acquire western education and embraced new professions. Its impact was minimal among the agricultural and services castes at lower levels of the hierarchy,

By 1901, human capital as captured by measures of literacy was documented in the colonial censuses. Apart from literacy recorded at the district level and aggregated at the province level, the colonial censuses documented literacy by caste. Table 4.4 shows the top two or three most literate castes in selected provinces. The table reports literacy and literacy in English. Three things stand out: first, there was a large gap between average literacy in a province and the literacy of the most literate castes; second, there was a large gap between male and female literacy; and third, castes with the highest literacy across provinces came from service sector occupations. The *Brahmans*, or the priests, had high literacy in every province. Other castes with high literacy were the trading castes and the castes in professions. All these groups belonged to the upper end of the caste hierarchy.

The highly literate upper castes could move into jobs that required tertiary education, such as government services, medicine, and law. In the highest level jobs in administrative and legal services, medical professions,

Table 4.4 *Highest literacy by caste in selected provinces*

	Number literate in 1,000		Number literate in English in 10,000	
	Male	Female	Male	Female
Assam	**67**	**4**	**87**	**<1**
Brahmans	517	27	592	8
Kayastha	471	56	910	9
Bombay	**116**	**9**	**60**	**8**
Vani (Gujarat)	776	158	709	5
Prabu	474	177	2,914	172
Brahman	580	54	1,026	10
Bengal	**67**	**4**	**35**	**2**
Baidya	648	259	3,039	85
Kayastha	560	66	1,323	33
Brahmans	467	26	737	5
Central Provinces	**54**	**2**	**18**	**2**
Bania	446	11	95	1
Brahman	365	9	337	2
Madras	**119**	**9**	**44**	**6**
Eurasian	729	710	7,150	6,951
Brahman	578	44	975	11
United Provinces	**57**	**2**	**18**	**3**
Kayastha	553	46	NA	NA
Cochin	**224**	**45**	**NA**	**NA**
Brahman (Malayali)	695	227	66	NA
Kshatriya (Malayali)	615	319	1,171	67
Nayyar	425	119	209	14
Mysore	**93**	**8**	**51**	**11**
Brahman	681	64	1,022	24
Digambara	410	21	79	NA
All India	**98**	**7**	**36**	**5**

Source: Census Report (1901, pp. 181–183)

and universities, three castes dominated: *Brahmans, Kayasthas, and Baidyas* (Census Report 1901, pp. 217–218). They were also among the most literate and had literacy in English. Several trading castes moved into industry as entrepreneurs, as we have seen in Chapter 3, and also into other modern commercial sectors, such as banking and retail. The high literacy in these castes relative to the rest of the population suggest the concentration of human capital in many service sector occupations. This is the starting point for thinking about India's service sector advantage.

4.3   Demand and Supply of Education

By the late nineteenth century, demand for education, and in particular for literacy in English, was high among the elites. The demand came mainly from the communities involved in urban occupations. The modernization of the economy, the development of new sectors, and the expanding civil service and other public services created demand for primary, secondary, and tertiary education.

The censuses show a large difference in literacy between urban and rural India. In 1901, 259 males and forty-nine females out of a thousand in large towns were literate, compared to ninety-eight males and seven females in rural India (Broadberry and Gupta 2010). However, demand for education was low, not just in the population engaged in agriculture, but also among workers in industry. In the cotton mills of Bombay, literacy was very low, as was the case in other industries. In its report, the Industrial Commission of 1916 found evidence that when children of fathers in artisanal jobs acquired primary education, they did not value manual occupations in industry and sought instead clerical jobs that required literacy (p. 109). As discussed in the previous section, the demand for education was mostly driven by certain service sector occupations. Chaudhary and Fenske (2023) asked if the development of the railway network in India created demand for education and found that the exposure to a railway line in a district, measured by the number of years of having a line, increased secondary school enrolment. The impact was mainly on male literacy and on literacy in English, but it was not broad-based.

In 1921, about 10 per cent of the population was literate and 1 per cent had literacy in English (Chaudhary 2010). The gap between male and female literacy was large: 17 per cent for men and 3 per cent for women. There were large differences in literacy across provinces. Bengal, Bombay, and Madras had some of the highest enrolment in schools (Chaudhary and Garg 2015). One unique feature of the education system was that, conditional on having access to primary education, demand for secondary education was high. Figure 4.1 shows the positive correlation between the literacy rate in 1921 and the share of workforce in the service sector.

Before the introduction of a uniform education system from the middle of the nineteenth century, religious schools provided education to specific groups using a group-specific curriculum. Patchy information from Bengal in 1811 put literacy at 4.3 per cent of the population. In comparison, the census of 1901 put literacy in Bengal at 6.7 per cent (Table 4.4). The EIC was mindful of the need to create a local elite that could be

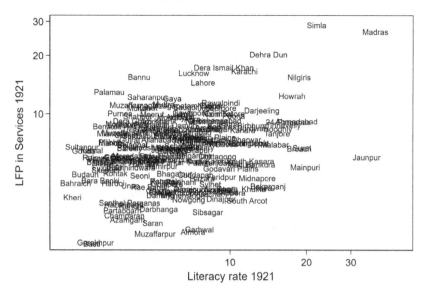

Figure 4.1 Relationship between literacy and share of the service sector in employment
Source: Data from Chaudhary and Fenske (2020)[4]

involved in the colonial administration. Nurullah and Naik (1951) have argued that all through the nineteenth century there were discussions in the policy circles and among Indian elites on the type of education that the country needed: western curriculum based, the language of education, and who should benefit from it. The social reformer Raja Ram Mohan Roy voiced his support for western science.

The new system combined publicly funded and managed schools with privately funded schools that also received financial aid from the government (Chaudhary 2015). The adoption of a uniform curriculum heralded a modern education system. Education spending came under the oversight of the provincial governments and was further decentralized to district and municipal boards. Under a decentralized system, allocation of funding was decided by those on the district and municipal boards. Indian elites had a presence on these boards and therefore their preferences shaped a substantial part of education spending. The boards decided where schools would be set up and what type of schools were needed. The preferences of the elites on the boards influenced

[4] I thank Latika Chaudhary and James Fenske for sharing the data.

which private schools would receive public funding. Chaudhary's (2009) important work on colonial education shows that the caste composition of districts had a major influence on the allocation of the education budget. The local elites responded to the demand from their communities for secondary schools. In districts with high caste diversity, there were fewer primary schools and a relatively larger share of private funding for education was directed to secondary schools (Chaudhary 2009).

Chaudhary et al. (2012) show that colonial India had one of the lowest spending on education per head of school age population when compared with other developing countries. It was lower in comparison to the Princely States in India, which were outside British administration. In comparison with other countries, India spent a low share of the education budget on primary education (Chaudhary 2009). Only one-third of the education budget was spent on primary schools between 1891/92 and 1916/17, while the USA spent more than 90 per cent of public education expenditure on primary education from 1850 to 1890. The USA began to expand secondary education when over 85 per cent of the population was able to read and write. In the United Kingdom public spending on primary education was 73 per cent and in Japan 84 per cent in 1890 (Chaudhary 2009).

Surprisingly, in India the share of the school age population enrolled in secondary schools was comparable to France, but lagged behind Brazil in primary school enrolment. Table 4.5 shows the relative share of enrolment in primary and secondary education. At the time, when most countries started with expanding primary education, Indian education policy prioritized secondary and higher education for the small number of children in primary schools creating inadequacies in the provision of schooling and development of human capital. Table 4.6 shows the prioritization of higher education over universal primary schooling. The share of spending on secondary and tertiary education was unusually high compared to other Asian countries, including Japan in 1930, with 60 per cent of the education budget allocated to secondary and tertiary education, when Japan and Indonesia spent less than 30 per cent on this and targeted expansion of primary education.

As Table 4.6 shows, this pattern of education spending has endured after independence. Spending per student in tertiary education was 86 per cent of per capita GDP in 2000 but only 14 per cent per student in primary education (Kochhar et al. 2006). Castello Climent et al. (2017) found that variations in economic development across Indian districts today can be explained by differences in access to higher education. I will argue in this chapter that the higher education bias in education in colonial India paved

Table 4.5 *Comparative enrolment rates (number enrolled per 1,000 school age population)*

	India	Brazil	Japan	France	UK
Primary					
1900	53	102	507	859	720
1910	78	123	599	857	729
1920	102	147	602	704	701
1930	142	215	609	803	745
Secondary					
1900	10	0	13	11	7
1910	14	5	74	14	21
1920	20	6	108	24	44
1930	34	8	165	32	58

Source: Chaudhary (2015, table 10.2)

Table 4.6 *Share of secondary and higher education in total government spending on education (%)*

	India	Indonesia	Japan
1890	61.2	18.8	14.8
1910	62.3	18.5	24.2
1930	59.5	21.4	30.8
1950	57.3	28.2	59.6
1970	75.5	36.2	62.9
1990	56.9	58.8	66.9

Source: Van Leeuwen (2007, pp. 276–284)

the way for concentration of human capital in service sector occupations and may explain India's productivity advantage in services.

Vocational training was available to a limited extent in the urban centres. Given the lack of technical knowledge among the industrial workers in the modern sectors, there was a shortage of technicians for the emerging industries. Initially most of these technicians were British (Report of Industrial Commission 1916–1918, pp. 104–105). Among the Indians, mostly Parsis had the qualifications to work as technicians in the cotton textile industry. Other groups gradually entered the occupation, but not in large numbers.

The Victoria Jubilee Technical Institute was set up in Bombay in 1887 to train workers for cotton mills, and from 1904 scholarships were available for workers to train in Europe and North America. However, the scheme was not very successful due to the barriers the visiting students faced in accessing technical training while abroad (Report of Industrial Commission 1916–1918, p. 107). The 1916 Industrial Commission noted that, outside India, training for new industrial skills was rarely available to Indians. Technical institutions were also set up in other parts of the country. Some were publicly funded and others relied on private initiatives (Report of Industrial Commission 1916–1918, p. 614). The scope of these initiatives remained limited and constrained by the lack of basic education among the industrial workers.

By 1901, four engineering schools had been set up under public initiatives in different parts of the country. There were other vocational and higher education institutions, such as agricultural and veterinary colleges, as well as medical schools. The numbers in attendance were small and the focus was on the needs of the public services and public works departments (Report of Industrial Commission 1916–1918, pp. 565–70). An Indian school of mines was set up in 1926 (Report of Industrial Commission 1916–1918, p. 501). Universities were established in Calcutta, Bombay, and Madras in the middle of the nineteenth century and the number of universities expanded in the course of the twentieth century.

As discussed, education spending in colonial India emphasized higher education rather that universal basic education. Consequently, the supply of education was skewed towards secondary and higher education that suited the demand from the elites. The British government in India showed little interest in universal primary education, even as policies to expand primary education were increasingly popular in Britain. The colonial government wanted to train a highly educated Indian elite, who could participate in the civil service and various administrative bodies. This is particularly significant as colonial policy went against creating broad-based human capital, a well-trodden path by that time in most developed countries in Europe and North America and also Asia's most successful economy, Japan. At a time when labour legislations in British industries were adopted in India without much delay, under pressure from British industrial interests, primary education did not become a priority despite various representations to the British administration in India and local initiatives. I will argue in Chapter 6 that the consequences of not prioritizing primary education had long term consequences for India's path of economic development, particularly in comparison to East Asia.

4.4   Structural Change

In 1875 nearly three-quarters of the Indian workforce was engaged in agriculture and the sector produced the largest share of national output. The share of agriculture in employment did not change much until 1950. The picture of the sectoral share in GDP is quite different. Table 4.7 shows the shares of different sectors over the twentieth century. The categories are primary, secondary, and tertiary. Agriculture is the main component of the primary sector and industry is the main component of the secondary sector. The tertiary sector is services. The decline of agriculture in GDP, the rising share of industry and services, and the persistence of a high share of agriculture in employment highlights big differences in labour productivity across agriculture and non-agriculture. Unlike in the developed countries and despite the growth in industry and services, few workers moved from low productivity agriculture to higher productivity industrial and service sectors.

Gollin (2014) re-evaluates the Lewis model in the context of the persistence of a large share of labour in agriculture in developing countries today and the productivity gap between agricultural and non-agricultural sectors. In the Lewis model, named after the Nobel Laureate, Arthur Lewis, the economy is divided into a subsistence level informal sector with 'unlimited surplus labour' and a formal modern sector. The shift of workers from the subsistence economy to the modern sector keeps wages low in the latter and encourages fast accumulation. Gollin argues that this was not the situation in the developing countries at the end of the twentieth century due to the frictions in factor markets. There is a large gap in wages and labour productivity between the non-agricultural

Table 4.7 *Changes in sectoral shares in GDP and employment in the twentieth century (%)*

	Primary		Secondary		Manufacturing	Tertiary	
	GDP	Employment	GDP	Employment	GDP	GDP	Employment
1900	66.2	75.0	10.8	10.6	10.3	23.0	14.4
1930	56.1	76.0	13.5	9.0	12.9	30.4	15.0
1950	50.4	73.6	15.8	10.2	12.0	30.0	16.2
1980	33.2	69.5	26.4	13.4	19.9	38.2	17.1
2000	22.6	64.2	30.9	13.9	23.4	45.5	21.0

Note: The small differences between Tables 4.1 and 4.7 arise due to differences in classification
Source: Sivasubramonian (2000, tables 2.8, 9.31, Appendix table 7(f) and 9 (d))

sector and the agricultural sector in developing countries. The average productivity of the non-agricultural sectors is relatively similar across developed and developing countries (Caselli 2005). Rodrik (2013) finds unconditional convergence in labour productivity in the manufacturing industry across a large number of countries between 1965 and 2005. This suggests a faster catch up to the technology frontier in modern manufacturing than for the economy as a whole. Countries adopt the latest technology in sectors like manufacturing. This technology is typically labour saving. Consequently, the transfer of labour from agriculture to non-agriculture tends to slow down and structural change in today's developing countries tends to follow a different path.

However, should this be the case for India, when the fastest growing sector is services? Many of the subsectors in services are in non-tradables and many of these sectors use labour more intensively relative to capital. The following section discusses the differences in labour productivity across the three main sectors: agriculture, industry, and services.

4.5   Historical Differences and Changes in Labour Productivity across Sectors

Figure 4.2 shows changes in sectoral output over the longer run. Industry and services grew faster that agriculture. In output per worker, the service sector already had an advantage during the colonial period, as

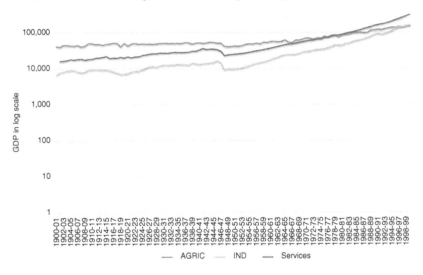

Figure 4.2 Sectoral GDP in 1948/49 prices (log scale)
Source: Sivasubramonian (2000, appendix table 7(f))

Table 4.8 *Changes in sectoral labour productivity (% per year)*

	Output per worker			
	Agriculture	Industry	Services	GDP
1872–1900	0.4	1.1	0.0	0.4
1900–1946	0.0	1.4	1.0	0.5
1950–1970	0.9	3.4	2.8	1.9
1978–2004*	1.4	2.5	3.5	3.3

Source: Broadberry and Gupta (2010)* Bosworth et al. (2007, table 3)

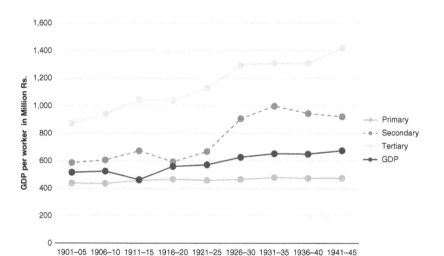

Figure 4.3 Output per worker by sector in million Rupees in 1948/49 prices (1901–1945)
Source: Author's calculations from Sivasubramonian (2000, tables 7.19, 2.11, 6.11)

Figure 4.3 shows. Output per worker in services was twice as high as in agriculture, but in industry it was only 25 per cent higher in 1901. The output and employment data from Sivasubramonian (2000) have been used by Broadberry and Gupta (2010) to calculate the average annual growth rates of labour productivity by sector over the twentieth century (see Table 4.8). Growth in output per worker put industry in the leading position until the late 1970s.

Output per worker in industry had begun to grow in the late nine-teenth century with the birth of the modern manufacturing sector, as discussed in Chapter 3, but the modern sector was too small to make an impact on the overall productivity of industry. Growth in output per worker in industry picked up as modern industry increased its share relative to the small-scale and artisanal industrial sector. Output per worker was stagnant in agriculture throughout this period. In services, growth in output per worker stagnated before 1900, as shown in Table 4.8. For the rest of the colonial period it was positive, but slower than in industry (see Table 4.8). Labour productivity growth in the economy as a whole was held back by stagnation in agriculture.

During the second half of the twentieth century, output per worker in agriculture grew, though slowly. Output per worker in industry and services grew faster. As Table 4.8 shows, growth in labour productivity in industry was faster than in services, not only in the colonial period, but also in the first thirty years after independence. This changed after 1978 and the service sector emerged as the fastest growing sector.

What explains the slower growth of the service sector between 1900 and 1946 and between 1950 and 1978, despite its productivity advantage? In the colonial period, the faster growth of industry reflects the rebalancing between the low productivity artisanal and small-scale industries and the higher productivity modern manufacturing. There were less significant changes in services. After 1950, under Nehruvian policies, the emphasis was on industrial development. High investment in this sector gave an advantage to industry relative to services. Economic reforms from the 1980s brought about productivity-enhancing changes in the private sector and the service sector began to catch up.

Table 4.9 reproduces the growth accounting exercise done by Bosworth, Collins and Virmani (2007). The paper disaggregates the sources of growth into the contributions of physical and human capital and the contribution of total factor productivity. The exercise shows that the contribution of physical capital was higher in industry, but the contribution of human capital was more important in the service sector. The contribution of total factor productivity in growth had been negative in agriculture and industry before 1980, but turned positive and increased significantly in all sectors following economic reforms. The service sector stands out in terms of the contribution of total factor productivity after 1980 (see Table 4.9). In this period India's total factor productivity growth in services was higher than that in China (Bosworth and Collins 2008). In terms of contribution to overall economic growth, it can be argued that, while China's growth is driven by manufacturing success, India's growth is led by the service sector. This is reflected in the difference in the pattern of structural change in India and China. Bosworth and Collins (2008) noted that India's development experience is very

Table 4.9 *Sources of growth in output per worker (1960–2004)*

	Output per worker	Contribution of		
		Physical capital	Human capital	TFP
Agriculture				
1960–1980	0.1	0.2	0.1	−0.1
1980–2004	1.7	0.4	0.3	1.1
Industry				
1960–1980	1.6	1.8	0.3	−0.4
1980–2004	3.0	1.6	0.3	1.1
Manufacturing				
1960–1980	**2.0**	**1.5**	**0.3**	**0.2**
1980–2004	**4.0**	**2.1**	**0.4**	**1.5**
Services				
1960–1980	**2.0**	**1.1**	**0.5**	**0.4**
1980–2004	**3.8**	**0.7**	**0.4**	**2.7**
India				
1960–1980	1.3	0.8	0.2	0.0
1980–2004	3.7	1.4	0.4	2.0

Source: Bosworth et al. (2007, tables 4 and 5)

different from that of China and other rapidly growing Asian economies, which have pursued manufacturing-led development. India's development path stands apart from the pattern of the structural change in most developed countries, but also in comparison to several fast-growing developing countries today, as shown in Table 4.1.

The policy of planned industrial development had prioritized more skill intensive sectors, rather than labour intensive sectors, in the early phase. The skills developed in the skill intensive industries could be used in the skill intensive services (Kochhar et al. 2006). The skill intensive services, such as banking and communication, have grown faster than other segments of the service sector. Singh (2012) shows that, within the service sector, subsectors like business services, communication, banking, hotels, and restaurants have shown an increase in growth in the 1980s and 1990s. Growth in other service subsectors, such as insurance, public administration, legal services, real estate, and personal services, slowed down in the 1990s. The fastest growing sectors are modern services like communications, business services, and services that are sold in the international market (Banga 2005; Eichengreen and Gupta 2011).

Eichengreen and Gupta (2011) point out that India's rapid growth in the service sector after 1990 is partly due to its unusually low share during the period of planning and even in the 1980s. They divide the service

Table 4.10 *Growth rates in selected services (% per year)*

	Share in 1980	1980s	1990s
Business services	0.3	13.5	19.8
Communications	1.0	6.1	13.6
Banking	3.4	11.9	12.7
Hospitality	0.7	6.5	9.3
Community services	4.3		8.4
Trade	11.9	5.9	7.3
Transport	3.8	6.3	6.9
Public administration and defence	6.0	7.0	6.0
Legal services	0.0	8.6	5.8
Personal services	1.1	2.4	5.0
Storage	0.1	2.7	2.0

Source: Gordon and Gupta (2004)

sector into three subgroups: traditional services, such as trade, transport and storage; traditional and modern services consumed by households, such as education, health, and hospitality; and modern services such as finance and information technology and communication. They show that, although service sector growth is spread across the groups, productivity growth has been fastest in the modern services. Gordon and Gupta (2004) found that the fastest growth was in the skill intensive business services, communications, and banking, but these sectors had a small share in GDP. Trade and public administration have larger shares and have grown at a slower pace (see Table 4.10). India's fast-growing service exports are also in these emerging sectors. Using evidence from the World Bank data, Banga (2005) suggests that the sectors such as business services, including software, show revealed comparative advantage in the activities that require high quality human capital. During 1990–1995 and 1996–2002, the share of software services in exports rose from 34 per cent to 60 per cent and India became a net foreign exchange earner in services after 1997–1998 (Banga 2005). Service sector exports have grown at about 20 per cent per year from the mid 1990s and accounted for 33 per cent of total exports in 2004, a very different composition of exports compared to China. The latter exports a growing volume of industrial goods (Bosworth and Collins 2008).

4.6   Human Capital and Service Sector Advantage

Does India enjoy an advantage in services in comparison to other developing countries? Consider the role of human capital. Kochhar et al.

(2006) suggest that the skewed education system that prioritized tertiary education was useful in the skill intensive industrial and service sectors. Demand for skilled workers has been high, while unskilled workers with basic education could not be absorbed in the fast-growing industrial sectors. Consequently, the movement of labour from agriculture to industry has remained low. From the 1990s, labour has moved from agriculture to the slow-growing, low-skill service sectors such as trade and construction, but the fastest growing service sectors have the same profile of labour demand as the skill intensive industries (Kotwal et al. 2011). These skill intensive services absorb little excess labour from agriculture.

Ramaswamy and Agrawal (2012) focus on urban India and find that the share of the service sector in employment was higher than the share in industry. Within services, trade and hospitality and financial and business services employed more people than industry. There was a difference in the human capital of workers in the two sectors in 2000. In manufacturing, 27 per cent of the male workers had secondary education and 14 per cent had tertiary education, while in services the numbers were 29 per cent and 21 per cent, respectively. Among female workers, only 4 per cent of the workforce in manufacturing in urban India had a college degree. In services the figure was 25 per cent. For female workers with secondary education, employment shares were 12 per cent in manufacturing and 20 per cent in services (Ramaswamy and Agrawal 2012). Educated women are better represented in service sector jobs. The manufacturing sector, on the other hand, absorbs workers with low levels of education. This is borne out by Figure 4.4. In 2001, the services sector had more workers with secondary and tertiary education than industry (see Figure 4.4).

Broadberry and Gupta (2010) break down comparative labour productivity levels for India and Britain by the three main sectors of agriculture, industry, and services. In the early 1870s, an average Indian agricultural worker produced slightly more than 10 per cent of the output produced by an average British agricultural worker. By the 1970s, this had fallen to around 2 per cent and it was even lower by the 1990s. The comparison of agricultural productivity is not meaningful, given the large differences in the share of employment in agriculture. More meaningful comparison can be made with respect to industry and services. Output per worker in the non-agricultural sectors, industry, and services was 18 per cent of the British level in 1871, rising to 25 per cent in 1930. The increase reflected the growth in modern, large-scale industry and declining importance of small-scale artisanal industry in this sector. The relative position of the service sector also showed a similar change. Since 1950, the relative performance of industry and services

Table 4.11 *Sectoral labour productivity in India relative to Britain*

	Agriculture	Industry	Services	GDP
1871–1973	11.2	18.2	18.1	15.1
1900/01	10.4	17.3	15.6	13.2
1910/11	11.1	24.2	17.7	14.4
1920/21	9.8	21.1	21.1	13.2
1929/30	8.3	25.3	25.2	14.2
1946/7	7.0	18.1	23.2	12.8
1950/51*	5.4	14.6	17.5	9.3
1960/61*	4.3	16.4	20.0	9.7
1970/71*	2.3	17.3	22.6	9.4
1980/81*	1.6	16.1	29.3	10.2
1990/91*	0.9	18.3	33.0	11.0
1999–2000*	1.0	15.8	32.8	11.4

Note: * Refers to India after independence
Source: Broadberry and Gupta (2010)

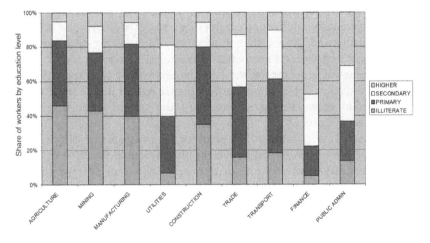

Figure 4.4 Human capital by sectors (2001)
Source: Broadberry and Gupta (2010)

has been quite different. The relative labour productivity in industry remained at around 15–18 per cent, but the Indian service sector has narrowed the gap with Britain (see Table 4.11). Indian labour productivity was one-third of the British level in 2000. The unusual performance of the service sector is not a recent phenomenon. The advantage the sector has enjoyed goes back to the colonial period and a historical perspective helps in understanding India's advantage in services. Earlier in the chapter I discussed the emphasis on secondary and tertiary education by the colonial administration. Caste-level literacy rates from 1901 shown in Table 4.4 show the high literacy rates among certain castes in service sector occupations. The demand for higher education was high among this group and they were able to move into public administration, public services, trade, and banking. In recent decades, as in colonial India, the highest concentration of human capital was in the service sector. A long run assessment of human capital in different sectors shows that the services sectors such as trade and public administration have always required a literate and numerate workforce. The biased emphasis on higher education has colonial origins and has provided an advantage to the service sector. The resulting concentration of human capital in services rather than manufacturing may explain India's service sector-led growth.

4.7   Conclusion

In this chapter, I have discussed the historical origins of India's service sector-led growth. Occupations that required literacy gave certain castes an advantage in moving to the emerging modern services that required educated workers. From the late nineteenth century, many of the upper castes shifted from their traditional occupations into the modern sectors, such as public administration, law, medicine, and education. Traders invested in modern industries. The demand for industrial workers in modern industries saw migration from rural to urban areas. Little changed in agriculture.

The colonial education system invested more in secondary and tertiary education without prioritising universal primary education, as in most countries in Europe, North America, and Japan in the nineteenth and early twentieth century. The concentration of human capital in the service sector gave this sector an advantage that had long term consequences and the bias towards higher education continued in independent India. The service sector has enjoyed higher labour productivity for over a century. India's service sector-led growth in recent decades has historical origins.

5   Region, Income, Caste, and Gender
Continuity and Change

In this chapter, I will look at four different aspects of inequality in India and assess the changes that have occurred over time and the continuity that still manifests in many aspects of economic and social life. These four aspects will be region, income, caste, and gender. The Indian subcontinent is diverse in geography, cropping pattern, and economic activity. Caste has defined occupation and access to opportunities in Indian society over centuries. Finally, the difference in the social and economic status of women from ancient times characterizes an important inequality: the preference for sons over daughter and a lower status of women in society.

The historical uneven development of regions has persisted in some dimensions and changed in some aspects. From 1950, policies have targeted aspects of these inequalities to bring about change. The abolition of the landlord system changed the dominant position of the traditional landowning groups. Industrial licensing, which was discussed in Chapter 3, considered the relative backwardness of regions in decisions on the location of new industries. Independent India implemented affirmative action in jobs and education for the lowest castes in Indian society from the 1950s. Changes in inheritance laws by different states opened the door to equal inheritance by women. More recently, various interventions have been made at the province level to introduce economic support for the girl child. This chapter takes a long view of changing inequalities as well as persistent inequalities for regions, groups defined by income, caste, and gender. I will start with the regional inequalities, followed by measures of income and wealth inequality and the changes from ancient inequality to inequality in modern India. The third section will emphasize caste inequality in access to jobs and education. Finally, I will discuss the unequal gender norms that have been highlighted in the literature on missing women.

5.1   Regional Inequality

From evidence based on travel writers and the surveys by Francis Buchanan Hamilton in the first decades of the nineteenth century, we get a glimpse of the differences in regional prosperity and deprivation. The prosperous regions in the seventeenth and eighteenth centuries were the urban centres, but this too was limited to certain groups: the nobility and wealthy merchants. The nobility and the merchant elites had amassed wealth and spent it on luxury consumption of non-agricultural goods. Artisans produced a wealth of industrial goods, including textiles, jewellery, and metal ware and the artisanal sector prospered in the urban centres. The image of a prosperous urban India has been held up as a symbol of industrial capability and prosperity of the nation.

The reality for the average Indian was quite different. Accounts of travellers from the fourteenth century discussed the regional differences, the opulence of the elites, but also pointed to the simple lifestyle of the average person based on consumption of food, the clothing they wore, and the dwellings where they lived. The picture from qualitative sources is one of urban prosperity among certain groups and rural poverty for most (Pelsaert 1978; Tavernier 1889; Bernier 1916). Today, this would be considered as an indicator of inequality in society. There would be similar descriptions of what is observed in India today in terms of the luxurious lifestyles of the rich and the destitution of a large number of people living below the poverty line. Evidence from seventeenth-century India indicates inequality of a larger magnitude.

The standard of living in rural India depended on agricultural productivity. The evidence on agricultural productivity differences is sketchy. Francis Buchanan surveyed different regions in eastern and southern India. His evidence on output per acre shows differences across the districts of Shahabad and Dinajpur in eastern India and Mysore and Canara in southern India. Sivramkrishna (2015) analyses data collected on Buchanan's journey through Mysore and Canara and finds that areas with higher productivity in land were more prosperous, but none of this evidence allows a systematic assessment of regional inequalities across the country because the surveys covered only a few districts. From the second half of the nineteenth century the available data allows a more systematic analysis of regional differences.

One of the first measures of regional inequality in India comes from the work of Caruana-Galizia (2013), who estimates regional income

Table 5.1 *Per capita provincial GDP in Rupees in 1948 prices*

	1881	1891	1901	1911
Assam	284	272	332	336
Bengal and states	195	195	190	158
Bombay and states	263	272	278	310
Central provinces and states	195	188	203	257
Cochin State	222	206	219	346
Hyderabad State	449	256	279	380
Madras and states	143	156	172	195
Mysore State	156	176	189	210
Punjab and states	180	187	221	276
Rajputana and states	221	278	260	278
Travancore	318	288	229	394
United Provinces and states	146	163	151	161

Note: States refer to princely states and are included in the estimates of
several provinces
Source: Caruana-Galizia (2013)

from 1875 to 1911 and shows that GDP per capita varied by province. Broadly speaking, Bombay Presidency had higher per capita GDP from 1881 relative to the eastern province of Bengal. This difference became larger over time as Bengal declined and Bombay grew (see Table 5.1). Other provinces that stand out as relatively prosperous were the princely states of Cochin, Travancore, and Hyderabad. GDP per capita in the northern province of Punjab grew over time, assisted by the canal construction. Here too the successful increase in agricultural productivity was an important factor. The poorest regions were the Madras Presidency and states and the United Provinces (see Table 5.1).

Roy (2014) has focused on the regional differences between British and princely states, regions of landlord and non-landlord systems, and geographical zones of coastal and riverine flood plains and the drylands. Roy finds that British states had lower revenue per square mile compared to the princely states, and within British states there were significant differences in revenue per capita. Revenue per capita was lower in the coastal and the floodplains compared to the drylands. This somewhat counterintuitive outcome may be explained in terms of lower investment in land and declining yields in densely populated fertile regions. Regions under the landlord system typically generated lower revenue per capita.

Figure 5.1 looks at the correlation between GDP per capita at the province level in 1911 and 2003. The correspondence is not precise given the changing borders and formation of new provinces. The graph shows a positive correlation between the colonial provinces and what is

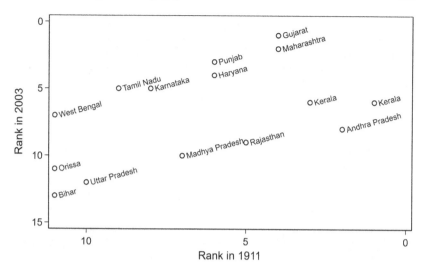

Figure 5.1 Correlation between GDP per capita for provinces (1911 and 2003)
Note: A lower rank indicates higher per capita GDP. Kerala is matched with the Princely States of Travancore and Cochin.
Source: Purfield (2006) for 2003 and Caruana-Galizia (2013) for 1911

roughly the equivalent province today. The richer provinces in 2003 were also richer in colonial India. The provinces of Bombay Presidency and Bombay States, which correspond to Maharashtra and Gujarat today, were the richest region in British India, though it ranked behind the princely states of Travancore, Cochin (Kerala today), and Hyderabad (Andhra Pradesh). Today both Maharashtra and Gujarat rank among the richest states in India and Kerala and Andhra Pradesh have fallen behind. The rise of Bombay Presidency as the industrial centre is discussed in Chapter 3. It differed from the other industrial centre, Bengal, in terms of the dominance of Indian commercial and industrial interests from the nineteenth century. Bengal, where the British commercial and industrial interests dominated, had one of the lowest per capita GDP in 1911 and shows an improved position in the ranking of per capita GDP in 2003. However, a comparison between Bengal Presidency and today's West Bengal is problematic as the geographical boundary of West Bengal, post partition, is very different from that of Bengal Presidency in colonial India. Although the industrial hub around Calcutta was prosperous, the agricultural regions in the rest of Bengal had gone into a decline.

Punjab and Haryana in 2003 were among the richest provinces. Punjab ranked sixth in 1911. The geographical borders of Punjab changed too as a result of the partition. Punjab had a dense irrigation network in colonial India and was the first region to see the fruits of the Green Revolution in the 1970s. The United Provinces in 1911 was one of the poorest regions and has remained relatively underdeveloped in 2003. The dominance of the upper castes among the economic elites and the conflict over political power in post-independence Uttar Pradesh did not lead to a path to development (Kohli 2012, p. 166).

Even when considering more recent changes in different regions, Bhattacharya and Sakthivel (2004) find no convergence between rich and poor provinces after the economic reforms. The more industrial provinces, Tamil Nadu, Maharashtra, and Gujarat, have grown faster than the less developed provinces, Bihar, Orissa, and Uttar Pradesh. Purfield (2006) finds a very stable pattern in ranking of provinces by GDP per capita between 1971 and 2003. Maharashtra and Gujarat are among the top four richest states together with Punjab and Haryana. The prosperity in the states of Maharashtra and Gujarat is not a recent phenomenon. As Figure 5.1 shows, the development of this region has origins in the colonial era. Punjab too has benefitted from the irrigation canals built in colonial India. Uttar Pradesh, Bihar, and Orissa at the lower end of economic development in 2003 were also poorer in 1911. Persistence of history has been discussed in many different contexts (Acemoglu et al. 2001; Nunn 2008; Dell 2010). The regional inequality in India can in part be associated with the impact of colonial policy in different regions.

5.2   Regional Differences in Poverty

To understand the regional inequality in colonial India, it is not sufficient to look at province level per capita GDP alone. One of the key measures of economic development is the poverty–headcount ratio, or how many people are below the poverty line as a share of the population. The poverty line is the minimum income required in a country to meet the basic needs of individuals: food, clothing, and shelter. In terms of daily requirement of calories of an average person, the poverty line considers 2400 calories to be a requirement in rural areas and 2100 calories in urban areas. Different countries adopt their own measure of what constitutes the minimum level of income. The World Bank uses a daily dollar rate as a measure for comparison across countries.

Another concept that is used to measure the incidence of poverty is the 'poverty gap index'. This is defined as the gap between mean income of people below the poverty line and the poverty line as a ratio of the poverty line. The larger the ratio, the more significant is the incidence of poverty. Most indicators of poverty are correlated with poor nutrition, access to education, and life expectancy.

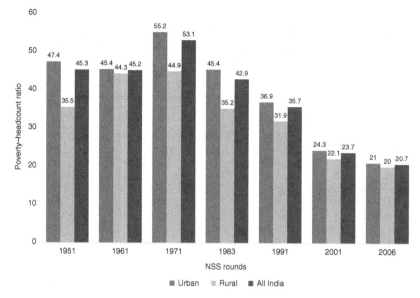

Figure 5.2 Poverty–headcount ratio (1951–2006) (measured in the various rounds of the National Sample Survey)
Source: Datt and Ravallion (2010)

The Indian National Congress had raised the issue of tackling poverty even before independence. The National Planning committee discussed a poverty line of Rs. 15 to Rs. 20 per person per month in 1944. Successive governments after independence specified poverty reduction as an objective and the five-year plans included it as a goal. The Planning Commission discussed figures of Rs. 20 to Rs. 25 per month in 1962. The numbers were revised over time. The Tendulkar Committee of 2005, headed by the well-known economist, adopted their own measure for urban and rural India at Rs. 578.80 per capita per month and Rs. 446.68 per capita per month, respectively.

The evidence on poverty from 1951 comes from the work of Gourav Datt and Martin Ravallian. Figure 5.2 shows the changes in the poverty–headcount ratio between 1952 and 2003. Until 1978, there were fluctuations, but no decline. The poverty–headcount ratio rose in the late 1960s following the agricultural crisis and began to decline from 1980 following the economic reforms. It declined slowly from 43 per cent in 1983 to 36 per cent in 1991 and 21 per cent in 2006 (see Figure 5.2). The slow decline particularly stands out in comparison to the share of the population that was pulled out of poverty in China since the 1980s, where the poverty–headcount ratio declined from 73 per cent in 1981 to 45 per cent in 1993 to 12 per cent in 2005 (Ravallion 2011).

Table 5.2 *Changes in poverty gap and poverty–headcount ratio*

	Poverty gap index		Poverty–headcount ratio (per cent)		
	1957–1960*	1990–1994*	1960*	1983**	2000**
Poor states					
Bihar	22.4	16.4	64.5	52.2	46.9
Uttar Pradesh	14.3	10.6	47.4	47.1	33.0
Orissa	20.3	7.4	60.9	65.3	46.3
Madhya Pradesh	19.4	12.7	56.7	49.8	38.8
Rajasthan	14.3	12.5	46.4	34.5	20.4
Middle income states					
Andhra Pradesh	22.9	7.7	65.1	28.9	18.8
West Bengal	13.7	6.5	50.3	54.8	32.1
Kerala	28.1	8.0	69.2	40.4	14.5
Karnataka	17.5	12.9	54.8	38.2	25.6
Rich States					
Tamil Nadu	26.2	11.0	69.7	51.7	21.5
Punjab	n.a	n.a	31.2	16.2	6.0
Haryana	n.a	n.a	31.2	21.4	11.8
Gujarat	18.6	9.6	56.8	32.8	15.5
Maharashtra	21.9	14.4	65.9	43.4	28.7

Source: *Datt (1998), **Ahluwalia (2000)

While the poverty–headcount ratio has declined everywhere in India, the richer states have been more successful in reducing poverty. The differences in decline in poverty across the provinces can be seen in Table 5.2. Kerala is a success story of poverty reduction among the middle-income provinces. West Bengal, too, has seen a significant decline in poverty. Among the rich provinces, Punjab, Haryana, Gujarat, and Maharashtra have seen large reductions in poverty between 1960 and 1980 and the trend has continued. Punjab had the lowest poverty–headcount ratio in 2000. Maharashtra has seen a slower decline compared to the other three rich states. The poor states have also seen a decline in the poverty–headcount ratio, but the numbers remained high even in 2000. The poverty gap index declined in all provinces, but the decline was slow in the poorer provinces.

Kohli (2014) points to the political divide across provinces that have successfully reduced poverty and those that did not do as well. Provinces such as Kerala and West Bengal adopted policies of redistribution under left wing governments. In the southern provinces there was a decline in the dominant position of the elites in politics from early twentieth

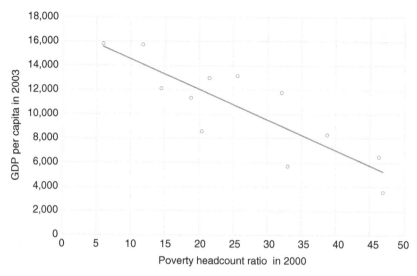

Figure 5.3A Correlation between per capita GDP for the provinces (2003) and poverty–headcount ratio (2000)
Source: Ahluwalia (2000)

century. By contrast, in the northern provinces of Uttar Pradesh and Bihar, the landowning elites and high caste groups held political power until recently and maintained their privileges (Kohli 2012, pp. 134–136).

Overall, there is a negative relationship between GDP per capita of the province and the poverty–headcount ratio (see Figure 5.3A). The relationship between per capita GDP growth post economic reform in the 1980s and 1990s and the poverty–headcount ratio is also negative (see Figure 5.3B). This suggests that growth has been one of the factors in pulling people out of poverty. However, relying on growth alone has not been adequate and poverty reduction differs across comparable provinces.

Ravallion and Datt (2002) show that, between 1960 and 1994, the decline in poverty across states depended on the increase in non-farm activity, but the responsiveness of poverty depended on the initial conditions in the rural economy. Provinces differed in poverty reduction due to initial differences in human capital and land distribution in 1960. More equal land distribution and higher literacy reduced poverty faster in response to rise in non-farm activity. Datt and Ravallion (2002) show that more than half the difference between Bihar and Kerala in the relationship between poverty–headcount ratio and non-farm output is attributable to the latter's substantially higher initial literacy rate. Female literacy, which was lower than male literacy everywhere, is a

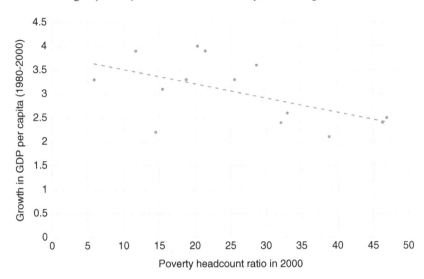

Figure 5.3B Correlation between per capita GDP growth for the provinces (1980–2000) and poverty–headcount ratio (2000)
Source: Bhattacharya and Sakthivel (2004) and Ahluwalia (2000)

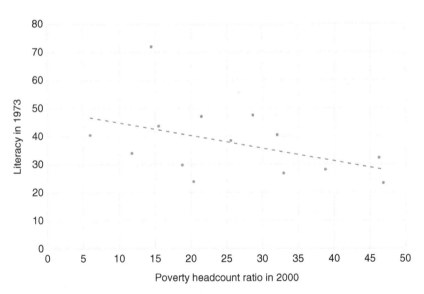

Figure 5.3C Correlation between literacy in 1973 and the poverty–headcount ratio for provinces (2000)
Source: Ahluwalia (2000)

good indicator of the differences in initial conditions. In Kerala, female literacy was 39 per cent in 1960 and in Bihar it was 7 per cent. Poverty–headcount ratio in 2000 had a negative relationship with literacy in 1973 (see Figure 5.3C). India has seen a much slower increase in literacy compared to several other countries, including China. In 2005, 22 per cent of men and 42 per cent of women were not literate and only 72 per cent of all primary school-age children were in education (Kohli 2014, p. 139).

Measures of poverty disguise some of the inequalities that have been slower to erode. Indian children show high levels of stunting (Jayachandran and Pande 2017). The share of the Indian population that consumes less-than-adequate calories rose from 65 per cent in 1983 to 76 per cent in 2005 (Kohli 2014, p. 138). This decline in calorie intake is across all income groups, despite rising incomes, and no long term changes in relative price of food (Deaton and Dreze 2009).

5.3   Income Inequality

Another way to think about distributional issues in a society is income or wealth inequality. Land inequality is often used as a measure of wealth inequality in agricultural economies and is measured using the Gini coefficient. The Gini coefficient lies between 0 and 100 as a measure of distribution of income or wealth in a population. The lower the value of the Gini coefficient, the more equal is the distribution of income and wealth or any other economic indicator of asset ownership. According to World Bank's most recent measures of income inequality, in 2014 South Africa had a Gini coefficient of 63 and in 2019 Brazil stood at 53. These are among the most unequal societies. By comparison, in 2011 the Indian Gini coefficient was lower at 36. South Korea's Gini coefficient was even lower at 31 in 2016. India ranks high at 82 in wealth Gini coefficient.

In their measurement of 'ancient inequality' Milanovic et al. (2010) suggest that in societies at a low level of development, when average income is very low, inequality is low as surplus above subsistence for the population is small. As income rises, the surplus increases and the scope for extraction of income above subsistence expands. They measure pre-industrial income inequality in twenty-eight societies starting from the Roman Empire to the year of Indian independence and distinguish between inequality between social groups and inequality within these groups. For India, the data is measured in two historical contexts. It compares inequality at the end of the Mughal Empire and at the end of British rule. In Mughal India they consider four economic groups: the nobility and zamindars, the rest of urban India (including occupational

Table 5.3 *Long-run between and within group income inequality in India*

	Between-group Gini	Within-group Gini
Mughal India 1750	38.5	48.9
India 1947	48.0	49.7
Average for 28 pre-industrial societies	44.8	45.7
India 2004	NA	32.6
Average for the modern counterparts		41.1

Source: Milanovic et al. (2010)

groups, merchants to sweepers), the village economy, and lastly, the tribal economy. The share of these groups in the population and in income is estimated. For 1947, there are many more occupational categories: British officials and traders, the nobility and Indian capitalists, petty traders, government and industrial workers, village rentiers, working land proprietors, share croppers and tenants, and landless peasants.

Table 5.3 shows the measure of inequality in India using two different Gini coefficients at three points in time, two historical and one more recent. The first measures between-group inequality and the second measures within-group inequality. Between-group inequality in Mughal India was lower than the average for twenty-eight societies (world) and also lower than the between-group inequality in India in 1947. Mughal India exhibited slightly higher within-group inequality compared to the average for the pre-industrial societies. This could be a result of the level of aggregation, but it is likely that there were bigger differences in assets owned within social groups, such as industrial interests and agricultural interests. However, the difference between industrial and agricultural interests in Mughal India was smaller. By 1947, the two measures of inequality looked similar. As Table 5.3 shows, within-group inequality was higher than the average for twenty-eight pre-industrial societies. In the modern counterparts of this group, India looks less unequal than the average for this group. On the other hand, India has been more unequal than Japan in the twentieth century. Inequality did not change significantly during colonial rule, with the top 1 per cent of income earners accounting for 15 per cent of the wealth in 1750 and 14 per cent in 1947 (Milanovic et al. 2010). In India after independence, the province level measures of the Gini coefficient in 1957–1960 and in 1990–1994 indicate lower levels of inequality than

Table 5.4 *Changes in province-level inequality in independent India*

	Rural Gini index		Urban Gini index	
	1957/60*	1990/1994*	1957/60*	1990/1994*
Poor states				
Bihar	29.8	22.4	31.2	31.7
Uttar Pradesh	30.9	28.1	37.5	32.7
Orissa	29.9	26.3	38.4	37.8
Madhya Pradesh	36.7	30.5	37.0	33.8
Rajasthan	36.5	28.0	32.0	29.6
Middle income states				
Andhra Pradesh	31.1	28.4	31.7	32.5
West Bengal	27.4	25.7	32.3	34.4
Kerala	34.7	30.7	30.5	37.1
Karnataka	34.8	26.5	33.8	34.6
Rich states				
Tamil Nadu	30.9	29.4	34.3	36.8
Punjab and Haryana	n.a	n.a	n.a	n.a
Gujarat	29.6	24.1	33.8	29.5
Maharashtra	29.2	30.2	35.5	34.9

Source: * Datt, 1998,

in the historical contexts. Rural Gini coefficients show some decline in all provinces, except Maharashtra (see Table 5.4).

Yet another measure of income inequality in colonial India comes from income tax records. The coverage of income tax in India has been limited historically and continues to be the case. It excludes agricultural incomes and all informal sector incomes. Although limited in scope, as only a small section of the population paid income tax, the data was collected systematically from 1885 and has been used by Alvaredo et al. (2017) to construct the regional share of top incomes. Alvaredo et al. (2017) and Banerjee and Piketty (2005) use the share of income earned by the top 0.1 per cent and 0.01 per cent of the income distribution as a measure of income concentration.

Their findings highlight two aspects of income concentration at the top level. Unlike in the African colonies, where European expatriates and settlers dominated top incomes, Indians were a significant share in the top 0.1 per cent of the income distribution (Alvaredo et al. 2021). This is likely to reflect the dominance of Indians in commercial and industrial activities. In Chapter 3, I have discussed the predominance of Indian entrepreneurs in one of the largest modern industrial sectors, the cotton textiles. Alvaredo et al. (2017) show that the Europeans accounted for not more than 40 per cent of those in the top 0.1 per cent of income distribution. Europeans, who served in the trading companies and other commercial activities, and those working for the government were paid high salaries. The wealth of the Indian urban elite in Bombay Presidency, today's Maharashtra and Gujarat, was already visible in the first decades of the twentieth century, and by 1947 an Indian elite dominated the top income groups.

A second insight from the data is that the entry of Indians in the top income group is also reflected in the changes in the share of provinces in top incomes. The Bengal Presidency had the largest concentration of top incomes in 1885. Bombay Presidency was the second largest (Alvaredo et al. 2017). British interests were dominant in Bengal, while Indian interests were more important in Bombay. The position of Bombay and Bengal Presidencies in income concentration switched over the next decades. At the time of independence, Bombay Presidency had the largest share in top incomes. As we saw in Chapter 3, Bombay and Bengal were the two most industrial regions and the income tax data covers the non-agricultural occupations.

Alvaredo et al. (2017) find a U-shaped pattern between 1885 and 1946 (see Figure 5.4). The top income share declined until the early 1920s and then rose again. The authors attribute the decline to slower growth of the modern non-agricultural sector in the early twentieth century. The faster growth of the new industries under Indian ownership may explain the rise from the 1920s.

Figure 5.4 shows a sharp decline in the share of top incomes after 1950. How did independent India deal with income inequality and how did this change over time? In Chapter 2 we discussed the abolition of the privileges enjoyed by the rulers of the princely states. The privy purse given to the 'princes' was proportional to the territory they handed over to the Indian Union (Roberts 1972). The Privy Purse Act of 1970 removed the compensation given to the 'princes'. The Nizam of Hyderabad was listed among the richest people in the world in 1937 by Time Magazine (Kumar 2020). The wealth of the ruling elites of the princely states was significant. The changes in taxation on wealth via the Estate Duty and Gift Tax Act of 1953 had an impact on wealth inequality as these taxes became more progressive between 1953 and 1991 (Kumar 2020).

Longer term evidence from 1922 come from Banerjee and Piketty (2005). They show that, after independence, there was another U-shaped evolution of the top income shares (Figure 5.4 combines data from 1885 with the data from 1922 to 2000). The falling share of top incomes in the first thirty years after independence was quite dramatic under the Nehruvian policies of public sector-led industrialization, where

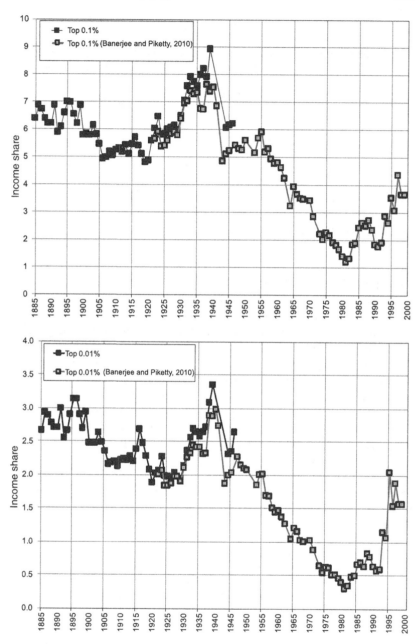

Figure 5.4 Changes in the top income shares (1885–2000)
Source: Alvaredo et al. (2017), figure 1, Copyright Elsevier

Table 5.5 *Share of growth captured by income groups (distribution of per adult pre-tax income)*

Income group	Share of growth captured (1951–1980)	Share of growth captured (1980–2015)
Total	100	100
Bottom 50 per cent	28	10.4
Middle 40 per cent	49	21.2
Next 9 per cent	24	40.0
Top 1 per cent	0.9	28.3
Top 0.1 per cent	−1.8	11.3
Top 0.01 per cent	−1.0	4.8
Top 0.001 per cent	−0.4	2.0

Source: Chancel and Piketty (2019)

regulations restricted the role of the private sector. Although economic planning did not put India on a high growth path, it reduced income concentration. The share of top incomes declined significantly.

After 1980, the share of top incomes began to rise again following removal of restrictions on private investment, but it did not go back to the 9 per cent share of the top 0.1 per cent in 1946. Colonial India shows higher inequality using income share of the top 0.1 per cent as a measure. The decline in inequality under the Nehruvian policies and its increase with economic reforms is convincingly shown in the work of Chancel and Piketty (2019). This is reproduced in Table 5.5, which shows that 28 per cent of the growth in income between 1951 and 1980 benefitted the bottom 50 per cent. The share declined to 10 per cent after 1980, while over 11 per cent of income growth went to the top 0.1 per cent. The middle forty per cent of the population have benefitted less from growth than in the comparable group in the USA, Europe and China (Chancel and Piketty 2019).

5.4   Caste Inequality

An important manifestation of inequality in India is through the hierarchy of the caste system. The occupational segregation by caste enforced through hereditary membership and endogamous marriage (Beteille 1965, p. 46) created inequality in wealth and social status. Occupation among Hindus was caste dependent and the notions of pollution and purity within the caste system prevented occupational and income mobility. Sociologists have debated if the salience of caste was a product of Hindu tradition (Dumont 1970) or an outcome of the colonial censuses (Dirks 2001). In his presidential address to the Indian History Congress of 1990, Vivekanand Jha pointed to discussion by the sociologists Karve and Malik on the locational segregation of occupation-based communities in the ancient civilization of Harappa (Jha 1991).

As discussed in Chapter 2, the Indian caste system comprises four *varnas*: Brahmans (the priests), Kshatriyas (the warriors), Vaishyas (the trading professionals), and Shudras (castes involved in other menial occupations). The occupation categories by subcastes or *jatis*, which are numerous, determined the community-specific norms of hierarchy and endogamous marriage conventions (Jodhka 2012). It is in this context that caste hierarchy was defined at the local level and continues to be the case. The term 'dominant caste' in a region was defined in terms of their socioeconomic strength (Vaid 2014). Outside the somewhat fluid configuration of economic power in the hands of upper and middle castes were the 'untouchable castes'. They were in occupations considered to be 'unclean', such as scavenging, cleaning, and organising funeral pyres.

5.5   Caste in Colonial India

Caste was mentioned as an economic and social category in the travel accounts of Francis Buchanan in 1807. Brahmans were at the top of this hierarchy and the Shudras at the bottom. The rulers of the princely states at the top of the political hierarchy were not necessarily Brahmans, but Kshatriyas (Bayly 2001). The economic dominance of upper and middle castes was varied across regions. Different caste groups could be the dominant caste in a region. Within-group hierarchy was not just specific to the Hindus, it permeated all religions in India. Bayly (2001) refers to the caste-like distinction between a Sikh cultivator and a trader in the Punjab (p. 18). The Muslims and the Christians had their own specific hierarchies. Although caste is not intrinsic to Islam, occupation-based hierarchies similar to the Hindu caste system existed in the Indian subcontinent (Ahmad and Chakravarti 1981). The Khoja and Bohra Muslims were involved specifically in trade and industry. Therefore, community-specific occupation built into the social structure a lack of social mobility.

Indian censuses from 1901 enumerated population, marital status, literacy, and infirmity by caste. It provided data on caste composition at the level of districts. The landlords were typically upper caste. Landowning peasants belonged to certain agricultural castes. Other service providers in the rural economy mostly belonged to the lower strata of caste hierarchy. The landless labourers came from the lower levels of the hierarchy. The land tenure systems entrenched the caste hierarchy. In landlord regions upper caste domination was stronger. The Punjab Land Alienation Act of 1901 specified that land could only be owned by agricultural castes to prevent land ownership passing into the hands of the non-cultivating castes. Cassan (2015) finds evidence of the manipulation of caste identity to be declared as an agricultural caste following the Act.

The traders came from specific castes and engaged in local and interregional trade and moneylending. These groups varied by region. The Marwari traders, who had migrated from Rajasthan, became important participants in grain trade and trade in other agricultural commodities in all regions. The Vanis in western India, the Chettiars in the south, and the Khatris in the north were the caste groups engaged in agricultural trade and moneylending. Several trading groups were involved in trade in raw cotton in western India and became industrial entrepreneurs, as discussed in Chapter 3. Their occupational shift from trade to industry used ties of caste and religion. This was first seen among the Hindu castes of Bhatias and Vanias and the minority religious groups of Parsis, Khoja Muslims, and Baghdadi Jews, who traded in raw cotton and set up the cotton textile industry in Bombay. In the aftermath of the First World War, the Marwari traders moved into the jute industry and, following the Great Depression, the Chettiars moved into a variety of industries. However, this pattern of occupational change was seen mainly among the trading groups, who belonged to the upper and middle castes. Brahmans and other upper castes moved into the high skilled professions in the modern sectors. Within the upper castes, therefore, there was mobility across occupations. The lack of mobility was most pronounced for the lowest castes, who had little access to occupations of the upper and middle castes.

Non-agricultural jobs in rural and urban India were caste based. Weavers and artisans typically belonged to certain castes. Caste and community was important in recruitment of industrial workers in the early phases of industrialization. Cotton and jute mills, as well as tea plantations, employed 'sirdars' or labour recruiters, who relied on community and caste networks of the native villages. Regional and sectoral labour markets were often defined by caste and linguistic groups (Das Gupta 1981). Within the industrial workspace different social groups had more interactions, but caste identities and segregation by jobs did not disappear within a firm. The constraint that certain jobs could only be done by certain castes introduced a lack of mobility.

Table 5.6 *Caste literacy by province (1931)*

	All	Hindu	Brahman	Caste with highest literacy	Lower castes
Assam	11.9	10.6	–	23.6 (Ahom)	3.1
Bengal	5.3	15.7	43.1	62.6 (Baidya)	5.0
Bihar and Orissa	6.9	5.5	19.2	36.2 (Kayastha)	0.6
Bombay	10.8	10.2	51.0	51.0 (Brahman)	2.8
Central Provinces and Berar	6.6	6.4	35.2	35.2 (Brahman)	1.5
Madras	10.8	10.4	54.3	54.3 (Brahman)	1.5
Punjab	6.3	9.6	15.1	27.6 (Khatri)	0.8
United Provinces	5.5	5.0	15.9	44.6 (Kayastha)	0.5
British India	9.3	8.4	33.4	33.4 (Brahman)	1.6

Source: Chaudhary (2015)

One measure of caste inequality in colonial India can be found in access to education. Indian literacy was very low compared to most countries in 1947, as we have seen in Chapter 4. But there was a large variation across social groups, in particular, across castes. The upper castes that include Brahmans, Khatriyas, and other professional groups had relatively high literacy compared to the lowest castes. Chaudhary (2015, pp. 166–68) shows that the literacy rate for Brahmans was 33 per cent in 1931, whereas for the lowest castes, the figure was 1.6 per cent.

The most literate caste was not always the Brahmans. Table 5.6 shows the province-level variation of literacy rates by upper castes and the literacy gap between the upper and the lower castes. Everywhere this gap was large and the common factor was the lack of access to education for the lowest castes. As I have discussed in Chapter 4, the allocation of education spending depended on district boards in which mainly upper castes were represented. Districts with higher caste diversity had fewer primary schools (Chaudhary 2009). Even when public schools were open to all social groups, the segregation of upper and lower castes prevented wider access to the children from the low castes (Chaudhary 2015, p. 174). The missionaries often stepped in to provide education to the children from low castes and tribes. Their impact was small.

A second measure of caste inequality in colonial India can be found in the work of Guntupalli and Baten (2006). Using a survey-based dataset on heights from all regions, they find significant differences in male stature by caste and religion. In the literature on living standards in history, heights are used as a proxy of well-being when systematic evidence on income and consumption is lacking. Although heights did

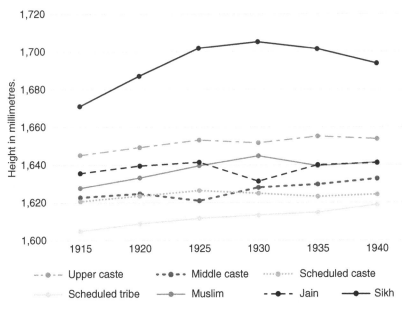

Figure 5.5 Differences in heights by social classes (1915–1940)
Source: Guntupalli and Baten (2006)

not change much over the first half of the twentieth century, the inter-group difference in heights across caste and religion is suggestive of economic inequality. Sikh men from the north were tallest. Jains, Muslim, and upper caste men were taller than the middle caste and lower caste men. As Figure 5.5 shows, the upper castes were taller than the lower caste social groups. The evidence on differences in height by occupation, which is correlated with caste, also provides suggestive evidence on economic inequality across social groups. The landlords were taller than other agricultural groups, traders and professionals were taller than weavers, potters, and other menial workers. The occupation-based difference in heights is indicative of inequality in income and consumption across castes.

5.6   Caste and Mobility after Independence

There are two ways to understand social mobility in the caste system (Vaid 2014). The first, following M. N. Srinivas's characterization of 'sanskritization', is the upward social mobility of a caste as a group adopting the conventions of a higher caste. The return migration of the

Gujarati Kanbis, a cultivating lower caste, who had migrated to Kenya in the first half of the twentieth century is an example of 'sankritization'. Upon their return, the group, which was now wealthier, had adopted Brahmanical customs and rose in the caste hierarchy under the caste name 'patidar' (Deshpande 2011, p. 53). The second path is an individual belonging to a particular caste moves out of the caste-based occupation. Similar to the historical example of occupational shift by caste groups from trade to industry (Gupta et al. 2022), there are examples of occupational change by caste groups in more recent times. Among them are the shift from agriculture to the garment industry in Tirupur by the Gounder community (Banerjee and Munshi 2004) and the shift by Kanbi Patels, a lower caste group involved in diamond cutting, to running the diamond sales network with the trading castes of Marwaris and Jains (Munshi 2011). Caste networks provided the valuable insurance in migration from rural to urban sectors (Munshi and Rosenzweig (2006).

India adopted one of the earliest interventions in affirmative active. This was enshrined in the Indian Constitution formulated in 1950. B. R. Ambedkar, an intellectual and political campaigner against the oppression of the caste system, was appointed the Law Minister by Nehru and asked to draft the new constitution of India. The new constitution guaranteed equal status to all social and religious groups and to men and women. The limited franchise introduced by the colonial government had given some Indians, both men and women, the right to vote in provincial elections. It required literacy and property ownership to be eligible to vote. Indian women had the right to vote well before Swiss women were enfranchised in 1978. The Indian Constitution after independence adopted universal adult franchise. The lowest castes in society were now eligible to exercise their political right.

Another new intervention was affirmative action in public education and public sector employment for the lowest strata of Indian society – the lowest castes or 'Dalits' and the tribal people. The government decreed that 20 per cent of jobs and university education was to be reserved for the scheduled castes and tribes, using the acronym SC/ST. A list of scheduled castes and tribes was announced, opening a door to upward mobility for these groups. In 1989, under the premiership of Vishwanath Pratap Singh, affirmative action was extended to 'other backward castes' or OBCs. The enumerated castes were mainly from the unprivileged social groups, but also included castes that had been lower down the caste hierarchy historically but had since then made economic gains. Over time the historical caste hierarchy saw changes both in economic sphere and in political space. Jaffrelot (2003) describes the emerging political competition between established political parties and the caste-based regional parties in the last decades of the twentieth century as a 'silent revolution' in Indian politics. Groups that had been underrepresented in the political system, particularly in northern India, made a claim on political representation. If the recording of caste by the colonial censuses had made caste socially and economically more salient (Dirks 2001), affirmative action made low caste identity more salient in the political space. Although Indian censuses stopped recording information by caste after independence, it remained an integral part of economic, social, and political life in India after independence. Social scientists have relied on survey-based evidence from the National Sample Surveys and National and Family Health Surveys to understand how caste inequalities have changed with policy interventions in the making of modern India.

What have been the economic and social consequences of this bold policy intervention? Vaid (2014) suggests that although the lowest castes experienced some changes in mobility, the overwhelming evidence is one of intergenerational continuity and persistence in inequality at the high and low ends of the caste distribution in occupations. The following section summarizes some of the main conclusions in the literature.

The structural change in the Indian economy has shifted jobs away from some traditional sectors and opened up new occupations for lower castes. The lower castes moved to lower and medium jobs in the new occupations, while high castes are in the upper tier jobs (McMillan 2005). Desai and Dubey (2012) distinguish between inequality of opportunity and inequality of outcome. The first relates to equality in opportunity to education and jobs and the second is conditional on acquiring the same education, are earnings or returns to education equal across castes? Using National Sample Survey data of 2006, Desai and Dubey (2012) find that scheduled castes and tribes are less likely to own land and have less education. Kijima (2006), using National Sample Survey data from 1983 to 1999, concluded that there was some improvements in literacy by occupational categories, but SC households earned lower returns to education and were still disadvantaged in obtaining well-paid jobs. While the first is an example of inequality of opportunity, the second is an example of inequality in outcome. Sectors such as mining, construction, and transport are relatively more open to lower castes, but they face barriers to entry in professional jobs in health, education, finance, and other high end services (Harriss-White et al. 2014, p. 67; Thorat and Newman 2010).

The expansion of primary education has improved access to school education for lower castes. However, there remain large differences in literacy. Based on National Family and Household Survey data 1992/3, 77.44 and 78.12 per cent of the schedules castes and scheduled tribes, respectively, had no education in 1992/93, in contrast with 59.2 per cent in other groups (Deshpande 2001). Using the National Sample Survey (NSS) of 2006, Desai and Dubey (2012) found that the upper caste men aged 25–49 had 8.18 years of education, while men in scheduled castes had 5.23 years. Hnatkovska, Lahiri, and Paul (2013) use NSS data up to 2004/05 to show that the gains during the past two decades have been more widespread and all sections of SC/ST households have made gains in literacy, leading to some convergence in literacy and occupational mobility between SC/ST and other castes. They argue, 'Indeed, it has now become far more likely that the son of a poor illiterate SC/ST cobbler would become a machine worker with middle or secondary school education having a much higher rank in his generation in income distribution than his father did in his generation' (Hnatkovska, Lahiri, and Paul 2013).

Bertrand, Hanna, and Mullainathan (2010) show that affirmative action successfully targets the underprivileged and has increased their presence at the cost of upper caste students. Affirmative action has increased college attendance of the targeted students, particularly at higher-quality institutions. The SC/ST students graduate at the same rate as others and enrol in competitive subjects, such as computer science and electronics (Bagde et al. 2016). Overall, the evidence suggests that the policy of affirmative action has had some success in improving access to higher education and in occupational mobility, although differences in labour market outcomes remain. The impact shows a difference at the high end and the low end of the labour market. Deshpande (2011) finds persistence rather than change in indicators of caste development. The economic reforms have not broken the correlation between upper castes and high-status professional jobs. Deshpande and Ramachandran (2019) find that the caste gap has narrowed in labour market outcomes in lower skilled jobs.

5.7   Gender Inequality

Cultural norms about women's role in society have created inequalities that are specific to India. Gender gaps in education and labour market outcomes exist in all societies today. Men earn more than women and have more skilled jobs. Women do a disproportionate share of housework and childcare and are less represented in high positions and in political space. Where India is an outlier is in the demographic deficit of women arising from the cultural norm of son preference and lower

Table 5.7 *Changing life expectancy at birth (1931–2001)*

Year	Male	Female
1901–1910	22.6	23.3
1911–1920	19.4	20.9
1921–1930	26.9	26.6
1931–1940	32.1	31.4
1941–1950	32.5	31.7
1951–1960	41.9	40.6
1961–1970	46.5	44.7
1971–1980	50.9	50.0
1981*	54	54
1991*	59	60
2001*	63	64

Source: Padmanabha (1981), Census series, * World Bank

social status for women from birth to end of life. Amartya Sen (1992) introduced the term 'missing women'. The number of men and women in a country are roughly equal. When the share of women falls short of 50 per cent, it points to the number of women who should have survived but are missing in the population. It is seen as an indicator of lack of care towards a girl child or unequal access to resources within the household for women as adults, leading to higher mortality among women relative to men. In this section, I focus on this specific aspect of gender inequality: the gender differential in the probability of survival, which is not biologically determined. The demographic deficit is the number of missing women.

In most societies, women live longer than men. In India, life expectancy at birth for women was lower than that of men between 1921 and the mid 1970s (see Table 5.7). The biological sex ratio at birth is 106 boys to every 100 girls. It reflects the physiological vulnerability of the male foetus. Male infants are also more vulnerable. Historically, male mortality at birth has been higher in most societies. In underdeveloped societies, male mortality at birth is even higher as a consequence of poor living standards and the poor health of the mother. Life expectation at birth for male children typically rise with economic development and changing disease environment.

In India, life expectancy at birth rose faster for males than for females from the 1920s to 1970s as Table 5.7 shows. After 1981, female life expectancy at birth edged above male life expectancy. Table 5.8 shows a significant regional variation. By 1971, life expectancy for males and

Table 5.8 *Changing life expectancy at birth by region (1931–1971)*

	1931			1971	
	Male	Female		Male	Female
North	29.1	27.0	North		
			Rajasthan	49.2	49.2
			Punjab	59.8	56.8
			Haryana	59.0	55.6
			Uttar Pradesh	45.4	40.5
West	29.2	29.9	West		
			Maharashtra	54.5	53.3
			Gujarat	48.8	48.8
			East		
East	27.9	28.1			
			West Bengal	56.4	58.0
			Bihar	54.2	51.5
			Orissa	46.0	45.3
			Central		
Central	30.7	32.3			
			Madhya Pradesh	46.3	47.6
			South		
South	33.4	35.1			
			Andhra Pradesh	48.4	40.3
			Karnataka	55.1	55.3
			Tamil Nadu	49.6	49.5
			Kerala	60.8	63.0

Source: Dyson (2019, tables 8.2 and 8.6)

females had risen in all regions but the regional variation in male and female life expectancy showed persistence.[1] The regions are divided into north, south, east, west, and central. Even in 1931, male life expectancy was higher in the north. The north has seen a persistent advantage for males, while in the other regions life expectancy at birth was more equal or there was a female advantage. I discuss the regional differences in sex ratio at birth in 1931 and then look at the changing sex ratio in the young over time. In recent decades in India, the sex ratio at birth is increasingly biased towards males compared to the biological norm. The developments in medical technology, amniocentesis in the 1980s, and ultrasound screening in the 1990s have increased parental choice and reduced the cost of choosing the sex of the unborn child, leading to prenatal sex selection.

[1] I compare 1931 with 1971, because from 1980 sex selection at birth was more feasible due to available technology.

Table 5.9 *Age-specific sex ratios in the age groups 0–15 by region (1931) (males per 100 females)*

Region/Province	Age groups			
	0–1	0–5	5–10	10–15
South				
Cochin	100.6	100.8	94.4	102.2
Travancore	100.9	101.0	102.9	103.1
Hyderabad	89.9	91.3	108.5	110.6
Mysore	96.5	96.2	99.9	10.6
Madras	96.5	96.7	101.8	104.2
West				
Bombay	99.8	99.1	111.5	116.3
Central Provinces and Berar	98.1	96.1	103.9	106.0
North				
Rajputana	98.8	99.0	113.7	120.3
United Provinces	99.8	99.3	116.0	122.6
Punjab	102.3	104.2	116.4	122.8
East				
Bihar & Orissa	98.2	95.3	108.7	112.6
Bengal	99.6	97.7	112.6	111.9
All India	98.8	97.9	109.9	113.6

Source: Bhaskar and Gupta (2007b)

What was the sex ratio in the young before availability of prenatal sex selection? Was colonial India different from India after independence? Table 5.9 reports the sex ratio in children from the census of 1931. The picture reveals that, in the age group 0–1, there were more females than males in all regions except in Punjab and Travancore and Cochin, the princely states which became the modern state of Kerala. It is interesting that the two regions that differed from this general picture did so for very different reasons. Qualitative evidence suggests that the relatively higher sex ratio among children below the age of one in Punjab reflects a strong son preference. By contrast, in Travancore and Cochin, the high sex ratio is likely to reflect the superior position of women within the household in this region and better health and nutrition of the mother, which lowered male mortality (Bhaskar and Gupta 2007b).

The Indian censuses noted that there was no systematic evidence of infanticide, suggesting that it was practised in a few communities. However, the census of 1901 referred to a widespread neglect of female children, even though the practice of infanticide was limited:

Even if there was no deliberate sign of hastening a girl's death, there is no doubt that as a rule, she receives less attention than would be bestowed on a son. She is less warmly clad, and less carefully rubbed with mustard oil as a prophylactic against the colds and chills to which the greater part of the mortality amongst young children is due, she is also probably not so well fed as a boy would be and when ill, her parents are not likely to make the same strenuous effort to ensure her recovery. (Report on the Census of India 1901, p. 116)

This is reflected in the deficit of girls that appeared more widely in the age group 5–10. The gap widened in the age group 10–15 and partly reflects high mortality at child birth for teenage mothers. Fenske et al. (2022) confirm that the sex ratio is most male biased in the age group 10–20 across regions and religions. In India, the average age at marriage in 1921 was 13 years and, consequently, the age at first birth was in the teenage years. High mortality at childbirth is, therefore, not surprising. Selective evidence from Madras Presidency based on hospital births shows high maternal mortality in teenage mothers (Fenske et al. 2022). The missing women in this age group also partly reflects under reporting in this age bin.

Table 5.10 shows the changing sex ratio in the young over the twentieth century. It provides a picture of persistence rather than change in regional differences. Regions that exhibited son preference in the colonial period continued to show a bias in the sex ratio in the age group 0–6. The male disadvantage at birth declined with economic development. In the regions that had exhibited son preference in the colonial period, the sex ratio became even more biased towards male children after 1980. This can be attributed to the new technology in sex-selective abortion, particularly the use of ultrasound technology after 1990. In all regions sex ratio at birth has increased over time, with the north and west seeing a dramatic rise. In particular, Punjab and Haryana stand out as a case of rapidly rising male bias in the sex ratio. Such an excess of males in the age group 0–6 can only be a result of prenatal sex selection. While the demographic deficit in the population below the age of six was due to a relative neglect for the girl child historically, the scope for active intervention with new technology has increased sex selective abortions. Abortion for birth control has been legal in India. Abortion for foetal sex selection has been illegal since 1994. However, anecdotal evidence and the male biased sex ratios at birth suggests that the practice flourishes. The extensive research in this field does not find evidence of sex selection at first birth, but its probability increases from the second birth if the first born is a girl child (Jha et al. 2006). Figure 5.6 shows the correlation between 0–10 sex ratio in 1931 and 0–9 sex ratio in 2011 using district-level data for greater accuracy. A strong positive correlation remains.

What accounts for the regional differences in son preference? The literature suggests various economic and social factors. Women's participation in economic activity may explain the north–south divide in the status of

Table 5.10 *Changing sex ratio in children 0–5 (1931) and 0–6 for all other years (males per 100 females)*[2]

Region/Province A	1931	Comparable regions/provinces after 1947	1971	1991	2001
South					
Cochin	100.6	Kerala	102.5	104.4	104.1
Travancore	100.9				
Hyderabad	89.9	Andhra Pradesh	100.6	101.6	102.8
Mysore	96.5	Karnataka	102.1	104.2	105.7
Madras	96.5	Tamil Nadu	100.9	105.5	106.2
West					
Bombay	99.8	Maharashtra	102.4	105.7	109.5
		Gujarat	106.5	107.8	113.2
Central Provinces and Berar	98.1	Madhya Pradesh	105.3	105.0	106.1
North					
Rajputana	98.8	Rajasthan	107.0	109.1	110.0
United Provinces	99.8	Uttar Pradesh	106.4	107.6	109.3
Punjab	102.3	Punjab	113.3	114.3	125.3
		Haryana	111.2	113.8	122.1
East					
Bihar & Orissa	98.2	Bihar		103.5	104.4	105.5
		Orissa	97.5	103.2	104.2
Bengal	99.6	West Bengal	97.7	103.5	104.2

Source: Gupta (2014)

women. Women work more in labour intensive agriculture and rarely use the plough, which requires physical strength (Boserup 1970). In wheat-growing regions of the north, women's participation is low. In rice cultivation, on the other hand, women's labour is important. It is in these areas that women enjoy higher social status (Bardhan 1974; Miller 1981). Carranza (2014) looks at the differences in soil quality that make agriculture more suitable for women's work as a predictor of son preference. However, Fenske et al. (2022) do not find a clear relationship between male-biased sex ratio and rice and wheat agriculture using district-level data in their analysis.

Son preference is pronounced in the higher castes in northern India based on qualitative evidence (Miller 1981). Hypergamy allows lower caste women to marry into the higher caste and move into the caste of the husband. High caste women are not permitted to marry below their caste status. Analysing district-level data from Punjab, Bengal, and

[2] The comparison of 0–10 in 1931 and 0–9 in 2011 is determined by the way the census data is reported.

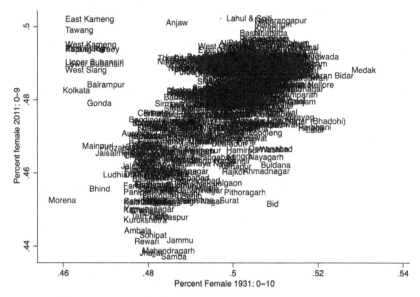

Figure 5.6 Correlation between 0–10 sex ratio (1931) and 0–9 sex ratio at the district level (2011)
Source Fenske et al. (2022)

Madras from the 1901 census, Chakraborty and Kim (2010) find son preference is strongest in the upper castes as reflected in the sex ratio in the age group 0–5.

There are explanations based on social conventions. Early censuses discussed the special position of sons in Hindu religion. Sons perform funeral rites. Son preference is stronger among Hindus compared to Muslims today. Fenske et al. (2022) found regional differences to be salient. Within a region, differences across religious groups in colonial India was not significant. Sex ratio among Hindus is more male biased today. Differences in attitude to sex-selective abortion may explain the emerging differences in sex ratio at birth among Hindus and Muslims in recent times (Bhalotra et al. 2018).

Marriage conventions are yet another factor that can explain the regional differences in son preference. Patrilocal marriage conventions require women to reside with the husband's family and sons provide insurance in old age. This custom prevails widely across all regions in India. Only a few communities, such as the Nairs of Kerala and the Khasi tribe in Assam, practice matrilocal marriage. Neither of these explanations can predict the strong regional divide. However, village exogamy was widespread in the north (Gould 1961) but not in the south. The marriage of a daughter in the north is typically arranged outside the village and married women lose close contact with the natal family, which may explain differences in the value of sons and daughters.

Patrilineal inheritance norms that stipulate inheritance down the male lineage is yet another explanation of preference for sons. Women are given a dowry at the time of marriage and the sons, who reside with the parents, inherit parental property. Dyson and Moore (1983) see inheritance and marriage customs as determinants of women's status. There is a north–south divide in inheritance. Property may be passed on to the daughters in the south, but only to sons in the north. Under the Hindu Succession Act of 1956, ancestral property could be inherited only by sons. Reforms were introduced in certain provinces, starting with Kerala in 1976, followed by Andhra Pradesh, Tamil Nadu, Maharashtra, and Karnataka over the next two decades. The legal reform opened up the way to inheritance by daughters. Roy (2015) found that, despite the change, parents continued to disinherit their daughters and gave higher dowries at marriage. Bhalotra et al. (2020) studied the effect of this legal change on parental preference for sons and daughters and found that in the regions that gave equal rights to daughters, there has been an increase in the sex ratio at birth in favour of the male child. The results point to the deep roots of inheritance norms and that son preference is hard to change.

This discussion focuses on the bias against the girl child and the large number of unborn girl children who would be counted among the 'missing women'. In colonial India, the largest deficit of women appeared in adolescence (see Figure 5.7). The pattern was the same in all regions (see Figure 5.7). Recent data, however, shows a different picture.

Anderson and Ray (2010) calculate the number of 'missing women' by age cohort for 2000. They found a significant number of missing females in the age group 0–4, but large numbers are also missing in the adult population due to maternal mortality and death from injury among women of child-bearing age and in older women above sixty. There is no clear pattern in the age group where the sex ratio is male biased across provinces, as shown in Table 5.11. Punjab and Haryana have a large share of missing girls at birth. Other provinces, such as Tamil Nadu and Kerala, have a large proportion missing in the oldest age group. The paper suggests that, although son preference and sex selection lead to 'missing women' in the population, other forms of unequal access to resources, such as nutrition and healthcare, may explain the significant numbers that are missing in the adult population.

Table 5.11 *Missing women in Indian provinces by age group (%)*

	At birth	0–15	15–45	45+
North				
Haryana	42.4	24.3	9.1	24.1
Punjab	59.5	12.1	4.3	24.0
Uttar Pradesh	14.2	31.7	22.0	32.0
West				
Maharashtra	12.3	15.1	12.7	59.9
Gujarat	25.8	24.2	14.7	35.3
East				
West Bengal	1.1	17.3	21.5	60.0
Bihar	6.1	40.8	14.8	38.2
Orissa	19.9	16.5	18.4	45.3
Central				
Madhya Pradesh	0	39.4	23.0	37.5
South				
Andhra Pradesh	17.1	14.0	15.8	53.4
Karnataka	16.6	16.7	14.0	56.2
Tamil Nadu	9.5	6.1	17.1	67.2
Kerala	20.3	4.4	6.1	69.3

Source: Anderson and Ray (2012)

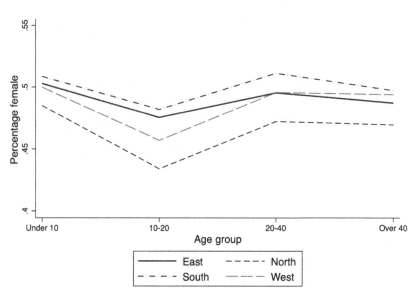

Figure 5.7 Missing women by age groups (1921) (per cent female in the population)
Source: Fenske et al. (2022)

5.8   Conclusion

This chapter has discussed four different inequalities in India and how they have changed or persisted over the long run. Regional inequalities in GDP per capita show a certain persistence. GDP per capita growth is negatively correlated with poverty–headcount ratio, although it is not the only factor that can explain changes in poverty. Income inequality shows a double U-shaped pattern over the twentieth century with a sharp decline in inequality under the Nehruvian policies of regulating the private sector. The share of the top 0.1 per cent in income rose with economic reforms from the 1980s but has not gone back to the high share of the colonial period.

The third inequality is related to caste. The chapter discusses the occupational segregation by caste in history and the slow change in caste inequality in Indian society despite affirmative action from the 1950s. The intervention has provided better access to education and jobs for the lowest castes, although progress remains limited.

Finally, the chapter discusses gender inequality in India over the twentieth century by focusing on the concept of 'missing women' and son preference, which can explain the big rise in the ratio of male children to female children. The skewed sex ratio in the age group 0–6 is specific to the north and more recently in the western provinces in India. There are a large number of missing women in the older age groups, showing that son preference is not the only factor to explain gender inequality. Intra-family allocation of resources reinforces unequal gender norms in India today. The chapter explores the cultural factors that have been suggested in the literature to explain the preference for sons and also discusses evidence on missing women by age groups historically and in recent times.

6   Colonial Development in a Comparative Perspective

India emerged from colonial rule after the Second World War at the same time as several other countries in Asia that had been ruled by Britain, the Netherlands, and Japan. Had colonialization led to underdevelopment? The picture was mixed. Malaysia and Singapore, both British colonies, were more prosperous in 1950 than in 1910. Korea and Taiwan, colonies of Japan, were better off in 1950 compared to 1910. India and Indonesia had stagnated (see Figure 6.1A). The difference in GDP per capita among the Asian colonies was not that significant in 1950, but over the next fifty years, big differences emerged in economic growth and industrialization. South Korea, Taiwan, and Singapore overtook the historically richer countries in Latin America (Figure 6.1B). The Latin American countries had become independent from Spanish and Portuguese Empires in the nineteenth century. The countries listed here had prospered with globalization in the late nineteenth century. After 1929, the larger economies became more inward looking and moved away from agriculture (Bértola and Ocampo 2012). The newly independent economies in Asia adopted policies for economic development in the second half of the twentieth century.

In the colonial period, the four economies of India, Indonesia, Korea, and Taiwan had looked quite similar, but after 1950 their paths of development diverged. South Korea and Taiwan were among the fastest growing economies in the world (see Figures 6.2A and 6.2B).

In this chapter, I explore the differences in colonial policy in India, Korea, and Taiwan that may have set them on different paths of growth and development. There were differences in terms of size, geography, population, and other initial conditions, but as colonies, all the countries fulfilled an economic role with respect to the imperial country. They started out as suppliers of raw material and a market for the industrial goods produced in the imperial country. During the world wars, they provided men for the battlefields and produced goods for the war effort. However, the state of the economy of the colonies at the time of independence was not the same. Acemoglu, Johnson, and Robinson (2001)

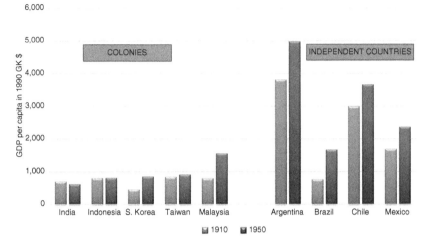

Figure 6.1A GDP per capita in the developing countries in Asia and Latin America in 1990 International Geary-Khamis dollars (1910–1950) Source: Maddison Data Project

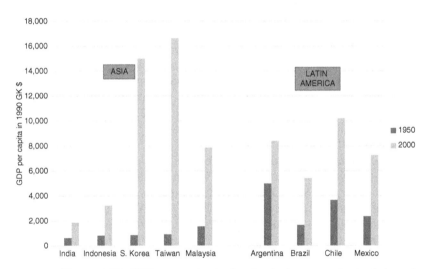

Figure 6.1B GDP per capita in the developing countries in Asia and Latin America in 1990 International Geary-Khamis dollars (1910–2000) Source: Maddison Data Project

distinguished between colonies where the Europeans settled and those where settlement was low. In the former, the colonizers introduced institutions that were conducive to development. In the latter, the institutions

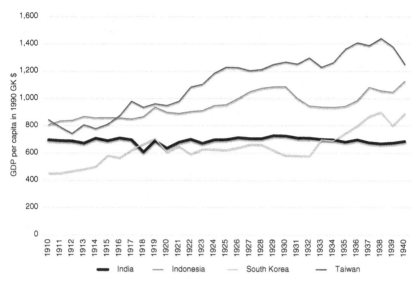

Figure 6.2A Change in GDP per capita in four colonial economies in
Asia in 1990 International Geary-Khamis dollars (the colonial period)
Source: The Maddison Project

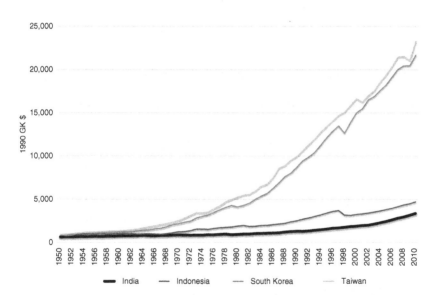

Figure 6.2B Post-colonial divergence: India, Indonesia, South Korea,
and Taiwan in 1990 International Geary-Khamis dollars
Source: Maddison Data Project

were extractive and impoverished the colony. Across the Asian colonies there are large differences in terms of settlement by the colonizers. Nowhere was settlement as large as in the case of Australia and New Zealand. Did proximity create a different context of colonization for Korea and Taiwan, which led to the adoption of different policies? Was Japan a different type of colonizer from Britain? This chapter will provide an overview of the Japanese colonization of Korea and Taiwan, the similarities and differences with British colonization of India, and compare the structure of these economies at the time of independence that laid the foundations for post-colonial development. In particular, the chapter will focus on a comparison between South Korea and India as these countries have been compared on many dimensions in the context of the different paths to economic development after independence.

The historical determinants of economic development after independence has received little attention in the literature. Instead the comparison between India and the East Asian countries has focused on the differences in policies of industrialization after independence. This chapter will focus on the differences in Japanese colonial policy in Korea and Taiwan and British policy in India that might have determined the path to be taken as the newly independent countries planned for development. The chapter will start with a discussion of the history of colonization of Korea and Taiwan. It will look at the industrial development in the two countries in comparison with India. It will discuss the pattern of agricultural development and offer a comparative perspective with India. The chapter will look specifically at the policies towards education and the growth of literacy in a comparative perspective. Finally, it will discuss the differences in structural change in the three Asian economies.

6.1   Development of Industries in the Colonies

India, Korea, and Taiwan were primarily agricultural at the time of colonization. However, over the first half of the twentieth century there was industrial development, and during the Second World War these industries consolidated their position and there was diversification in production. Korea, in particular, had become an industrial offshoot of Japan, catering to the war effort and began to export manufactured goods to Japan.

Indian industries too had consolidated their position during the First World War. During the interwar years, Indian industrial interests were growing in importance and demanded tariffs to protect their interests in the home market, as discussed in Chapter 3. India was at the centre of the competition in the textile market between Britain and Japan after the First World War as Japan increasingly encroached into Britain's market share in India. The policy of Imperial Preference targeted Japanese access to the Indian market. British multinational corporations entered in new industries in the 1930s, which were supportive of tariffs and shared common concerns with the import substituting Indian industries.

I will argue in this chapter that industrialization proceeded at a similar pace in India, Korea, and Taiwan. At the time of independence, the three countries did not look as different in the share of industry in GDP as they did thirty years later. However, in 1950 the three countries looked very different in agricultural development and investment in human capital. The initial conditions of low land inequality and high primary school enrolment in 1960 put South Korea and Taiwan on a growth path (Rodrik 1995). The East Asian economies had a higher level of literacy at the time of independence. The distribution of land was modelled on Japan and more equal compared to India. These conditions were missing in India.

6.2 Economic Interdependence in the Colonies

6.2.1 Korea

Unlike India, Korea was isolated from the rest of the world until 1876. Traditional agriculture was practised widely, artisanal production catered to the village economy, and internal and external trade was limited (Chung 2006, chap. 2). When the economy began to open up to outside influence after 1876 under a treaty with Japan, Japan became the main trading partner selling modern industrial goods, such as cotton textiles, and importing rice. Korea became a protectorate of Japan in 1905 and formally a colony in 1910. Before colonization, 50 per cent of Japanese exports to Korea was cotton textiles. British textiles had a large share of the market. After the conquest of Korea, British cotton textiles were replaced almost entirely by exports from Japan (Duus 1984). The colonization process involved building an infrastructure for trade. Investment in ports, railways, and banking integrated the Korean economy into the Japanese economic system (Chung 2006, chap. 3). Rice was at the heart of the policy of colonization. Korean rice, though more expensive than rice from South East Asia, was preferred in Japan and imports from Korea were large when harvests failed (Duus 1984).

As a colonizer, Japan sought to tie Korea in this international division of labour producing agricultural goods. At the same time Korea was seen as a useful location for Japanese industrial investment. This coincided with Japan's military ambition in East Asia. Suh (1978) divides the colonial period into three parts: 1910–1919, when agricultural development was prioritized; 1920–1929, when foundations of new industries were laid; and 1939 onwards, when Korea became a part of Japan's war effort. In the first period, as with the British administration's efforts to define property rights in land in India, Japan began colonization of Korea with a nationwide cadastral survey and created a land tenure system that gave ownership rights and tax liabilities to cultivators. This marked the first difference between India and Korea in terms of land concentration. The Japanese state regulated Japanese investment in industry in Korea to create complementarity in specialization by sector (Suh 1978, pp. 2–3). In the second period, there was an effort to increase rice yields as this was Korea's main export to Japan. Production of other agricultural raw materials, such as raw cotton and silk, were also developed. There was a large increase in yields in agriculture as a result of the use of commercial fertilizers and improved seeds. Output more than doubled between 1915 and 1940 (Chung 2006, chap. 4). During this time, Japanese investment in industrial firms was permitted and Japanese-owned firms were set up in new industries. In the third period, Japan began to invest in war-related industries, which processed metals and produced chemicals. Japan's involvement in the war made northern Korea an attractive location to build industrial and mining capacity (Boestel et al. 1999, p. 188).

Processed food had been the largest sector in manufacturing. It produced 32 per cent of output and the chemical industry accounted for 17 per cent in 1931. By 1940 the respective shares were 20 per cent and 36 per cent. The overall share of light industry producing consumer goods in 1931 was 67 per cent, but declined to 50 per cent. By 1940 industries producing intermediate goods produced half of the manufacturing output (Suh 1978, table 4). After the end of the colonial rule and the Korean war that followed, Korea was divided into two countries. The independent state of South Korea was largely dependent on agriculture that employed three-quarters of the labour force. The more industrial region in the north was in a different country.

6.2.2   Taiwan

Taiwan was a trading post of the Dutch East India Company in the seventeenth century. When Taiwan came under Chinese rule in 1685, its economic significance as a trading port declined. In 1895, the country came under Japanese rule. It was an agricultural economy, producing rice, tea, and sugarcane. There had been some migration from China, but the economy comprised of isolated rural communities and there was little trade (Cha 2002). The Japanese integrated the internal market and established infrastructure for external trade by building railways, unifying the currency, and setting up the Bank of Taiwan. As in the case of Korea, the Japanese government conducted a cadastral survey to confer property rights to unregistered land and this generated a large increase in land revenue (Ho 1975). Taiwan was important as a source of agricultural production, in particular rice and tea, and the Japanese government invested to increase productivity in the cultivation of these crops (Cha 2002).

In the initial phase of colonial rule, agricultural growth was 2–2.5 per cent. After 1920, it increased to 3.8 per cent and labour productivity in agriculture was 88 per cent higher in 1935 compared to 1910 (Ho 1975). Taiwan supplied agricultural products to the Japanese market and the main industry that developed was sugar. Metal working and chemical industries developed during the war, but were not as important as in Korea (Ho 1975).

6.3   Industrial Development in a Comparative Perspective

Did the Japanese view industrial development in East Asia differently? In Chapter 3, I argued that, until the First World War, there was little interest on the part of the colonial government or British business to develop industries that were not producing goods for export. In the nineteenth century, Britain saw India as a market for industrial goods. Even if Empire trade was not that large in Britain's total trade (O'Brien 1982), the colonial market was of significant importance in specific industries, in particular cotton textiles. The cotton textiles industry in Britain sold 60 per cent of its output in foreign markets (Clark et al. 2014), and 60 per cent of demand for cotton textiles in India was met by import from Britain in 1880.

Lancashire lobbied all through the nineteenth century to stop the growth of an import substituting industry in India and competition in the Indian markets. The attitude of the colonial government towards Indian industrialization changed during the First World War, when industrial capability in the colony assumed importance. British administrators became more open to tariffs for import substituting industries. However, Britain did not see India as a place to relocate industries, despite lower wage costs and strategic reasons. The exception was jute. The two industries that attracted British investment were tea and jute – both processed agricultural products that were cultivated in India. Both industries sold in the export market. A jute industry in India was closer to the source of raw materials and faced lower labour costs.[1] British investment in Indian industry was confined mainly to export sectors until the 1930s, when foreign direct investment was channelled through multinational companies in a few import substituting industries.

In Korea, Japanese investment in industry was a significant component of industrial investment. Large Japanese investments were made in companies incorporated in Korea, apart from direct investment by Japanese companies that opened subsidiaries (Chung 2006, chap. 4). In 1943, over 78 per cent of private investment and 22 per cent of public investment came from Japan. Over 83 per cent of private investment was in firms incorporated in Korea (see Table 4.2). In India, the largest share of British investment was in companies incorporated in Britain, such as tea and the railways. Chung (2006) estimated the share of total investment in GDP at over 10 per cent, a significant increase from less than 0.5 per cent of GDP in 1910, and argued that the Japanese contribution to the rising investment was substantial.

Korean investment in incorporated companies was small to begin with and increased over time. Most of the Korean investment in industry was in smaller unincorporated companies. Chung claims the technology used in Korean-owned firms mostly lagged behind the technology in Japanese-owned firms. The Japanese firms were more capital intensive. Chung points out that the modern technology of Japanese firms had spillover effects on local firms. Kim and Park (2008) question the view that all of the productivity growth in industry between 1910 and 1940 was in the Japanese-owned firms and occurred from 1930. They show that labour productivity in Korean firms began to rise early in the colonial period. Table 6.1 shows the share of Japanese investment by sector and the contribution of Japanese human capital in industrial development by sector.

The share of mining and manufacturing in GDP at 4–5 per cent was smaller than in India in 1910, but by 1940 it had increased to 26 per cent. As Table 6.1 shows, Japanese investment dominated the Korean manufacturing industry, both in terms of authorized capital and technical personnel. Except in machinery, Japanese investment was dominant in all sectors. In the share of technical personnel, the Japanese technicians had a sizeable presence, but in metal and chemical industries their presence was dominant. Both these industries were important in the war effort. The Japanese residents in Korea were mainly engaged in urban

---

[1] Dundee in Scotland had been the centre of the jute industry. It imported raw jute from India. Once jute firms were set up in Calcutta with British capital, its locational advantage made Calcutta the centre of jute manufacturing.

Table 6.1 *Share of Japanese investment and human capital in Korea (1940) (%)*

	Share of Japanese technical personnel	Share of Japanese authorised capital	Total in million Yen
Printing	76	57.1	3.5
Metal	89	98.4	379.1
Machinery	75	58	146.6
Chemical	89	99.6	277.3
Gas and electrical appliances	81*	100	553.0
Ceramics	52	100	53.2
Textiles	73	84.5	90.6
Wood products	68	89.5	52.5
Processed food	64	92.3	79.1
Total	81	94.1	1725.4

Note: * includes gas, electricity, and water supply
Source: Suh (1978, table 8 and 9)

activities. Over 70 per cent of the Korean population were in agriculture in 1940, but the Japanese expatriates, who made up 3 per cent of the population, were engaged in government, manufacturing, transport, and communication (Suh 1978, p. 19).

In Taiwan, Japanese immigration brought in the technical and commercial skills needed in industry and services. The share of Japanese immigrants was around 5 per cent but they were overrepresented in skilled jobs. 30 per cent of the clerical workers, 45 per cent of professional workers, and over 70 per cent of the government employees and technicians were Japanese (Ho 1975). Japanese involvement played a role in the development of the agricultural technology.

Indian investment was large in cotton textiles, iron steel, and several other import substituting industries, such as sugar and food processing (Chapter 3). There is less systematic evidence on the presence of British technicians in the industrial sectors in India. Entrepreneurs from Indian trading communities were dominant in the cotton mills in Bombay in early twentieth century. However, there was an overwhelming presence of the British and the highly educated Parsis among the technical personnel (see Table 6.2).

In colonial India and in colonial Korea and Taiwan, the modern manufacturing industry was the fastest growing sector starting from a low base. Table 6.3 shows the composition of the manufacturing industry and growth across sectors in manufacturing in Korea and Taiwan.

Table 6.2 *Skilled personnel in Bombay cotton textile industry*

	Directors	Mill managers		Skilled workers		Engineers	
	1925	1895	1925	1895	1925	1895	1925
European	24	27	28	54	78	23	15
Parsi	49	20	32	71	113	32	77
Hindu	77	4	11	36	32	4	23
Muslim	19	2	5	1	1	1	2
Baghdadi Jew	6	2	8		2	1	2

Source: Rutnagur (1927, pp. 297–311, p. 249)

Table 6.3 *Growth and composition of manufacturing industries (%)*

	Share of manufacturing output					
	Korea			Taiwan		Growth
	1914–1916	1936–1940	Growth 1913–1939	1914–1916	1936–1940	1913–1939
Food	35	27	7.27	70	73	6.06
Textiles	13	18	7.96	1	2	6.64
Chemicals	12	30	12.5	20	11	3.21
Non-metallic minerals	3	3	12.95	1	2	8.49
Metals	16	11	6.85	2	5	10.82
Machinery	2	3	8.47	1	2	13.03
All manufacturing			8.12			5.94

Source: Suh (1978, tables 2 and 3)

Food industries had a dominant share of industrial output in both countries, particularly in Taiwan. Metal and chemical industries had a sizeable share of industrial output in Korea. In Taiwan, these industries were less important.

Geography may have played its part in the nature of colonial involvement in industry. Nakajima and Okazaki (2018) looked at the effect of proximity of the colonies on Japan. Colonial interdependence led to increased economic activity in the regions close to Korea. Proximity might have allowed easy relocation of resources to Korea in response to lower wages or the introduction of industrial regulation in Japan and led to industrial development in the colonies. Involvement of Japanese entrepreneurs and skilled workers in industry in Korea and Taiwan was widespread. Thousands of Japanese workers settled and worked in Korea. In the 1930s, the share of foreign population in Korea and Taiwan were between 3–5 per cent of the population (Booth 2007, p. 20). The share of the British expatriates in India was well below 1 per cent.

6.4   Commodity Trade

During the colonial period, Korea's trade increased faster than GDP. The share of exports to Japan increased from 74 per cent to 92 per cent and imports from Japan increased from 62 per cent to 88 per cent between 1910 and 1940. Manufactured goods were the main component in these imports and exports were mainly food and raw materials until 1925. By 1940 manufactured goods had a sizeable share of exports (see Table 6.4A).

Taiwan's exports to Japan, on the other hand, comprised mainly of agricultural products (see Table 6.4B), and the share of agricultural exports, mainly rice and sugar, increased over time. Processed sugar was almost half of all agricultural exports and Japanese companies invested in sugar. The first large sugar refinery was set up with Japanese capital (Ho 1975).

Table 6.4A *Composition of exports from Korea to Japan*

	1915	1925	1940
Unprocessed food	18.4	64.9	27.5
Processed food	0.5	2.2	4.3
Raw materials	9.9	10.1	20.8
Semi manufactures	10.9	12.1	29.6
Finished manufactured	60.3*	10.7	17.7

* *Finished manufactured were mainly artisanal products*
Source: Suh (2020, table 6)

Table 6.4B *Composition of exports from Taiwan to Japan*

	1910–1919	1920–1929	1930–1939
Unprocessed food	77.3	82.9	84.5
Processed food	–	0.1	0.1
Raw materials	9.5	8.4	7.6
Manufactured goods	13.0	8.5	7.5

Source: Ho (1975, table 3)

The share of trade in GDP had similarly increased in colonial India, although Britain was less reliant on India for imports and exports. Britain's share of exports from India in 1865 was 69 per cent and declined to 23 per cent by 1914. Britain's share in imports declined from 84 per cent in 1865 to 61 per cent in 1914. (Statistical abstracts for British India for respective years) Britain's share increased again in the 1930s with Imperial Preference in trade within the Empire (Arthi et al. 2024). Manufactured goods were not important in Indian exports unless they were non-competing imports. In 1811, 33 per cent of India's exports had been handloom-produced cotton textiles, but in 1935 the figure was less than 2 per cent. The main manufactured export from India was jute products with a share of 15 per cent in 1935. Exports of raw cotton and jute, tea, and food grains were close to 60 per cent (see Table 2.3 in Chapter 2). India and Korea had a different trading relationship with the respective imperial countries. British industries did not view India as a place to relocate their production facilities. India was either a source of non-competing manufactured goods or a place to set import substituting industries for the domestic market, when tariffs were introduced in the 1930s.

6.5   Agricultural Development in a Comparative Perspective

In another important aspect, British policy in India differed significantly from Japan's policy in East Asia. This was with respect to agricultural development. Japan relied on imports from the colonies for an essential food grain and therefore increasing yield in rice cultivation was seen as imperative. By the early twentieth century, Japan had a large non-agricultural sector and self-sufficiency in food was given up for importing food. Yield per acre in rice in Japan was stagnating and Japan used colonization as a means of acquiring new land that could supply agricultural products to Japan, in particular rice (Ho 1975). Large tracts of land were brought under rice cultivation in Korea and Taiwan. Japan invested to improve land productivity in rice cultivation in the colonies. The first step was to introduce the Japanese varieties of rice that had higher yield. These varieties required intensive use of water and fertilizer and building an irrigation infrastructure was a priority for the policymakers. In 1950, about 60 per cent of cultivated land was under rice. Korea and Taiwan followed the Japanese path of increasing agricultural productivity through greater use of labour input and fertilizer rather than mechanization (Hayami and Ruttan 1971).

East Asia looked very similar to Japan in terms of the use of land for rice cultivation as well as in land ownership. Even before the land reforms of the 1950s, the land owning gentry did not own large tracts of land. Much of the land belonging to non-cultivating landlords had been redistributed to cultivating owners (Ho 1975). The land reforms of the 1950s improved land distribution even more (Boestel et al. 2013, p. 77). Introduction of better seeds and double cropping raised agricultural productivity. Table 6.5A shows the changes in fertilizer use and expansion in double cropping of land. Both contributed to agricultural growth and both depended on the availability of irrigation. As the table shows, by 1925, 59 per cent of the land was irrigated in Korea and 70 per cent in Taiwan. This increased further over the next decade. In Taiwan, adoption of new technology was rapid. By the 1920s, there had been a substantial investment in irrigation, which created the conditions for adoption of high yielding varieties in rice and sugarcane (Ho 1975). The Japanese introduced two institutional changes: the reform of the land tax and development of agricultural associations. The cadastral survey had increased the number of landowners with legal ownership and improved inheritance rights and the sale of land. The land tax reform created incentives for landowners to improve land productivity (Myers and Ching 1964).

Ho (1975) argues that in Taiwan, the colonial government provided two unconventional inputs: agricultural science and modern institutions that paved the way for agricultural development. The agricultural associations created links between landowners, cultivators and agricultural experimental stations and the number of such associations increased rapidly. This improved information flow and dissemination of new technology, and adoption of new types of seeds (Myers and Ching 1964). Farmers organizations assisted in dissemination and adoption of new technology and the cooperatives assisted by providing access to credit and distribution of fertilizers. Neither of these inputs were widely available in the cultivation of food crops in India. Agricultural research centres existed but focused on improving yields in raw cotton and other cash crops.

Kang and Ramachandran (1999) show that in Korea irrigation expanded at 18 per cent a year and use of chemical fertilizer increased at 22 per cent per year. The total investment in irrigation and roadbuilding in the rural areas was 30–45 per cent of total revenue during this period.

In order to improve agricultural yields, Japan as a colonizer differed from the British in India.[2] While yield per acre in rice cultivation in the Japanese colonies improved, in India yield per acre in food grains stagnated, particularly in rice cultivation. Table 6.5A shows that indicators of improvements in agriculture in Korea and Taiwan, the share

---

[2] This is not to suggest that Japan was a benevolent colonizer, but rather it suited Japan's imperial interest to invest in agriculture.

Table 6.5A *Changes in agricultural production in Korea and Taiwan*

	Korea			Taiwan		
	Share of cultivated land (%)		Fertilizer	Share of cultivated land (%)		Fertilizer
	Irrigated area	Double cropping	per hectare	Irrigated area	Double cropping	per hectare
1920		16	1.3	57	67	12
1925	49	17	3.4	70	71	20
1930	59	22	12	88	74	33
1935	69	26	28	78	65	55

Source: Myers and Saburo (1984, tables 2 and 3)

Table 6.5B *Changes in agricultural production in Korea and Taiwan*

Period	Crop output (index)	Crop acreage (index)	Labour input (index)	Fertilizer input (index)	Percentage irrigated are under paddy	Percentage of paddy land using HYV	Rice yield kg/ hectare
Korea							
1915–1919	100	100	100	100	NA	39	1,384
1920–1924	110	107	101	168	17	64	1,407
1925–1929	114	112	106	457	22	73	1,553
1930–1934	129	116	100	736	26	77	1,823
1935–1939	145	118	97	1129	28	85	2,084
Taiwan							
1910–1914	85	92	98	59	33	NA	1,330
1915–1919	100	100	100	100	37	NA	1,413
1920–1924	108	103	97	123	42	2	1,468
1925–1929	139	112	100	167	48	18	1,642
1930–1934	170	121	102	218	55	29	1,808
1935–1939	202	130	111	315	59	46	2,052

Source: Ho (1975, table 2). Sugar yields in Taiwan increased from 25.390 in 1901–1914 to 70,332 in 1935–1939

of irrigated land, the share of double cropped land, and the per hectare use of fertilizer increased between 1920 and 1935. Table 6.5B confirms these patterns for acreage under rice and shows that increase in productivity rather than increase in acreage account for the increase in agricultural production. This is a contrast with the developments in Indian agriculture under colonial policies. As I have shown in Chapter 2, the last fifty years of British rule was characterized by agricultural stagnation.

Investment in irrigation in India was a contrast to the colonial policy in East Asia. Irrigation covered less than 20 per cent of land under cultivation in 1935, compared to 69 per cent in Korea and 78 per cent in Taiwan. Irrigation received only a small part of total spending from revenues and was a small part of capital expenditure (see discussion in Chapter 2). India's agricultural stagnation was a failure of colonial policy to invest in the largest sector of the economy. Increases in yield per acre occurred in irrigated areas of the canal colonies in Punjab and Sind and favourably affected wheat and cotton yields. This was not the case for most rice growing regions and consequently Indian rice yields remained well below the levels in East Asia.

The difference between the two regions in the colonial interdependence was that Japan supplemented food availability through imports, whereas Britain's trade in agricultural products from India involved opium, tea, and cotton. Tea was a mass consumption good in Britain, but was consumed in small quantities. Opium was traded to buy tea from China and declined in importance as India replaced China as the tea producer. During the American Civil War, India became the main supplier of raw cotton to British industries, but lost market share once the war ended. India as a colony was not as important in British trade and not important at all as a supplier of essential food grains. The difference in geographic proximity and the consequent differences in the economic relationship appears to explain the differences in the policies of Britain and Japan as colonizers in Asia.

6.6   Investment in Education

Japan as a colonizer viewed education in the colonies very differently from the British in India. As discussed in Chapter 4, British policy towards education focused on creating an English-speaking elite, who could run the administrative services. At a time when Britain moved towards universal primary schooling, in India education spending did not prioritise primary education and a disproportionate share of the budget was spent on secondary education. For those who had access to primary education, the enrolment in secondary and tertiary education was high, even in comparison to several European countries as well as Japan (see Chapter 4). Japan adopted a different policy in the colonies where primary education was still low and prioritized expanding primary education.

Go and Park (2019) discuss the availability of schooling in Korea and Taiwan before colonization. They argue that private education was more common in Korea than in Taiwan. These were mainly traditional schools run privately and westernized education offered by missionaries. On the eve of colonization, enrolment in private schools in Korea was 7 per cent and mainly among boys. The enrolment in private schools in Taiwan was 3 per cent in 1895. The education policy of the colonial government was to segregate it by ethnicity. Children of Japanese immigrants had more favourable access to education and typically could avail of primary, secondary, and tertiary education. However, 'common' public schools were open to the local population and this was limited to primary education (Go and Park 2019).

Enrolment of children aged 5 to 14 in 'common' public schools in Korea and Taiwan increased during colonial rule. Taking into account private and public schools, Kimura (1993) estimates that primary school enrolment rate for boys went up to 70 per cent in 1940 in colonial Korea and that access to education for boys was not confined to the elites and middle classes. Girls, however, rarely received any form of education. More recent evidence comes from Go and Park (2019), who consider public school enrolment. In 1943, nearly 50 per cent of school age children from all social classes in Taiwan were enrolled in schools compared to just under 30 per cent in Korea (Go and Park 2019). Figure 6.3A shows the differences in enrolment in the two countries. Figure 6.3B shows the large difference in the enrolment rate between boys and girls, particularly in Korea. Go and Park (2019) discuss the reasons for the differences in expansion of schooling in the two countries. One reason for the slower growth in Korea could have been the availability of private education on a larger scale and its expansion during the initial years of the colonial period. The share of private schools increased until 1920 and then declined. By the 1930s, only 5 per cent of the school age children were in private schools.

There were also differences in the funding of schools. Both countries charged fees and relied on local support, but schools in Taiwan charged lower fees and had more financial support from provincial governments. The Japanese colonies made a bigger push to public education in the initial phase of colonialization. The greater scope of public education in Taiwan appears to have accounted for faster growth in primary education. In 1960, literacy rates in both countries were well above what would have been predicted on the basis of their per capita incomes (Rodrik 1995).

The Japanese colonies in East Asia looked far superior in their primary school expansion in comparison to India under British rule. The enrolment rate in colonial India was one of the lowest in the world (see Chapter 4). The reliance on private funding for schools

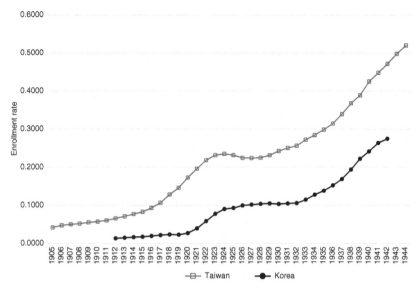

Figure 6.3A Public school enrolment in Korea and Taiwan

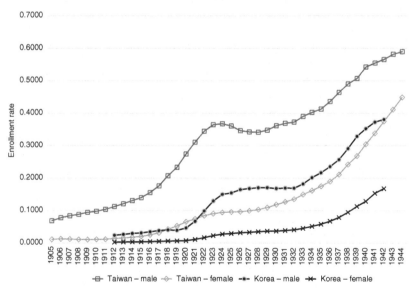

Figure 6.3B Gender gap in school enrolment in Korea and Taiwan
Source: Go and Park 2019[3]

[3] I thank Sun Go for sharing the data from his paper.

increased the influence of the elites, who were in local bodies and did not prioritise spending on primary education. In Indonesia, a Dutch colony, the priority was primary education. The enrolment rate in primary school was 22 per cent in 1940 (Booth 1998, p. 275), which was low in comparison to East Asia but higher than in British India at just over 15 per cent. The increase in the provision of secondary education in Indonesia began after 1970 (Van der Eng 2010). In 1950, India spent 58 per cent of the education budget on secondary and tertiary education. In Indonesia, the figure was 28 per cent (see Table 4.6 in Chapter 4).

6.7   Colonial Origins of Economic Development after 1950

Korea was divided into north and south along the 38th parallel in 1945 under the supervision of the Soviet Union and the USA. The Korean war that followed in 1950–1953 solidified the division of the two countries into two different economic systems. The north came under a communist system and South Korea's capitalist economy saw one of the fastest growths in the world. In colonial Korea, the north had been more industrial and more developed. Per capita GDP in the north and the south were roughly the same in 1910. In 1940, South Korea's GDP per capita was 70 per cent of that of North Korea (Kim 2021). Under the new policies in independent South Korea, the spectacular growth of the next four decades transformed the country from one of the low income countries to one of the richest emerging economies.

This impressive performance occurred under state-directed industrialization, which provided incentives to the private sector to invest in industries that were prioritized for development. The initial policies supported import substitution in industries by introducing multiple exchange rates and tariffs that allowed easier access to import of capital goods and raw materials, but made import of consumer goods more expensive. Unlike India's efforts to develop a domestic capital goods sector, South Korea relied on imports and started to develop industries, where the economy could gain a competitive advantage in the export market. The move from import substitution to export promotion began early in the 1960s, when the government unified the exchange rate and provided for export subsidy and easy access to import and credit to industrial sectors that were prioritized. In the early phase, the industries that developed were mainly consumer goods. From 1973 six capital intensive intermediate and capital goods industries, such as steel, non-ferrous metal, machinery, shipbuilding, electronic, and chemical industries, became the priority sectors

Table 6.6 *Sectoral distribution of GDP and employment in South Korea and Taiwan after 1950 (%)*

		South Korea				
	GDP			Employment		
Years	Agriculture	Industry	Services	Agriculture	Industry	Services
1955	39.3	9.7	51.0			
1960	38.0	12.0	50.0	79.5	5.4	15.1
1970	31.1	20.4	48.5	50.5	14.3	35.2
1980	17.8	25.3	56.9	34.0	22.6	43.4
1990	9.1	29.7	61.2	18.3	27.3	54.4
		Taiwan				
	GDP			Employment		
	Agriculture	Industry	Services	Agriculture	Industry	Services
1952	32.2	19.7	48.1	56.1	16.9	27.0
1961	27.4	26.8	46.0	49.8	20.9	29.3
1970	15.5	36.8	47.7	36.7	27.9	35.4
1980	7.7	45.8	46.6	19.5	42.5	38.0
1990	4.2	41.2	54.6	12.9	40.8	46.3

Source: Boestel et al. (1999, p. 77)

for development (Kim 2021). Export subsidies were given to support these industries to became competitive in the world market. The condition was that within a certain time a specified share of output would be exported.

Table 6.6 shows the success of the industrialization policy as the share of industry increased sharply in GDP and employment. Table 6.7 shows the high share of gross fixed capital formation in GDP in Korea relative to India and the increase in the share of manufacturing in gross fixed capital formation across the three countries. While India pushed up the investment rate in manufacturing in the 1950s under the second five year plan, South Korea raised the investment rate in the 1970s. The increase in the investment in industry was sustained in East Asia but declined in India.

Table 6.8 shows yet another difference between India and East Asia in terms of the rates of growth in exports. In the colonial period and even in the 1950s, India and South Korea did not look very different in the share of exports in GDP. Their paths diverged after 1960 as South

Table 6.7 *Gross fixed capital formation and the share of manufacturing (%)*

	Share of fixed capital formation in GDP 1973–1997 (%)*	Share of manufacturing in gross fixed capital formation (%)				
		1950	1960	1970	1980	1990
India	20	11.6	27.8	27.5	12.5	10.4
South Korea	31	13	15	17	28.3	32.3
Taiwan	24	19.5	23.5	36.1	29.0	25.7

Source: Amsden (2001, table 6.3, p. 131*)

Table 6.8 *Growth of exports (1950–1990) (%)*

	1950–1960	1960–1970	1970–1980	1980–1990	1990–1995
India	0.4	3.7	17.3	7	11.7
South Korea	1.3	39.8	37.2	15.0	26.3
Taiwan	6.5	23.2	28.6	14.8	20.3

Source: Amsden (2001, table 7.1, p. 162)

Korea embraced an export-led strategy, while India was to remain committed to policies of import substitution. The share of manufactured goods in exports rose from 5 per cent in 1960 to 35 per cent by the early 1970s (Yoo 2017). The failure to make a transition to a more open economy after the initial phase of an inward looking development strategy was a factor in the slowdown in industrial growth in India. Rodrik (1995) and Young (1995) attribute Korea's success to the high rate of capital accumulation. India's investment rate was low in comparison.

Kohli (1994) raised an important question: How can we think of the political economy of high growth countries? He explored Korea's colonial history to understand how it might have impacted on the post-war growth experience. Kohli argues that the origins of the Korean economic miracle lies in the Japanese lineage. Japan experienced modern economic growth after the Meiji restoration of 1868. Japanese developmental policies were applied to the context of the colonies. Similar interventions were made in modernizing agriculture, industry, and infrastructure.

Kohli (2004) argues that Korea was perhaps the only example where the colony exported manufactured goods to the imperial power by the 1930s. As pointed out earlier in this chapter, the geographical proximity may have been a factor that allowed the adoption of similar practices in the colonies. The proximity may have assisted the development of complementary industries in the colony and generated skills and technological knowledge that could be used effectively in independent South Korea. The education system made access to primary school widespread and produced a literate workers for industries.

Booth (1999) suggests that the Japanese colonies in East Asia evolved differently to the European colonies in South-East Asia. The high literacy of Korea and Taiwan was an outcome of Japanese policy to raise human capital of the workforce. The independent governments build on this legacy. An equal distribution of income and wealth has been highlighted as a favourable initial condition in East Asia (Rodrik 1995). Here too the Japanese intervention in the land tenure systems in Korea and Taiwan created more equal distribution of land ownership than what had emerged in the landlord system under British colonial policy in India.

6.8   Structural Change

Figures 6.4A, 6.4B and 6.4C show the pattern of structural change in India, South Korea, and Taiwan over the twentieth century. The sectors are classified as primary, secondary, and tertiary, to use comparable data, broadly capturing agriculture, industry, and services.[4] All three countries started with a high share of agriculture and other primary sector activities in GDP at over 60 per cent. The share of the secondary sector in GDP was similar in India and South Korea in 1950, but in South Korea the primary sector contributed less to output and the share of the service sector was larger. From 1950 the decline in the share of the primary sector accelerated and the share of industry and mining increased. In 2000, the primary and secondary sectors had the same share in GDP in India. In South Korea, the share of the primary sector had declined to 4 per cent and the secondary sector produced one-third of GDP. The share of the secondary sector was larger in Taiwan compared to India and Korea in 1950 and increased to over half the national output by 1980. The share of the primary sector declined dramatically. In 2000, the two East Asian countries looked remarkably similar. However, in India, the secondary sector remained much smaller and the pattern of structural change

---

[4] Primary sector includes, agriculture, finishing, and forestry. Secondary sector includes, mining, manufacturing, and construction. Tertiary sector includes all services.

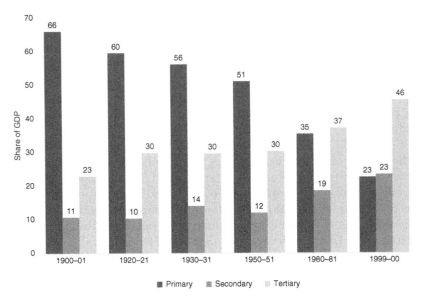

Figure 6.4A Structural change in India (1900–2000)
Source: Sivasubramonian, 2000. Appendix tables 7(f) and 9 (d)

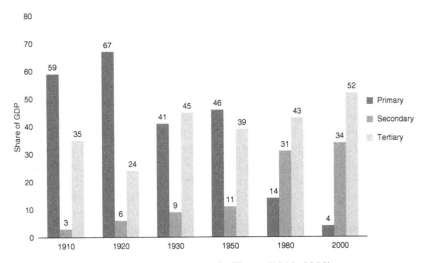

Figure 6.4B Structural change in Korea (1910–2000)
Source: Long run Historical Statistics in Korea and Taiwan.
(Hitotsubashi University)

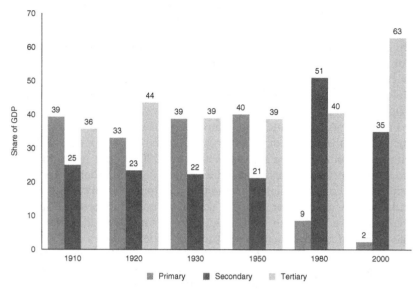

Figure 6.4C Structural change in Taiwan (1910–2000)
Source: Long run Historical Statistics in Korea and Taiwan.
(Hitotsubashi University)[5]

showed the growing importance of the tertiary sector. The relatively high share of agriculture in India is yet another difference.

The figures show the relative weakness of the secondary sector in India after 1950. This was particularly true in manufacturing. Unlike India, East Asia followed an infant industry policy of protecting domestic industry only in the 'learning' phase (Perkins and Tang 2017) and moved early towards export-promoting policies in the manufacturing industry.

India's post-independence growth performance is seen as a failure in comparison to the East Asian successes. Growth in output per worker in South Korea and Taiwan was just below 6 per cent per year between 1960 and 1994, more than double of the average for South Asia at 2.3 per cent per year (Collins et al. 1996). Growth in physical capital per worker was around 3 per cent per year compared to South Asia's 1 per cent per year and growth in human capital per worker was over 0.06 per cent per year compared to South Asia's 0.03 per cent per year (Collins et al. 1996). Collins et al. (1996) argue that external conditions explain very little of the growth difference between South

---

[5] I thank Kyoji Fukao for making the data available.

and East Asia. Education is a more important explanatory variable. In South Korea and Taiwan, the average years of education of the workforce rose from 3.2 in 1960 to over 8 in 1994. In India, the change was from 1.3 to 3.4. Public expenditure on education in South Korea was twice as high as in India in 1970. The long-run consequences of colonial policy may have contributed to the different paths of development followed in South and East Asia.

Figures 6.5A, 6.5B and 6.5C shows the differences in sectoral productivity in the three countries under colonial rule. India started out with an advantage in the service sector. In 2000, output per worker in the tertiary sector was higher in India. In East Asia, although the tertiary sector started out with higher productivity, output per worker in the secondary sector rose faster and this sector became the most productive sector in the economy in 1940. Figures 6.5B and 6.5C show the colonial origins of an advantage in industrial activities in Korea and Taiwan. Indian advantage in services is shown in Figure 6.5A. I have argued in this chapter that the policies of extending primary education provided an advantage to industry in Korea and Taiwan. The emphasis on higher education for some groups and the concentration of human capital in services in India discussed in Chapter 4 provided an advantage to this sector relative to industry.

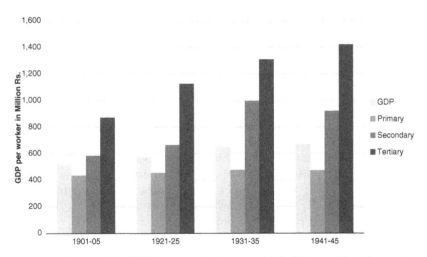

Figure 6.5A GDP per worker in colonial India in million Rupees in 1948–49 prices (1905–1945)
Source: Author's calculations from Sivasubramonian (2000)

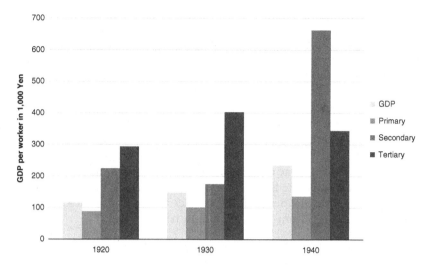

Figure 6.5B GDP per worker in colonial Korea in 1,000 Yen in 1935 prices
Source: Long run Historical Statistics in Korea and Taiwan. (Hitotsubashi University)*

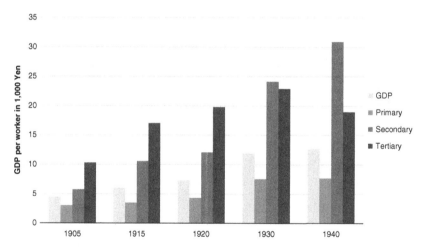

Figure 6.5C GDP per worker in colonial Taiwan in 1,000 Yen in 1935 (1905–1940)
Source: Long run Historical Statistics in Korea and Taiwan. (Hitotsubashi University)[6]

[6] I thank Kyoji Fukao for making the data available.

6.9   Conclusion

The slow growth in India in the post-independence decades is a relative failure when compared to the rapid growth seen in East Asia. In this chapter I have shown that the share of industry in GDP in the three countries at the time of independence did not look that different. Thirty years later, the industrial sector in the East Asian economies accounted for a much larger share of GDP. Colonial policies towards extension of primary education created a literate workforce for industry. In India, this was missing. The concentration of human capital in the service sector and not in industry is one of the big differences between India and South Korea and Taiwan. The literature has often emphasized the differences in policies after independence. Looking back at colonial policies provides a different perspective on East Asia's industrial success.

Conclusion
The Myths and the Realities of India's Long-Run Development

The first three decades after the independence of India in 1947 have been seen as a failure of growth. A regulated economy led to inefficiency and low growth. The architect of Indian planning, Prime Minister Jawaharlal Nehru, did not put India on an East Asian path. The historical perspective taken in this book analyzes the post-independence decades in terms of the context of policy making, the growth and development of the Indian economy before independence, and the legacy of historical institutions and economic policy. At the time of independence, India was one of the poorest countries in the world. The globalized economy in the British Empire had not seen prosperity. For decades, the economy had been through stagnation. Agriculture, in particular food production, had stagnated in most parts of the country. In 1947 India had a small but modern industrial sector.

The question that I raised in the book is: How did India get there? Did connections with the global economy of the British Empire lead to impoverishment? How did the regulated economy and the loss of global connections in independent India compare? What are the myths and the realities of the connections to the global market?

C.1   Myths of the Market in a Colonial Economy

Markets functioned well under colonial rule and restrictions hindered market activity after independence. The literature has myths on both sides. 'Colonialization was beneficial with rising trade and investment' (Ferguson 2004) is one. 'Colonial rule was extractive and reduced pre-colonial prosperity' (Tharoor 2018) is another. Ferguson in his book *Empire: How Britain Made the Modern World* (2004) writes,

Average incomes rose by only 14 per cent between 1757 and 1947, while British incomes rose by 347 per cent... Even if the British rule did not increase Indian incomes, things might have been much worse under a restored Mughal regime. (p. 117)

187

According to this statement, India fared better under British rule compared to the state of the economy under the Mughals. It claims that colonization integrated India into the global economy and provided transport networks and access to Britain's capital market. I have argued in this book and provided empirical evidence that Indian GDP per capita stagnated in the globalized economy of colonial India. Growth picked up after independence in a regulatory regime as India moved towards protecting the economy from trade and foreign capital and Indianization of the industrial sector and restrictions on private investment.

A different view of the global market comes from the recent book *The Inglorious Empire* by Sashi Tharoor (2018):

Britain's industrial revolution was built on the destruction of Indian textile industries. The textiles were an emblematic case in point: The British set about systematically destroying Indian manufacturing and exports… Ironically, the British used Indian raw material and exported the finished product back to India and the rest of the world adding the industrial equivalent of adding insult to injury. (p. 216)

Looking at empirical evidence systematically tells a different story. I have argued in Chapter 2 that decline of the traditional industry was hard to stop. The labour saving technology of the industrial revolution gave British industry an advantage in the world market. As prices of machine-made textiles tumbled, British goods displaced Indian imports in the British market first, then in the third markets, and finally in the Indian market. The effect of the decline in the traditional textile industry was localized and did not have a large effect on the economy. The estimated decline in industrial employment ranges from over 50 per cent (Bagchi 1976; Twomey 1983) to 28 per cent (Ray 2009) in Bengal, which was the centre of the textile industry at this time. The decline in industrial employment spanned over 30 years in the nineteenth century. Per capita consumption of textiles in India increased as imports were cheaper.

From 1880, cotton textiles were produced by an emerging modern industry using British technology imported by Indian entrepreneurs. This industry was set up by Indian entrepreneurs in competition with Lancashire and without any state support. It began to regain market share from imports of British goods. Industrial growth during the first half of the twentieth century was not trivial.

Chapter 1 shows that India was relatively prosperous in 1600 under the reign of Akbar, as shown by the estimates of GDP per capita. At $682 India was well over the subsistence income level of $400 in 1600. The decline in income began from the middle of the seventeenth century, well before colonization. It coincided with the arrival of the European

trading companies and the dramatic rise in textile exports. I have argued
that the share of the textile industry was too small to counter the decline
in per capita output in agriculture. By the nineteenth century the decline
in GDP per capita turned into stagnation. Although trade increased
from the middle of the nineteenth century, it did not turn economic
stagnation into growth.

When India was integrated into the global economy of the British
Empire, policies of the colonial administration to develop a modern
transport system and introduce property rights in land did not reverse
the decline in yield per acre in land in most parts of the country. It did
not stop stagnation in incomes in the largest sector of the economy.
Yield per acre in 1910 was lower than in 1600. GDP per capita tracked
agricultural output per capita. As the economy approached an ecological crisis, irrigation covered only 20 per cent of the land under cultivation. The Nationalist historians have criticized the railways as serving
colonial interests. Though the lines initially linked the agricultural hinterland to the ports, over time the network became denser and linked
markets within the country. It reduced price fluctuations in response to
weather shocks and brought benefits to isolated communities. However,
evidence confirms that the colonial economy spent too little on irrigation compared to the spending on the railways, which can explain agricultural stagnation. The investment rate in the colonial economy was
only 7 per cent of GDP.

Despite the links with the British capital markets, few industries
received British investment before the First World War. The railways
and tea were the main beneficiaries. While British capital flowed to
export oriented sectors, Indian investment dominated the import substituting sectors, in particular, the cotton textiles industry. Community
networks of Indian merchants had accumulated enough wealth in trade
and informal banking to invest in the modern cotton textile industry.
The largest British investment in India was the railways, but it created
few backward linkages with the industry as in other countries, drawing
the criticism that the colonizers did not develop a capital goods industry. Large-scale modern industry saw the fastest growth in output per
worker as the industrial sector rebalanced between the modern and the
traditional sectors.

The colonial administration introduced a modern education system. Universities in the metropolitan cities created an elite with literacy in English. But who were educated? At the time of independence
only 17 per cent of the population was literate. There was a large gap
between male and female literacy and only 142 out of 1,000 school age
children were at school in 1931, one of the lowest in the world. Public

investment in education was one of the lowest in the world. It was lower than in other British colonies and other underdeveloped countries, such as Brazil and Mexico, and also lower than in the princely states. India spent a large share of education budget on secondary and tertiary education rather than primary education for all. This had consequences for human capital in different sectors. Most of the educated workers were in services, while most industrial and agricultural workers were not literate. This had implications for productivity growth in these sectors. The higher education bias of colonial education policy persisted in independent India and is one of the factors that may have given the service sector an advantage at the cost of a competitive industrial sector.

C.2   The Transition from a Colonial Economy

India moved from an open economy to one of the most regulated economies of the world. The new government in independent India embraced self-sufficiency as the means to develop the economy. Industrial development was at the core of this policy, as in many other parts of the underdeveloped world. Many countries in Latin America, newly independent countries in Asia, and Africa turned away from global connections too. India moved from an open economy to one of the most regulated economies of the world. The strategy paid off for a short period as industrial growth increased. The investment rate more than doubled within ten years. Agricultural growth turned positive for the first time in half a century with investment in new infrastructure. The Green Revolution that followed in agriculture had a large impact on many sectors of the economy and society. However, as industrial growth rate began to decline, economic reforms were introduced. Under the reforms, Indian growth more than doubled. The economic reforms have been seen as a turning point in India's economic growth since independence. However, a historical perspective makes the low growth of the Nehruvian period a turning point from stagnation of the colonial period to modern economic growth.

C.3   A Myth of the Market

It has been argued that India was stuck in a low growth regime due to the regulatory policies (Ahluwalia 1991; Panagariya 2008). India's growth was low in comparison to the fast-growing economies in East Asia, but not in comparison to the long-run trend. There was an efficiency cost of regulation, but planned development had put the economy on a growth path. The trebling of investment rate within two decades compensated for the loss of efficiency (Delong 2003). Pro-business reforms gradually

removed industrial regulation from 1980 and put India on a higher
growth path (Rodrik and Subramaniam 2005). Pro-market reforms from
the 1990s followed. A long view sees the turning point of the Nehruvian
period in the context of colonial policies and its impact on the economy.
The historical perspective in this book also helps to rethink some of
the views on regional development today. The high GDP per capita of
some regions, such as Maharashtra and Gujarat, show historical persistence. The Bombay Presidency in colonial India was one of the most
prosperous regions. The regions that were under the landlord system
are more underdeveloped in several dimensions today compared to non-
landlord regions. The advantage in literacy by certain castes due to their
traditional occupations had provided these groups an advantage in the
new occupations in colonial India and the inequality in access to new
opportunities after 1950 showed persistence. It also helps in understanding India's advantage in the service sector.

Comparisons have been made with East Asia as a critique of the
Nehruvian policies. As South Korea and Taiwan gained independence
from Japan, they too turned to import substitution in the 1950s in
order to develop the industrial sector. In 1950, India, South Korea,
and Taiwan did not look very different in terms of the share of industry in GDP. However, the strategy of import substitution differed
across these countries. While India focused on capital goods production, South Korea and Taiwan developed industries that gained international competitiveness. A historical perspective in this book brings
colonial legacy into the discussion, as a factor that influenced the different outcomes.

The investment in agriculture in the Japanese colonies raised agricultural productivity and created different conditions for movement of
workers from agriculture to industry. This was aided by widening access
to primary education in the Japanese colonies. Both South Korea and
Taiwan had a literate workforce that could work in the emerging industries after independence. The education level of the workforce increased
rapidly from the 1950s. Most workers in Indian industries had no education as access to primary education had been limited under British policies. India has a concentration of educated workers in the service sectors
and has moved towards a service sector-led growth. The different paths
of development in the two East Asian economies and India have colonial
origins. In this book I have focused on factors from history that account
for policies and outcomes in independent India. The regulatory regime
in independent India marked a reversal of fortune from stagnation under
the global economy of the British Empire to economic growth under
state-directed development.

References

Abū 'l-Fazl [1595] (1927). *The Ā' īn–i-Akbarī*. Translated into English by H. Blochman. New Delhi: Low Price Publications.

Acemoglu, D., Johnson, S., and Robinson, J. A. (2001). 'The colonial origins of comparative development: An empirical investigation'. *American Economic Review*, *91*(5), pp. 1369–1401.

Aggarwal, A. (2022). *Three essays on the economic and political causes and consequences of migration in Asia*. Unpublished PhD thesis, University of Warwick.

Agnihotri, I. (1996). 'Ecology, land use and colonization: The canal colonies of Punjab'. *Indian Economic and Social History Review*, *33*(1), pp. 37–58.

Ahluwalia, I. J. (1991). *Productivity and Growth in Indian Manufacturing*. Delhi: Oxford University Press.

Ahluwalia, M. S. (2000). 'Economic performance of states in post-reforms period'. *Economic and Political Weekly*, *35*, pp. 1637–1648.

Ahmad, S. S. and Chakravarti, A. K. (1981). 'Some regional characteristics of Muslim caste systems in India'. *GeoJournal*, *5*(1), pp. 55–60.

Ali, I. (1987). 'Malign growth? Agricultural colonialism and the roots of backwardness in Punjab'. *Past and Present*, *114*(1), pp. 110–132.

Allen, R. C. (2001). 'The Great Divergence in European wages and prices from the middle ages to the First World War'. *Explorations in Economic History*, *38*(4), pp. 411–447.

(2007). 'India in the Great Divergence', in Hatton, T. J., O'Rourke, K. H., and Taylor, A. M. (eds.), *The New Comparative Economic History: Essays in Honor of Jeffrey G. Williamson*. Cambridge, MA: MIT Press, pp. 9–32.

(2009). *The British Industrial Revolution in Global Perspective*. Cambridge University Press.

Alvaredo, F., Bergeron, A., and Cassan, G. (2017). 'Income concentration in British India, 1885–1946'. *Journal of Development Economics*, *127*, pp. 459–469.

Alvaredo, F., Cogneau, D., and Piketty, T. (2021). 'Income inequality under colonial rule evidence from French Algeria, Cameroon, Tunisia, and Vietnam and comparisons with British colonies 1920–1960'. *Journal of Development Economics*, *152*, 102680.

Amsden, A. H. (2001). *The Rise of 'The Rest': Challenges to the West from Late-Industrializing Economies*. Oxford University Press.

Anderson, S. and Ray, D. (2010). 'Missing women: Age and disease'. *The Review of Economic Studies*, *77*(4), pp. 1262–1300.

(2012). 'The age distribution of missing women in India'. *Economic and Political Weekly*, 47, pp. 87–95.

Anstey, V. (1929). *The Economic Development of India*. Longmans, Green and Company.

Appadurai, A. (1993). 'Number in the colonial imagination', in Breckenridge, C. A. and van der Veer, P. (eds.), *Orientalism and the Postcolonial Predicament: Perspectives on South Asia*. Philadelphia: University of Pennsylvania Press, pp. 314–339.

Arasaratnam, S. (1987). 'Writing the history of the Indian Ocean 1500–1800'. *Asian Studies Review*, 11(1), pp. 32–35.

Arthi, V., Lampe, M., Nair, A., and O'Rourke, K. H. (2024). 'Deliberate surrender? The impact of interwar Indian protection'. *The Economic Journal*, 134(657), pp. 23–47.

Asher, S., Campion, A., Gollin, D., and Novosad, P. (2022). 'The long-run development impacts of agricultural productivity gains: Evidence from irrigation canals in India'. *Working Paper*.

Baden-Powell, B. H. (1896). 'The Origin of Zamindari Estates in Bengal'. *The Quarterly Journal of Economics*, 11(1), pp. 36–69.

Bagchi, A. K. (1972). *Private Investment in India 1900–39*. Cambridge: Cambridge University Press.

(1976). 'De-industrialization in India in the nineteenth century: Some theoretical implications'. *The Journal of Development Studies*, 12(2), pp. 135–164.

(1983). *The Political Economy of Underdevelopment*. Cambridge: Cambridge University Press.

(1997). *The Evolution of the State Bank of India, Volume 2: The Era of the Presidency Banks, 1876–1920*. London and New Delhi: SAGE Publications.

Bagde, S., Epple, D., and Taylor, L. (2016). 'Does affirmative action work? Caste, gender, college quality, and academic success in India'. *American Economic Review*, 106(6), pp. 1495–1521.

Bairoch, P. (1997). 'New estimates on agricultural productivity and yields of developed countries, 1800–1990', in Bhaduri, A. and Skarstein, R. (eds.), *Economic Development and Agricultural Productivity*. Edward Elgar Publishing, pp. 45–64.

Baker, C. J. (1984). *An Indian Rural Economy, 1880–1955: The Tamilnad Countryside*. Oxford: Clarendon Press.

Balakrishnan, P. (2010). *Economic Growth in India*. Oxford: Oxford University Press.

Balakrishnan, P. and Parameswaran, M. (2007). 'Understanding economic growth in India: A prerequisite'. *Economic and Political Weekly*, 42, pp. 2915–2922.

Banerjee, A. and Iyer, L. (2005). 'History, institutions, and economic performance: The legacy of colonial land tenure systems in India'. *American Economic Review*, 95(4), pp. 1190–1213.

Banerjee, A. and Munshi, K. (2004). 'How efficiently is capital allocated? Evidence from the knitted garment industry in Tirupur'. *The Review of Economic Studies*, 71(1), pp. 19–42.

Banerjee, A. and Piketty, T. (2005). 'Top Indian incomes, 1922–2000'. *The World Bank Economic Review*, 19(1), pp. 1–20.

Banerjee, A. V., Gertler, P. J., and Ghatak, M. (2002). 'Empowerment and efficiency: Tenancy reform in West Bengal'. *Journal of political economy*, *110*(2), pp. 239–280.

Banga, R. (2005). 'Critical issues in India's service-led growth', Working Paper No.171 Indian Council for Research on International Economic Relations, New Delhi.

Barber, W. J. (1975). *British Economic Thought and India, 1600–1858: A Study in the History of Development Economics*. Oxford: Clarendon Press.

Bardhan, P. K. (1974). 'On life and death questions'. *Economic and Political Weekly 9*(32/34), pp. 1293–1304.

Bardhan, P. and Mookherjee, D. (2011). 'Subsidized farm input programs and agricultural performance: A farm-level analysis of West Bengal's green revolution 1982–95'. *American Economic Journal: Applied Economics*, *3*, pp. 186–214.

Bardhan, P., Mookherjee, D., and Kumar, N. (2012). 'State-led or market-led green revolution? Role of private irrigation investment vis-a-vis local government programs in West Bengal's farm productivity growth'. *Journal of Development Economics*, *99*(2), pp. 222–235.

Barker, R., Herdt, R. W., and Rose, B. (1985). *The Rice Economy of Asia (Vol. 2)*. Manila: International Rice Research Institute and Washington, DC: Resources for the Future.

Bayly, C. A. (1983). *Rulers, Townsmen and Bazaars: North Indian Society in the Age of British Expansion, 1770–1870*. Cambridge: Cambridge University Press.

Bayly, S. (2001). *Caste, Society and Politics in India from the Eighteenth Century to the Modern Age (Vol. 3)*. Cambridge University Press.

Becker, S. O., and Woessmann, L. (2009). 'Was Weber wrong? A human capital theory of protestant economic history'. *The Quarterly Journal of Economics*, *124*(2), pp. 531–596.

Beckert, S. (2015). *Empire of Cotton: A Global History*. Vintage.

Bernier, F. (1916). *Travels in the Mogul Empire: AD 1656–1668*. H. Milford: Oxford University Press.

Bértola, L. and Ocampo, J. A. (2012). *The Economic Development of Latin America since Independence*. Oxford: Oxford University Press.

Bertrand, M., Hanna, R., and Mullainathan, S. (2010). 'Affirmative action in education: Evidence from engineering college admissions in India'. *Journal of Public Economics*, *94*(1–2), pp. 16–29.

Besley, T. and Burgess, R. (2000). 'Land reform, poverty reduction, and growth: Evidence from India'. *The Quarterly Journal of Economics*, *115*(2), pp. 389–430.

Beteille, A. (1965). *Caste, Class and Power*. Berkeley and Los Angeles: University of California Press.

Bhagwati, J. N. and Desai, P. (1970). *India, Planning for Industrialisation: Industrialisation and Trade Policies since 1951*. London: Oxford University Press for the OECD.

Bhalla, G. S. and Singh, G. (2010). 'Growth of Indian agriculture: A district level study'. *Planning Commission, Government of India*. Available at: http://planningcommission.nic.in/reports/sereport/ser/ser_gia2604.pdf.

Bhalla, G. S. and Tyagi, D. S. (1989). 'Spatial pattern of agricultural development in India'. *Economic and Political Weekly*, *24*, pp. A46–A56.

Bhalotra, S. R., Clots-Figueras, I., and Iyer, L. (2018). 'Religion and abortion: The role of politician identity'. *IZA Discussion Paper No. 11292*.

Bhalotra, S. R., Brulé, R., and Roy, S. (2020). 'Women's inheritance rights reform and the preference for sons in India'. *Journal of Development Economics*, *146*, p. 102275.

Bharadwaj, P., Fenske, J., Kala, N., and Mirza, R. A. (2020). 'The Green revolution and infant mortality in India'. *Journal of Health Economics*, *71*, p. 102314.

Bhaskar, V. and Gupta, B. (2007a). 'India's development in the era of growth'. *Oxford Review of Economic Policy*, *23*(2), pp. 135–142.

(2007b). 'India's missing girls: Biology, customs, and economic development'. *Oxford Review of Economic Policy*, *23*(2), pp. 221–238.

Bhattacharya, B. B. and Mitra, A. (1990). 'Excess growth of tertiary sector in Indian economy: Issues and implications'. *Economic and Political Weekly*, *25*, pp. 2445–2450.

Bhattacharya, B. B. and Sakthivel, S. (2004). 'Regional growth and disparity in India: Comparison of pre- and post-reform decades'. *Economic and Political Weekly*, *39*, pp. 1071–1077.

Bhattacharya, N. (1985). 'Lenders and Debtors: Punjab Countryside, 1880–1940'. *Studies in History*, *1*(2), pp. 305–342.

Bloom, N., Mahajan, A., McKenzie, D., and Roberts, J. (2010). 'Why do firms in developing countries have low productivity?' *American Economic Review*, *100*(2), pp. 619–623.

Blyn, G. (1966). *Agricultural Trends in India 1891–1947: Output, Availability and Production*. Philadelphia: University of Pennsylvania Press.

Boestel, J., Francks, P., and Kim, C. H. (1999) *Agriculture and Economic Development in East Asia: From Growth to Protectionism in Japan, Korea and Taiwan*. Taylor & Francis Group.

(2013). *Agriculture and Economic Development in East Asia: From Growth to Protectionism in Japan, Korea and Taiwan*. Abingdon, Oxon: Routledge.

Bogart, D. and Chaudhary, L. (2015a). 'Off the rails: Is state ownership bad for productivity?' *Journal of Comparative Economics*, *43*(4), pp. 997–1013.

(2015b). 'Railways in colonial India: An economic achievement?', in Chaudhary, L., Gupta, B., Roy, T., and Swamy, A. V. (eds.), *A New Economic History of Colonial India*. Abingdon, Oxon: Routledge, pp. 140–160.

Booth, A. (1998). *The Indonesian Economy in the Nineteenth and Twentieth Centuries: A History of Missed Opportunities*. London: Macmillan Press Limited.

(1999). 'Initial conditions and miraculous growth: Why is South East Asia different from Taiwan and South Korea?' *World Development*, *27*(2), pp. 301–321.

Booth, A. E. (2007). *Colonial Legacies: Economic and Social Development in East and Southeast Asia*. University of Hawaii Press.

Bose, S. (eds.) (1994). *Credit, Markets and the Agrarian Economy*. Delhi: Oxford University Press.

Boserup, E. (1970). *Woman's Role in Economic Development*. Routledge.

Bosworth, B. and Collins, S. (2008). 'Accounting for growth: Comparing China and India'. *Journal of Economic Perspectives*, 22(1), pp. 45–66.

Bosworth, B., Collins, S., and Virmani, A. (2007). 'Sources of growth in the Indian economy', in Collins, S., Bosworth, B., and Panagariya, A. (eds.), *India Policy Forum, 2006–07*. Washington, DC: Brookings Institution Press, pp. 1–69.

Botticini, M. and Eckstein, Z. (2005). 'Jewish occupational selection: Education, restrictions, or minorities?' *Journal of Economic History*, 65, pp. 922–948.

(2006). 'Path dependence and occupations', in Durlauf, S. and Blume, L. (eds.), *New Palgrave Dictionary of Economics*. New York: Palgrave Macmillan, pp. 1–10.

Bouchon, G. and Lombard, D. (1987). 'The Indian Ocean in the fifteenth century', in Gupta, A. D. and Pearson, M. N. (eds.), *India and the Indian Ocean 1500–1800*. Delhi: Oxford University Press, pp. 46–70.

Breman, J. (1999). 'Industrial labour in post-colonial India. I: Industrializing the economy and formalizing labour'. *International Review of Social History*, 44(2), pp. 249–300.

Brennig, J. (1986). 'Textile producers and production in late-nineteenth century Coromandel'. *Indian Economic and Social History Review*, 23(4), pp. 333–356.

(1990). 'The textile trade of 17th Century Northern Coromandel', in Subrahmanyam, S. (ed.), *Markets and State in early Modern India*. Delhi: Oxford University Press, pp. 66–89.

Broadberry, S., Custodis, J., and Gupta, B. (2015). 'India and the Great Divergence: An Anglo-Indian comparison of GDP per capita, 1600–1871'. *Explorations in Economic History*, 55, pp. 58–75.

Broadberry, S. and Gupta, B. (2006). 'The early modern Great Divergence: Wages, prices and economic development in Europe and Asia, 1500–1800'. *Economic History Review*, 59(1), pp. 2–31.

(2009). 'Lancashire, India and shifting competitive advantage in cotton textiles, 1700–1850: The neglected role of factor prices'. *Economic History Review*, 62, pp. 279–305.

(2010). 'The historical roots of India's service-led development: A sectoral analysis of Anglo-Indian productivity differences, 1870–2000'. *Explorations in Economic History*, 47(3), pp. 264–278.

(2015). 'Indian economic performance and living standards: 1600–2000', in Chaudhary, L., Gupta, B., Roy, T., and Swamy, A. V. (eds.), *A New Economic History of Colonial India*. Abingdon, Oxon: Routledge, pp. 15–32.

Buchanan, F. H. (1807). *A Journey from Madras through the Countries of Mysore, Canara, and Malabar*. (Vols. 1–3). London: T. Cadell & W. Davies.

Burgess, R. and Donaldson, D. (2010). 'Can openness mitigate the effects of weather shocks? Evidence from India's famine era'. *American Economic Review*, 100(2), pp. 449–453.

Captivating History. (2020). *Ancient Mediterranean Civilizations: A Captivating Guide to Carthage, the Minoans, Phoenicians, Mycenaeans, and Etruscans*.

Carranza, E. (2014). Soil endowments, female labor force participation, and the demographic deficit of women in India. *American Economic Journal: Applied Economics*, 6(4), 197–225.

Caruana-Galizia, P. (2013). 'Indian regional income inequality: Estimates of provincial GDP, 1875–1911'. *Economic History of Developing Regions*, 28(1), pp. 1–27.

Caselli, F. (2005). 'Accounting for cross-country income differences'. *Handbook of Economic Growth*, 1, pp. 679–741.

Caselli, F. and Gennaioli, N. (2013). 'Dynastic management'. *Economic Inquiry*, 51(1), pp. 971–996.

Cassan, G. (2015). 'Identity-based policies and identity manipulation: Evidence from colonial Punjab'. *American Economic Journal: Economic Policy*, 7(4), pp. 103–131.

Castelló-Climent, A., Chaudhary, L., and Mukhopadhyay, A. (2018). 'Higher education and prosperity: From Catholic missionaries to luminosity in India'. *The Economic Journal*, 128(616), pp. 3039–3075.

Cha, M. S. (2002). 'The colonial origins of Korea's market economy', in Latham, A. J. H., and Kawakatsu, H. (eds.), *Asia Pacific Dynamism 1550–2000*. London: Routledge, pp. 100–117.

Chakrabarty, D. (1989). *Rethinking Working-Class History: Bengal 1890–1940*, Princeton University Press.

Chakraborty, T. and Kim, S. (2010). 'Kinship institutions and sex ratios in India'. *Demography*, 47(4), 989–1012.

Chakravarty, S. (1987). *Development Planning: The Indian Experience*. Oxford: Clarendon Press.

Chancel, L. and Piketty, T. (2019). 'Indian income inequality, 1922–2015: From British Raj to Billionaire Raj?' *Review of Income and Wealth*, 65, pp. S33–S62.

Chandavarkar, R. (1994). *The Origins of Industrial Capitalism in India: Business Strategies and the Working Classes in Bombay 1900–1940*. (Cambridge South Asian Studies, number 51.) New York: Cambridge University Press.

Chandra, S. (1982). 'Standard of living 1: Mughal India', in Raychaudhuri, T. and Habib, I. (eds.), *The Cambridge Economic History of India, Volume 1: c. 1200–1750*. Cambridge: Cambridge University Press, pp. 458–471.

Chapman, S. (1992). *Merchant Enterprise in Britain: From Industrial Revolution to World War I*. Cambridge: Cambridge University Press.

Chaudhuri, K. N. (1978). *The Trading World of Asia and the English East India Company, 1660–1760*. Cambridge: Cambridge University Press.

Chaudhary, L. (2009). 'Determinants of primary schooling in British India'. *The Journal of Economic History*, 69(1), pp. 269–302.

(2010). 'Taxation and educational development: Evidence from British India'. *Explorations in Economic History*, 47(3), pp. 279–293.

(2015). Caste, colonialism and schooling: Education in British India. In *A New Economic History of Colonial India* (pp. 161–178). Routledge.

Chaudhary, L. and Fenske, J. (2020). 'Did railways affect literacy? Evidence from India' *CAGE working paper 529*.

(2023). 'Railways, development, and literacy in India'. *The Journal of Economic History*, 83(4), 1139–1174.

Chaudhary, L. and Garg, M. (2015). 'Does history matter? Colonial education investments in India'. *The Economic History Review*, 68(3), pp. 937–961.

198   References

Chaudhary, L., Gupta, B., Roy, T., and Swamy, A. V. (2015). 'Agriculture in colonial India', in Chaudhary, L., Gupta, B., Roy, T., and Swamy, A. V. (eds.), *A New Economic History of Colonial India*. Abingdon, Oxon: Routledge, pp. 100–116.

Chaudhary, L., Musacchio, A., Nafziger, S., and Yan, S. (2012). 'Big BRICs, weak foundations: The beginning of public elementary education in Brazil, Russia, India, and China'. *Explorations in Economic History*, 49(2), pp. 221–240.

Chaudhary, L. and Swamy, A. V. (2017). 'Protecting the borrower: An experiment in colonial India'. *Explorations in Economic History*, 65, pp. 36–54.

Chibber, V. (2003). *Locked in Place: State-Building and Late Industrialization in India*. Princeton: Princeton University Press.

Chung, Y. I. (2006). *Korea under siege, 1876–1945: Capital formation and economic transformation*. Oxford University Press.

Clark, G., O'Rourke, K. H., and Taylor, A. M. (2014). The growing dependence of Britain on trade during the Industrial Revolution. *Scandinavian Economic History Review*, 62(2), 109–136.

Collins, S. M., Bosworth, B. P., and Rodrik, D. (1996). 'Economic growth in East Asia: Accumulation versus assimilation'. *Brookings Papers on Economic Activity*, 1996(2), pp. 135–203.

Crafts, N. F. (1989). 'British industrialization in an international context'. *Journal of interdisciplinary history*, 415–428.

Damodaran, V., Hamilton, J., and Allan, R. (2019). 'Climate signals, environment and livelihoods in the long seventeenth century in India', in Mukherjee, A. (ed.), *A Cultural History of Famine*. Abingdon, Oxon: Routledge, pp. 52–70.

Dar, A. (2019). 'All is water: Technological complementarities and path dependence in Indian agriculture'. Mimeo.

Darling, M. (1925). *The Punjab Peasant in Prosperity and Debt*. H. Milford: Oxford University Press.

Das Gupta, R. (1976). 'Factory Labour in Eastern India: Sources of Supply, 1855–1946 Some Preliminary Findings'. *The Indian Economic & Social History Review*, 13(3), 277–329.

(1981). Structure of the labour market in colonial India. *Economic and Political Weekly*, 1781–1806.

Datt, G. (1997). *Poverty in India and Indian States*. Washington, DC: International Food Policy Research Institute.

(1998). *Poverty in India and Indian states: An update. Food Consumption and Nutrition Division Discussion Paper 47*. Washington, DC: International Food Policy Research Institute.

Datt, G. and Ravallion, M. (2002). 'Is India's economic growth leaving the poor behind?' *Journal of Economic Perspectives*, 16(3), pp. 89–108.

(2010). 'Shining for the poor too?' *Economic and Political Weekly*, 45, pp. 55–60.

Datta, K. L. (1914). *Report on the Enquiry into the Rise of Prices in India, 1*, Superintendent Government Printing (Calcutta).

Datta, M. K. (2017). 'Irrigation in India: The post-Green Revolution experi-
ence, challenges and strategies', in Goswami, B., Bezbaruah, M. P., and
Mandal, R. (eds.), *Indian Agriculture after the Green Revolution*. Abingdon,
Oxon: Routledge, pp. 96–111.

Datta, R. (2019). 'Subsistence crises and economic history: A study of
eighteenth-century Bengal', in *A Cultural History of Famine*, Abingdon,
Oxon: Routledge, pp. 37–51.

Deaton, A. and Drèze, J. (2009). 'Food and nutrition in India: Facts and inter-
pretations'. *Economic and Political Weekly*, 44(7), pp. 42–65.

De la Croix, D., Doepke, M., and Mokyr, J. (2018). 'Clans, guilds, and markets:
Apprenticeship institutions and growth in the preindustrial economy'. *The
Quarterly Journal of Economics*, 133(1), pp. 1–70.

Dell, M. (2010). 'The persistent effects of Peru's mining mita'. *Econometrica*,
78(6), pp. 1863–1903.

Delong, J. B. (2003). 'India since independence: An analytic growth narrative',
in Rodrik, D. (ed.), *In Search of Prosperity*. Princeton: Princeton University
Press, pp. 184–204.

Desai, A. V. (1972). 'Population and standards of living in Akbar's Time'. *Indian
Economic and Social History Review*, 9(1), pp. 43–62.

(1978). 'Population and standards of living in Akbar's Time: A second look'.
Indian Economic and Social History Review, 15(1), pp. 53–79.

Desai, S. and Dubey, A. (2012). 'Caste in 21st century India: Competing narratives'. *Economic and Political Weekly*, 46(11), p. 40.

Deshpande, A. (2001). 'Caste at birth? Redefining disparity in India'. *Review of
Development Economics*, 5(1), pp. 130–144.

(2011). *The Grammar of Caste: Economic Discrimination in Contemporary India*.
New Delhi: Oxford University Press.

Deshpande, A. and Ramachandran, R. (2019). 'Traditional hierarchies and
affirmative action in a globalizing economy: Evidence from India'. *World
Development*, 118, pp. 63–78.

Dhawan, B. D. and Yadav, S. S. (1997). 'Public investment in Indian agriculture:
Trends and determinants'. *Economic and Political Weekly*, 32, pp. 710–714.

Dirks, N. (2001). *Castes of Mind: Colonialism and the Making of Modern India*.
Princeton: Princeton University Press.

Donaldson, D. (2018). 'Railroads of the Raj: Estimating the impact of transportation infrastructure'. *American Economic Review*, 108(4–5), pp. 899–934.

(2019). 'Comparative advantage and agricultural trade'. *Agricultural Economics*,
50, pp. 29–40.

Dumont, L. (1970). 'Religion, politics, and society in the individualistic uni-
verse'. Proceedings of the Royal Anthropological Institute of Great Britain
and Ireland (1970), pp. 31–41.

Dutt, R.C. (1902). *The Economic History of India in the Victorian age*, 7th ed.
London: Routledge and Kegan Paul, Ltd., 1952

(1906). *The Economic History of India Under Early British Rule.*, Vol. 1. London:
K. Paul, Trench, Trübner.

Dutta, M.K. (2017). 'Irrigation in India: The post-Green Revolution experience, challenges and strategies' In Goswami, B., Bezbaruah, M.P., and

200   References

Mandal, R. (eds), *Indian Agriculture after the Green Revolution*, Routledge. pp. 96–111.
Duus, P. (1984) 'Economic Dimensions of Meiji Imperialism: The Case of Korea, 1895–1910' in Myers, R., and Peattie, M. (eds.). *The Japanese Colonial Empire, 1895–1945*. Princeton, NJ: Princeton University Press.
Dyson, T. (2019). 'The population history of Asia', in *Oxford Research Encyclopedia of Asian History*.
Dyson, T. and Moore, M. (1983). On kinship structure, female autonomy, and demographic behavior in India. *Population and Development Review*, 35–60.
Eichengreen, B. and Gupta, P. (2011). 'The service sector as India's road to economic growth (No. w16757)'. National Bureau of Economic Research.
Fan, S., Hazell, P., and Throat, S. K. (2000). 'Impact of public expenditure on poverty in rural India'. *Economic and Political Weekly*, 35(40), pp. 3581–3588.
Fenske, J., Gupta, B., and Neumann, C. (2022). 'Missing women in Colonial India', CEPR Discussion Paper No.17189.
Ferguson, N. (2004). *Empire: How Britain Made the Modern World*. Penguin UK.
Findlay, R. and O'Rourke, K. H. (2009). *Power and Plenty*. Princeton: Princeton University Press.
Foster, A. D. and Rosenzweig, M. R. (1996). 'Technical change and human-capital returns and investments: Evidence from the green revolution'. *The American Economic Review*, 86, pp. 931–953.
(2004a). 'Agricultural productivity growth, rural economic diversity, and economic reforms: India, 1970–2000'. *Economic Development and Cultural Change*, 52(3), pp. 509–542.
(2004b). 'Technological change and the distribution of schooling: Evidence from Green-Revolution India'. *Journal of Development Economics*, 74(1), pp. 87–111.
Frankel, J. A. and Romer, D. (1999). 'Does trade cause growth?' *American Economic Review*, 89, pp. 379–399.
Fukazawa, H. (1982). 'Standard of living 2: Maharashtra and the Deccan', in Raychaudhuri, T. and Habib, I. (eds.), *The Cambridge Economic History of India, Volume 1: c. 1200–1750*. Cambridge: Cambridge University Press, pp. 471–477.
Go, S. and Park, K. J. (2019). 'Universal public schooling in Colonial Korea and Taiwan', in Mitch, D. and Cappelli, G. (eds.), *Globalization and the Rise of Mass Education*. Palgrave Studies in Economic History. Cham: Palgrave Macmillan.
Gollin, D. (2014). 'The Lewis model: A 60-year retrospective'. *Journal of Economic Perspectives*, 28(3), pp. 71–88.
Gordon, J. and Gupta, P. (2004). 'Understanding India's services Revolution', *IMF Working Paper Series*, Number 171, Washington, DC.
Goswami, O. (1982). 'Collaboration and conflict: European and Indian capitalists and the jute economy of Bengal, 1919–39'. *The Indian Economic & Social History Review*, 19(2), pp. 141–179.
(1990). 'The Bengal famine of 1943: Re-examining the data'. *Indian Economic and Social History Review*, 27(4), pp. 445–463.

Gould, H. A. (1961). 'A further note on village exogamy in North India'. *Southwestern Journal of Anthropology*, *17*(3), pp. 297–300.

Great Britain, East India (Irrigation). (1904). *Report of the Indian irrigation commission, 1901–1903. Part I*. General Parliament, House of Commons.

Guha, R. (1963). *A Rule for Property in Bengal: An Essay on the Idea of the Permanent Settlement*. Paris: Moulton & Co.

Guha, S. (1985). *The Agrarian Economy of the Bombay–Deccan 1818–1941*. Delhi: Oxford University Press.

Guntupalli, A. M. and Baten, J. (2006). The development and inequality of heights in North, West, and East India 1915–1944. *Explorations in Economic History*, *43*(4), 578–608.

(2009). 'Measuring gender well-being with biological welfare indicators', in Harris, B., Gálvez, L., and Machado, H. (eds.), *Gender and Well-being in Europe. Historical and Contemporary Perspectives*. Farnham: Ashgate, pp. 43–45.

Gupta, B. (1997). Collusion in the Indian tea industry in the great depression: An analysis of panel data. *Explorations in Economic History*, *34*(2), 155–173.

(2001). 'The international tea cartel during the great depression, 1929–1933'. *The Journal of Economic History*, *61*(1), pp. 144–159.

(2005). 'Why did collusion fail? The Indian Jute industry in the interwar years'. *Business History*, *47*, pp. 532–552.

(2011). 'Wages, unions, and labour productivity: Evidence from Indian cotton mills'. *Economic History Review*, *64*(S1), pp. 76–98.

(2014). 'Discrimination or social networks: Industrial investment in Colonial India'. *Journal of Economic History*, *74*, pp. 141–168.

(2018) 'South Asia in the World Economy: 1600–1950' in Riello, G. and Roy, T. (ed.), *Economic Global History*. Bloomsbury, 2018.

(2019). 'Falling behind and catching up: India's transition from a colonial economy'. *The Economic History Review*, *72*(3), 803–827.

(2021) 'From free trade to regulation: The political economy of India's Development' in Broadberry, S. and Fukao, K. (ed.), *The Cambridge Economic History of the Modern World*. Cambridge University Press.

Gupta, B and Roy, T. 'From Artisanal Production to Machine tools: Industrialization in India over the long run' in O'Rourke, K. H. and Williamson, J. G. (2017). *The Spread of Modern Industry to the Periphery Since 1871* (p. 410). Oxford University Press.

Gupta, B., Mookherjee, D., Munshi, K., and Sanclemente, M. (2022). 'Community origins of industrial entrepreneurship in Colonial India'. *Journal of Development Economics*, *159*, pp. 1–19.

Gupta, B. and Swamy, A. V. (2017). 'Reputational consequences of labour coercion: Evidence from Assam's tea plantations'. *Journal of Development Economics*, *127*, pp. 431–439.

Habib, I. (1969). 'Potentialities of capitalistic development in the economy of Mughal India'. *The Journal of Economic History*, *29*(1), pp. 32–78.

(1976). 'Notes on Indian textile technology in the seventeenth century', in De, B. (ed.), *Essays in Honour of Professor S. C. Sarkar*. People's Publishing House New Delhi, pp. 182–183.

(1982a). 'Population', in Raychaudhuri, T. and Habib, I. (eds.), *The Cambridge Economic History of India, Volume 1: c.1200–c.1750.* Cambridge: Cambridge University Press, pp. 163–171.

(1982b). 'North India', in Raychaudhuri, T. and Habib, I. (eds.), *The Cambridge Economic History of India, 1, c.1200–c.1750.* Cambridge: Cambridge University Press, pp. 235–249.

Haider, N. (2004, August). 'Prices and wages in India (1200–1800): Source material, historiography and new directions'. In *Utrecht conference 'Towards a global history of prices and wages'* (2004).

Hamilton, F. (1833). *A Geographical, Statistical, and Historical Description of the District, or Zila, of Dinajpur, in the Province, or Soubah, of Bengal.* Asiatic Society.

Harriss-White, B., Vidyarthee, K., and Dixit, A. (2014). 'Dalit and Adivasi participation in India's business economy'. *Journal of Social Inclusion Studies, 1*(1), pp. 76–105.

Hatekar, N. and Dongre, A. (2005). 'Structural breaks in India's growth: Revisiting the debate with a longer perspective'. *Economic and Political Weekly, 40*(14), pp. 1432–1435.

Hayami, Y. and Ruttan, V. W. (1971). *Agricultural Development: An International Perspective* (pp. xiv+-367).

Haynes, D. E. (2012). *Small Town Capitalism in Western India: Artisans, Merchants, and the Making of the Informal Economy, 1870–1960* (Vol. 20). New York: Cambridge University Press.

Heston, A. (1983). 'National income', in Kumar, D. and Desai, M. (eds.), *The Cambridge Economic History of India, Volume 2: c.1757–c.1970.* Cambridge: Cambridge University Press, pp. 463–532.

Hnatkovska, V., Lahiri, A., and Paul, S. B. (2013). 'Breaking the caste barrier intergenerational mobility in India'. *Journal of Human Resources, 48*(2), pp. 435–473.

Ho, S. P. (1975). 'The economic development of colonial Taiwan: Evidence and interpretation'. *The Journal of Asian Studies, 34*(2), pp. 417–439.

Hurd, J. (1975). 'Railways and the expansion of markets in India, 1861–1921'. *Explorations in Economic History, 12*(3), pp. 263–288.

(1983). 'Railways', in Kumar, D. and Desai, M. (eds.), *The Cambridge Economic History of India, 2, c.1757–c.1970.* New Delhi: Orient Longman, pp. 737–761.

Jaffrelot, C. (2003). 'India: Caste stronger than religion?', IIAS Newsletter, *32*.

Jayachandran, S. and Pande, R. (2017). 'Why are Indian children so short? The role of birth order and son preference'. *American Economic Review, 107*(9), pp. 2600–2629.

Jha, P., Kumar, R., Vasa, P., Dhingra, N., Thiruchelvam, D., and Moineddin, R. (2006). 'Low male-to-female sex ratio of children born in India: National survey of 1· 1 million households'. *The Lancet, 367*(9506), 211–218.

Jha, R. (2007). 'Investment and subsidies in Indian agriculture'. *ASARC Working Paper 2007/03*, Australian National University, Canberra.

Jha, V. (1991). 'Social stratification in ancient India: Some reflections'. *Social Scientist, 19*, 19–40.

Jodhka, S. S. (2012). *Caste. Oxford India Short Introductions*. New Delhi: Oxford University Press.

Kaiwar, V. (1994). 'The colonial state, capital and the peasantry in Bombay Presidency'. *Modern Asian Studies, 28*(4), pp. 793–832.

Kang, K., and Ramachandran, V. (1999). 'Economic transformation in Korea: Rapid growth without an agricultural revolution?' *Economic Development and Cultural Change, 47*(4), 783–801.

Kelkar, V. L. and Kumar, R. (1990). 'Industrial growth in the eighties: Emerging policy issues'. *Economic and Political Weekly, 25*, pp. 209–222.

Khanna, T. and Yafeh, Y. (2007). 'Business groups in emerging markets: Paragons or parasites?' *Journal of Economic Literature, 45*(2), pp. 331–372.

Kidron, M. (1965). 'Excess imports of capital and technology in the private sector'. *The Economic Weekly, 24*, pp. 705–707.

Kijima, Y. (2006). 'Caste and tribe inequality: Evidence from India, 1983–1999'. *Economic Development and Cultural Change, 54*(2), pp. 369–404.

Kim, D. (2021). 'The great divergence on the Korean peninsula (1910–2020)'. *Australian Economic History Review, 61*(3), 318–341.

Kim, D. and Park, K. J. (2008). 'Colonialism and industrialisation: Factory labour productivity of colonial Korea, 1913–37'. *Australian Economic History Review, 48*(1), pp. 26–46.

Kimura, M. (1993). 'Standards of living in colonial Korea: Did the masses become worse off or better off under Japanese rule?'. *The Journal of Economic History, 53*(3), 629–652.

(2012). 'A Cliometric revolution in the economic history of Korea: A critical review'. *Australian Economic History Review, 52*(1), pp. 85–95.

Kiyokawa, Y. (1983). 'Technical adaptations and managerial resources in India: A study of the experience of the cotton textile industry from a comparative viewpoint'. *Developing Economies, 21*, pp. 97–133.

Kochhar, K., Kumar, U., Rajan, R., Subramanian, A., and Tokatlidis, I. (2006). 'India's pattern of development: What happened, what follows?' *Journal of Monetary Economics, 53*(5), pp. 981–1019.

Kohli, A. (1994). 'Where do high growth political economies come from? The Japanese lineage of Korea's "developmental state"'. *World Development, 22*(9), pp. 1269–1293.

(2004). *State-directed Development: Political Power and Industrialization in the Global Periphery*. New York: Cambridge University Press.

(2006). 'Politics of economic growth in India, 1980–2005, Part 1: 1980s'. *Economic and Political Weekly, 41*, pp. 1251–1259.

(2012). *Poverty Amid Plenty in the New India*. Cambridge, UK: Cambridge University Press.

(ed.) (2014). *India's Democracy: An Analysis of Changing State-society Relations (Vol. 913)*. Princeton: Princeton University Press.

Kotwal, A., Ramaswami, B., and Wadhwa, W. (2011). 'Economic liberalization and Indian economic growth: What's the evidence?'. *Journal of Economic Literature, 49*(4), pp. 1152–1199.

Kremer, M. (1990). 'Population growth and technological change: One million B.C. to 1990'. *The Quarterly Journal of Economics, 108*(3), pp. 681–716.

(1993). 'Population growth and technological change: One million BC to 1990'. *The Quarterly Journal of Economics*, *108*(3), 681–716.

Kudaisya, M. (2010). 'Marwari and Chettiar Merchant's, C. 1850s–1950s: Comparative trajectories', in *Chinese and Indian Business*. Brill, pp. 85–119.

Kumar, A. (1995). 'Colonial requirements and engineering education: The public works department, 1847–1947', in Macleod, R. and Kumar, D. (eds.), *Technology and the Raj*. New Delhi, London: SAGE, pp. 216–234.

Kumar, D. (1998). *Colonialism, Property and the State*. Delhi: Oxford University Press.

Kumar, D. (1987). 'The forgotten sector: Services in Madras Presidency in the first half of the nineteenth century'. *Indian Economic History Review*, *24*, pp. 367–393.

Kumar, R. (2020). 'Top Indian wealth shares and inheritances 1966–1985'. *Cliometrica*, *14*(3), 551–580.

Kurosaki, T. (2003). 'Specialization and diversification in agricultural transformation: The case of West Punjab, 1903–92'. *American Journal of Agricultural Economics*, *85*(2), pp. 372–386.

(2017). *Comparative Economic Development in India, Pakistan and Bangladesh: Agriculture in the Twentieth Century*. Tokyo: Maruzen Pub.

Kuznets, S. (1971). Simon Kuznets Prize lecture.

Lockwood, D. (2012). *The Indian bourgeoisie: A political history of the Indian capitalist class in the early twentieth century*. Bloomsbury Publishing.

Ludden, D. (1999). *The New Cambridge History of India IV.4: An Agrarian History of South Asia*. Cambridge: Cambridge University Press.

(2005). *Agricultural Production and South Asian History*. Oxford University Press.

Macdonell, A. A. (1914). 'The early history of caste'. *The American Historical Review*, *19*(2), 230–244.

Maddison, A. (1995). *Monitoring the World Economy, 1820–1992*. Paris: Organisation for Economic Co-operation and Development.

Mahadevan, R. (1978). 'Immigrant entrepreneurs in Colonial Burma – An exploratory study of the role of Nattukottai Chettiars of Tamil Nadu, 1880–1930'. *The Indian Economic & Social History Review*, *15*(3), pp. 329–358.

Markovits, C. (2002). *Indian Business and Nationalist Politics 1931–39*. Cambridge: Cambridge University Press.

Maurer, N. and Sharma, T. (2001). 'Enforcing property rights through reputation: Mexico's early industrialization, 1878–1913'. *Journal of Economic History*, *61*(4), pp. 950–973.

McAlpin, M. B. (1974). 'Railroads, prices, and peasant rationality: India 1860–1900'. *The Journal of Economic History*, *34*(3), pp. 662–684.

McCloskey, D. N. (1972). 'The enclosure of open fields: Preface to a study of its impact on the efficiency of English agriculture in the eighteenth century'. *The Journal of Economic History*, *32*(1), pp. 15–35.

McMillan, A. (2005). *Standing at the Margins: Representation and Electoral Reservation in India*. Oxford University Press.

Milanovic, B., Hoff, K., and Horowitz, S. (2010). 'Turnover in power as a restraint on investing in influence: Evidence from the post-communist transition'. *Economics & Politics*, *22*(3), pp. 329–361.

Miller, B. D. (1981). *The Endangered Sex: Neglect of Female Children in Rural North India*. Cornell University Press.

Mitchener, K. J. and Weidenmier, M. (2008). 'Trade and empire'. *The Economic Journal*, *118*(533), pp. 1805–1834.

Mohan, R. (2006). 'Agricultural credit in India: Status, issues and future agenda'. *Economic and Political Weekly*, *41*, pp. 1013–1023.

Mokyr, J. (2009). *The Enlightened Economy: Britain and the Industrial Revolution, 1700–1850*. Yale University Press.

   (2015). 'Progress, useful knowledge and the origins of the industrial revolution', in Greif, A., Kiesling, L., and Nye, J. V. C. (eds.), *Institutions, Innovation, and Industrialization: Essays in Economic History and Development*. Princeton: Princeton University Press, pp. 33–67.

Moosvi, S. (1973). 'Production, consumption and population in Akbar's Time'. *Indian Economic and Social History Review*, *10*(2), pp. 181–195.

   (1977). 'Note on professor Alan Heston's "Standard of Living in Akbar's Time: A Comment"'. *Indian Economic and Social History Review*, *14*(3), pp. 397–401.

   (2008). *People, Taxation, and Trade in Mughal India*. New Delhi: Oxford University Press.

   (2015). *The Economy of the Mughal Empire c. 1595: A Statistical Study*. New Delhi: Oxford University Press.

Moreland, W. H. (1923). *India at the Death of Akbar: An Economic Study*. London: Macmillan.

   (1923). *From Akbar to Aurangzeb: A Study in Indian Economic History*. London: Macmillan.

Morris, M. D. (1965). *The Emergence of an Industrial Labour Force in India*. Berkeley: University of California Press.

   (1967). 'Values as an obstacle to economic growth in South Asia: An historical survey'. *The Journal of Economic History*, *27*(4), 588–607.

   (1983). 'Growth of large-scale industry to 1947', in Kumar, D. and Desai, M. (eds.), *The Cambridge Economic History of India, Volume II*. Delhi: Cambridge University Press, 1982. pp. 553–676.

Mukerjee, M. (2011). *Churchill's Secret War: The British Empire and the Ravaging of India During World War II*. Penguin.

Mukherjee, R. (1967). *The Economic History of India, 1600–1800*. Allahabad: Kitab Mahal.

Munshi, K. (2011). 'Strength in numbers: Networks as a solution to occupational traps'. *The Review of Economic Studies*, *78*(3), pp. 1069–1101.

   (2019). 'Caste and the Indian economy'. *Journal of Economic Literature*, *57*(4), pp. 781–834.

Munshi, K. and Rosenzweig, M. (2006). 'Traditional institutions meet the modern world: Caste, gender, and schooling choice in a globalizing economy'. *American Economic Review*, *96*(4), pp. 1225–1252.

Myers, R. H., and Ching, A. (1964). 'Agricultural development in Taiwan under Japanese colonial rule'. *The Journal of Asian Studies*, *23*(4), 555–570.

Myers, R. H., and Saburo, Y. (1984). 'Agricultural Development in the Empire'. in Myers, R., and Peattie, M. (eds.). *The Japanese Colonial Empire, 1895–1945*. Princeton, NJ: Princeton University Press.

Nagaraj, R. (1990). Industrial growth: Further evidence and towards an explanation and issues. *Economic and Political Weekly*, 2313–2332.
   (2003a). 'Foreign direct investment in India in the 1990s: Trends and issues'. *Economic and Political Weekly*, 38, pp. 1701–1712.
   (2003b). 'Industrial policy and performance since 1980: Which way now?' *Economic and Political Weekly*, 38, pp. 3707–3715.
Nakajima, K. and Okazaki, T. (2018). 'The expanding Empire and spatial distribution of economic activity: The case of Japan's colonization of Korea during the pre-war period'. *The Economic History Review*, 71(2), pp. 593–616.
Naoroji, D. (1878). *Poverty of India*. London: Printed by Vincent Brooks, Day and Son.
Narain, D. (1965). *Impact of Price Movements on Areas under Selected Crops in India (1900–1939)*. Berkeley: University of California Press.
Nath, M. (2022). 'Credit risk in colonial India'. *The Economic History Review*, 75(2), pp. 396–420.
Nomura, C. (2014). 'The origin of the controlling power of managing agents over modern business enterprises in colonial India'. *The Indian Economic & Social History Review*, 51(1), pp. 95–132.
Nunn, N. (2008). 'The long-term effects of Africa's slave trades'. *The Quarterly Journal of Economics*, 123(1), pp. 139–176.
Nurullah, S., and J. P. Naik. *A History of Education in India (During the British Period)*. London: Macmillan, 1951.
O'Brien, P. (1982). 'European economic development: The contribution of the periphery'. *The Economic History Review*, 35(1), 1–18.
O'Brien, P., Griffiths, T. P., and Hunt, P. (1991). 'Political components of the industrial revolution: Parliament and the English cotton textile industry, 1660–1774'. *Economic History Review*, pp. 395–423.
O'Grada, C. (2008a). 'The ripple that drowns? twentieth -century famines in China and India as economic history'. *The Economic History Review*, 61(S1), 44, pp. 5–37.
   (2008b). 'Sufficiency and sufficiency and sufficiency': Revisiting the Bengal Famine of 1943–44', available at: www2.warwick.ac.uk/fax/soc/economics/newsevents/conference.
Oonk, G. (2001). 'Motor or millstone? The managing agency system in Bombay and Ahmedabad, 1850–1930'. *The Indian Economic & Social History Review*, 38(4), 419–452.
Padmanabha, P. (1981). 'Census of India, 1981: Salient Features'. *India International Centre Quarterly*, 8(3/4), 207–218.
Panagariya, A. (2004). Growth and Reforms during 1980s and 1990s. *Economic and Political Weekly*, 2581–2594.
   (2008). *India: The Emerging Giant*. New Delhi: Oxford University Press.
Parthasarathi, P. (1998). 'Rethinking wages and competitiveness in the eighteenth century: Britain and South India'. *Past and Present*, 158(1), pp. 79–109.
   (2001). *The Transition to a Colonial Economy: Weavers, Merchants and Kings in South India, 1720–1800*. Cambridge: Cambridge University Press.
   (2011). *Why Europe Grew Rich and Asia Did Not: Global Economic Divergence 1600–1850*. Cambridge: Cambridge University Press.
Pascali, L. (2017). 'The wind of change: Maritime technology, trade, and economic development'. *American Economic Review*, 107(9), pp. 2821–2854.

Patel, K. (1963). *Rural Labour in Industrial Bombay*. Bombay: Popular Prakashan.

Pelsaert, F. (1925). *Jahangir's India, the Remonstrantie of Francisco Pelsaert*. Cambridge: W. Heffer & Sons.

Pelsaert, F. (1978). *A Dutch Chronicle of Mughal India*. Pakistan: Sang-e-Meel Publications.

Perkins, D. H. and Tang, J. P. (2017). 'East Asian industrial pioneers: Japan, Korea, and Taiwan', in *The Spread of Modern Industry to the Periphery since 1871*. Oxford: Oxford University Press, pp. 169–196.

Persaud, A. (2019). 'Escaping local risk by entering indentureship: Evidence from nineteenth -century Indian migration'. *The Journal of Economic History*, *79*(2), pp. 447–476.

Pomeranz, K. (2000). *The Great Divergence: China, Europe, and the Making of the Modern World Economy*. Princeton, NJ: Princeton University Press.

Prakash, O. (1976). 'Bullion for goods: International trade and the economy of early eighteenth century Bengal'. *The Indian Economic & Social History Review*, *13*(2), pp. 159–186.

Pray, C. E. (1984). 'The impact of agricultural research in British India'. *Journal of Economic History*, *44*(2), pp. 429–440.

Purfield, C., and Schiff, J. A. (2006). 'Is economic growth leaving some states behind'. In *India Goes Global*. International Monetary Fund, p. 12.

Ram, K. (1984). 'The Indian working class and the peasantry: A review of current evidence on interlinks between the two classes', in Das, A. N., Nilkant, V., and Dubey, P. S. (eds.), *The Worker and the Working Class: A Labour Studies Anthology*. Delhi: Public Enterprises Centre for Continuing Education, pp. 181–186.

Ramaswamy, V. (1985). *Textiles and Weavers in Medieval South India*. New Delhi: Oxford University Press.

Ramaswamy, K. V. and Agrawal, T. (2012). '*Services-Led Growth, Employment and Job Quality: A Study of Manufacturing and Service-Sector in Urban India*. Indira Gandhi Institute of Development Research, Mumbai.

Rani, U. and Unni, J. (2004). 'Unorganised and organised manufacturing in India: Potential for employment generating growth'. *Economic and Political Weekly*, *39*, pp. 4568–4580.

Ravallion, M. (2011). 'A comparative perspective on poverty reduction in Brazil, China, and India'. *The World Bank Research Observer*, *26*(1), pp. 71–104.

Ravallion, M. and Datt, G. (2002). 'Why has economic growth been more pro-poor in some states of India than others?' *Journal of Development Economics*, *68*(2), pp. 381–400.

Ray, D. (1998). *Development Economics*. Princeton, NJ: Princeton University Press.

Ray, I. (2009). 'Identifying the woes of the cotton textile industry in Bengal: Tales of the nineteenth century'. *The Economic History Review*, *62*(4), pp. 857–892.

(2011). *Bengal Industries and the British Industrial Revolution (1757–1857)*. Routledge.

Renuka, M. (2003). 'Productivity growth in Indian agriculture: The role of globalization and economic reform'. *Asia Pacific Development Journal*, *10*(2), pp. 57–72.

Report of the Bombay Mill-Owner's Association, for the year 1889; Bombay.

Report of the Indian Irrigation Commission, 1916–18, Government of India, Calcutta.

Report on the Census of India 1901

Roberts, N. A. (1972). 'The supreme court in a developing society: Progressive or reactionary force? A study of the privy purse case in India'. *The American Journal of Comparative Law, 20*(1), 79–110.

Rodrik, D. (1995). 'Getting interventions right: How South Korea and Taiwan grew rich'. *Economic Policy, 10*(20), pp. 53–107.

    (2013). 'Unconditional convergence in manufacturing'. *The Quarterly Journal of Economics, 128*(1), pp. 165–204.

Rodrik, D. and Subramaniam, A. (2005). 'From Hindu growth to productivity surge: The mystery of the Indian growth transition'. *IMF Staff Papers, 52*, pp. 193–228.

Rothermund, D. (1993). *An Economic History of India*. Routledge.

Roy, B. (1996). *An Analysis of Long-Term Growth of National Income and Capital Formation in India (1850–51 to 1950–51)*. Calcutta: Firma KLM Private.

Roy, S. (2015). 'Empowering women? Inheritance rights, female education and dowry payments in India'. *Journal of Development Economics, 114*, pp. 233–251.

Roy, T. (2006). *The Economic History of India 1857–1947*, Second Edition. Delhi: Oxford University Press.

    (2002). 'Economic history and modern India: Redefining the link'. *Journal of Economic Perspectives, 16*(3), pp. 109–130.

    (2007). 'A delayed revolution: Environment and agrarian change in India'. *Oxford Review of Economic Policy, 23*(2), pp. 239–250.

    (2008). 'Knowledge and divergence from the perspective of early modern India'. *Journal of Global History, 3*(3), pp. 361–387.

    (2010). 'Economic conditions in early modern Bengal: A contribution to the divergence debate'. *Journal of Economic History, 70*(1), pp. 179–194.

    (2011). *The Economic History of India 1857–1947*, Third Edition. Delhi: Oxford University Press.

    (2013). *An economic history of early modern India*. Routledge.

    (2014). 'Geography or Politics? Regional Inequality in Colonial India', *European Review of Economic History*, 18(3), 306–323.

    (2018). *A Business History of India: Enterprise and the Emergence of Capitalism from 1700*. New York: Cambridge University Press.

Rudner, D. W. (1994). *Caste and Capitalism in Colonial India: The Nattukottai Chettiars*. Berkeley: University of California Press.

Rungta, S. (1985). 'Bowreah cotton and Fort Gloster Jute Mills, 1872–1900'. *The Indian Economic & Social History Review*, 22(2), pp. 109–137.

Rutnagur, S. M. (1927). *Bombay Industries: The Cotton Mills*. Bombay: Indian Textile Journal.

Sarkar, J. (2010). 'Ownership and corporate governance in Indian firms. Corporate governance: An emerging scenario'. *National Stock Exchange of India Ltd*, pp. 217–267.

Sen, A. (1977). 'Starvation and exchange entitlements: A general approach and its application to the great Bengal famine'. *Cambridge Journal of Economics, 1*(1), pp. 33–59.

    (1992). 'Missing women'. *BMJ: British Medical Journal, 304*(6827), 587.

Sen, S. (1999). *Women and Labour in Late Colonial India: The Bengal Jute Industry*. Cambridge University Press.

Sengupta, N. (1985). 'Irrigation: Traditional vs modern'. *Economic and Political Weekly, 20*, pp. 1919–1938.

Singer, H. W. (1989). 'Terms of trade and economic development', in *Economic Development*. Palgrave Macmillan UK, pp. 323–328.

Singh, B. (2012). 'Is the service-led growth of India sustainable?'. *International Journal of Trade, Economics and Finance, 3*(4), 316.

Sivasubramonian, S. (2000). *National Income of India in the Twentieth Century*. New Delhi: Oxford University Press.

(2004). *The Sources of Economic Growth in India, 1950–1 to 1999–2000*. New Delhi: Oxford University Press.

Sivramkrishna, S. (2009). 'Ascertaining living standards in Erstwhile Mysore, Southern India, from Francis Buchanan's journey of 1800–01: An empirical contribution to the Great Divergence debate'. *Journal of the Economic and Social History of the Orient, 52*(4–5), pp. 695–733.

(2015). *In Search of Stability: Economics of Money, History of the Rupee*. New Delhi: Manohar.

Srinivasan, T. N. and Tendulkar, S. D. (2003). *Reintegrating India with the World Economy*. Washington, DC: Institute of International Economics.

Statistical Abstract for British India. (1905). 'Statistical abstract relating to British India from 1894–95 to 1903–04'. London: Her Majesty's Stationary Office.

Stein, B. (1982). 'South India: Some general considerations of the region and its early history'. *The Cambridge Economic History of India, 1*, 14–42.

Stokes, Eric. (1959). *The English Utilitarians and India*. Oxford: Clarendon Press.

Stone, I. (1984). *Canal Irrigation in British India: Perspectives on Technological Change in a Peasant Economy*. Cambridge: Cambridge University Press.

Subrahmanyam, S. (1990). 'Rural industry and commercial agriculture in late seventeenth-century south-eastern India'. *Past & Present, 126*, pp. 76–114.

Suh, S.-C. (1978). *Growth and Structural Changes in the Korean Economy, 1910–1940*. Cambridge: Harvard University Press.

(2020). *Growth and Structural Changes in the Korean Economy, 1910–1940*. Cambridge, MA: Brill.

Swamy, A. V. (2011). 'Land and law in Colonial India', in Ma, D. and van Zanden, J. (eds.), *Law and Long-Term Economic Change*. Redwood City: Stanford University Press, pp. 138–157.

Sweeney, S. (2011). *Financing India's Imperial Railway, 1875–1914*. London: Pickering & Chatto.

Syrquin, M. (1988). 'Patterns of structural change'. *Handbook of development economics, 1*, 203–273.

Tavernier, J. (1889). *Travels in India*. United Kingdom: Macmillan and Company.

Tharoor, S. (2018). *Inglorious Empire: What the British Did to India*. Penguin UK.

Thatcher, W. S. (1926). 'WH Moreland and Prop. P. Geyl. Jahangir's India: Being the Remonstrantie of Francisco Pelsaert'. *The Economic Journal, 36*(142), pp. 268–269.

Thorat, S. and Newman, K. (2010). 'Economic discrimination: Concept, consequences, and remedies', in Thorat, S. and Newman, K. (eds.), *Blocked by*

Caste: Economic Discrimination in Modern India. New Delhi, India: Oxford University Press.

Timberg, T. A. (1978). *The Marwaris: From Traders to Industrialists*. New Delhi: Vikas.

Tomlinson, B. R. (1981). 'Colonial firms and the decline of colonialism in eastern India 1914–47'. *Modern Asian Studies*, 15(3), pp. 455–486.

(2013). *The Economy of Modern India: From 1860 to the Twenty-first Century*. Cambridge: Cambridge University Press.

Tripathi, A. and Prasad, A. R. (2009). 'Estimation of agricultural supply response by cointegration approach'. *The Indian Economic Journal*, 57(1), pp. 106–131.

Tripathi, D. (1967). 'Opportunism of free trade: Lancashire Cotton Famine and Indian cotton cultivation'. *The Indian Economic and Social History Review*, 4(3), pp. 255–263.

(1971). 'Indian entrepreneurship in historical perspective: A reinterpretation'. *Economic and Political Weekly*, 6, pp. M59–M66.

(1981). *The Dynamics of a Tradition: Kasturbhai Lalbhai and His Entrepreneurship*. New Delhi: Manohar.

(1987). *State and Business in India: A Historical Perspective*. Delhi: Manohar.

(1997). *Historical Roots of Entrepreneurship in India and Japan: A Comparative Perspective*. New Delhi: Manohar.

(2004). *The Oxford History of Indian Business*. New Delhi: Oxford University Press.

Tripathi, D. and Mehta, M. (1990). *Business Houses in Western India*. London: Jaya Books.

Tulpule, B. and Datta, R. C. (1988). 'Real wages in Indian industry'. *Economic and Political Weekly*, 23, pp. 2275–2277.

Twomey, M. J. (1983). 'Employment in nineteenth century Indian textiles'. *Explorations in Economic History*, 20(1), pp. 37–57.

Vaid, D. (2014). 'Caste in contemporary India: Flexibility and persistence'. *Annual Review of Sociology*, 40, pp. 391–410.

Van der Eng, P. (2010). 'The sources of long-term economic growth in Indonesia, 1880–2008'. *Explorations in Economic History*, 47(3), pp. 294–309.

Van Leeuwen, B. (2007). *Human capital and economic growth in India, Indonesia and Japan: A quantitative analysis, 1890–2000*. Ph.D. Dissertation, Utrecht University.

Van Zanden, J. L. (1999). 'Wages and the standard of living in Europe, 1500–1800'. *European Review of Economic History*, 3(2), pp. 175–197.

Van Zanden, J. L. and Marks, D. (2013). *An Economic History of Indonesia: 1800–2010*. Routledge.

Visaria, L. and Visaria, P. (1983). 'Population (1757–1947)'. in Kumar, D. (ed.), *The Cambridge Economic History of India, 2*. Cambridge, UK: Cambridge University Press, pp. 463–532.

Wallack, J. (2003). 'Structural breaks in Indian macroeconomic data'. *Economic and Political Weekly*, 38, pp. 4312–4315.

Weber, M. (1967). *The Religion of India: The Sociology of Hinduism and Buddhism*. Translated and Edited by Hans H. Gerth and Don Martindale. Free Press.

Whitcombe, E. (1972). *Agrarian Conditions in North India, Uttar Pradesh: 1860–1900*. Berkeley: University of California Press.

Wolcott, S. (1994). 'The perils of lifetime employment systems: Productivity advance in the Indian and Japanese textile industries, 1920–1938'. *Journal of Economic History*, *54*, pp. 307–324.

Wolcott, S. and Clark, G. (1999). 'Why nations fail: Managerial decisions and performance in Indian cotton textile, 1890–1938'. *Journal of Economic History*, *59*, pp. 397–423.

Yoo, J. (2017). 'Korea's rapid export expansion in the 1960s: How it began'. *KDI Journal of Economic Policy*, *39*(2), 1–23.

Young, A. (1995). 'The Tyranny of numbers: Confronting the statistical realities of the East Asian growth experience'. *Quarterly Journal of Economics*, *110*(3), pp. 641–680.

Index

Printed in the United States
by Baker & Taylor Publisher Services